Glencoe Publishing Co., Inc.
17337 Ventura Boulevard
Encino, California 91316

Collier Macmillan Canada, Ltd.

Printed in the United States of America

ISBN 0-02-659850-7

1 2 3 4 5 6 7 8 9   86 85 84 83 82

EFFECTIVE SPEECH

Richard W. Clark

Glencoe Publishing Co., Inc.
Encino, California

Acknowledgments

Broomheads & Neals: From The "Mary Celeste" by L. du Garde Peach. From Radio Plays. Used by permission of Reed International and Broomheads & Neals.

Curtis Brown, Ltd.: For "Don't Cry, Darling, It's Blood All Right." From Verses from 1929 On by Ogden Nash. Copyright © 1934, 1959 by Ogden Nash. Reprinted by permission of the Estate of Ogden Nash and Curtis Brown, Ltd.

Chicago Tribune–New York News Syndicate, Inc.: From Prime Time. Reprinted by permission of the Chicago Tribune–New York News Syndicate, Inc.

City News Publishing Co., Inc.: From "The Absurdity of Eternal Peace," by Benito Mussolini. From Vital Speeches of the Day. Used by permission of City News Publishing Co., Inc.

Executors of L. du Garde Peach Royalties Trust: From The "Mary Celeste" by L. du Garde Peach. From Radio Plays. Used by permission of IPC Magazines and the Executors of L. du Garde Peach Royalties Trust.

Field Newspaper Syndicate: From "Campaign '80: It's Empty—but It's Got Style" by Bob Greene. © 1980 by Field Enterprises, Inc. Reprinted courtesy of Field Newspaper Syndicate.

Harper & Row, Publishers, Inc.: For "My Grandmother Would Rock Quietly and Hum" (excluding one stanza), by Leonard Adamé in From the Barrio: A Chicano Anthology by Luis Omar Salinas and Lillian Faderman. Copyright © 1973 by Luis Omar Salinas and Lillian Faderman. Reprinted by permission of Harper & Row, Publishers, Inc.

Olwyn Hughes Literary Agency: For "Mushrooms." From The Colossus and Other Poems by Sylvia Plath. Published by Faber & Faber, London. © 1967 by Ted Hughes. Used by permission of Olwyn Hughes Literary Agency.

Jefferson Communications, Inc.: From Shoe. Reprinted by permission of Jefferson Communications, Inc., Reston, Virginia.

Barbara Jordan: From "Who Then Will Speak for the Common Good?" From 1976 Democratic Convention Keynote Address. Used by permission of Barbara Jordan.

Alfred A. Knopf, Inc.: For "Mushrooms." From The Colossus and Other Poems by Sylvia Plath. Used by permission of Alfred A. Knopf, Inc.

Little, Brown and Company: For "Don't Cry, Darling, It's Blood All Right." From Verses from 1929 On by Ogden Nash. Copyright 1934 by The Curtis Publishing Company. By permission of Little, Brown and Company.

Macmillan Publishing Co., Inc.: For "The Song of Wandering Aengus." From The Collected Poems of W. B. Yeats by William Butler Yeats. Copyright 1906 by Macmillan Publishing Co., Inc., renewed 1934 by W. B. Yeats. Reprinted with permission of Macmillan Publishing Co., Inc.

New Directions Publishing Corp.: For "Not Waving but Drowning." From Selected Poems of Stevie Smith. Copyright © 1964 by Stevie Smith. Reprinted by permission of New Directions.

The New York Times: © 1938 by The New York Times Company. Reprinted by permission of The New York Times.

Random House, Inc.: From *Act One* by Moss Hart. Used by permission of Random House, Inc.

The Register and Tribune Syndicate, Inc.: From *The Family Circus* by Bil Keane. Reprinted courtesy The Register and Tribune Syndicate, Inc.

Lyle Stuart Inc.: From *The Great Comedians*. Copyright © 1968 by Larry Wilde. Published by arrangement with Lyle Stuart.

Viking-Penguin Inc.: From "The Open Window." From *The Complete Short Stories of Saki* (H. H. Munro). Copyright 1930, © renewed 1958 by The Viking Press, Inc. Reprinted by permission of Viking-Penguin Inc.

World Book-Childcraft International, Inc.: From *The World Book Encyclopedia*. © 1981 World Book-Childcraft International, Inc.

The author gratefully acknowledges the assistance of Peter Bogdanoff in gathering materials for the Handbook of Contest Speaking.

Contents

PART 1

The Communication Process

1. You the Communicator

2. Communicating with Others

3. Active Listening

A Case Study

In 1979 Sperry Univac, the computer division of the Sperry Corporation, launched an advertising campaign with the slogan "We understand how important it is to listen." As part of this campaign, speech teacher Lyman K. Steil was hired to conduct listening seminars to make Sperry employees more efficient and persuasive. These are some of Steil's observations about listening:

- Most people spend 80 percent of their waking hours communicating with others, and half of that time is spent listening. Yet most of us listen at only 25 percent of our ability.
- If each member of the 100-million-member American work force makes only one ten-dollar listening error a year, there is a yearly waste of one billion dollars.
- Dramatic disasters, such as plane crashes and fatal hotel fires, are often caused by people not listening to instructions.
- Small talk is an important (but neglected) area of speech. Making and listening to small talk helps people establish personal relationships, which are essential to good business relationships.

THINK AND DISCUSS

One purpose of the Sperry advertising campaign was to improve the company's public image. In what way do you think the slogan and seminars might help this image?

Do you think Steil is correct when he says people listen at only 25 percent of their ability? How would you compare your listening habits with those of the average person?

Do you believe small talk is as important a part of communication as Steil says it is? How would you evaluate your own ability to make small talk?

In Part One, "The Communication Process," you will learn more about the problems discussed in this Case Study. You will study how and why people communicate, and how you can become an active listener.

1 You the Communicator

Communication is the act of telling our ideas to others, and listening while they tell their ideas to us. In order to communicate effectively with others, you must first understand yourself. You must know your own strengths and weaknesses, and your likes and dislikes. You must be aware of how people react to you when you speak. You should be aware of how they react to your voice and gestures as well as how they react to what you say.

We communicate primarily with our voices. An effective communicator speaks in a clear, pleasant voice, with enough variety to hold the listeners' interest. Good articulation and correct pronunciation are also important parts of using your voice.

After working through this chapter, you should be able to

- know yourself better as a communicator
- understand how other people see you
- speak so that you can be understood
- use your voice effectively

The Speaking Skills lessons in this chapter will help you understand the people you communicate with. In these lessons, you will learn to

- observe other people
- become aware of prejudices that may result from your observations
- respect your listeners' intelligence and feelings

The Skills for Success lessons will show you how communication skills can help you choose a career. In these lessons, you will learn to

- analyze your career interests
- explore careers in communications

1.1 Knowing Yourself as a Communicator

Observing Other People

The way we communicate with other people is affected by the things we observe about them. A person's age, background, clothes, and way of speaking may cause us to assume certain things about him or her. This may lead us not to speak to this person, or to speak only about certain subjects or using certain words. Some of our observations of people may give us valuable information about them. Other observations may be based on prejudice or fear. Here are some questions to ask yourself about people:

1. *Age.* Am I assuming that this person is too young to understand me, or too old to be interested in what I have to say? How can I learn what people are really like, so that age difference will matter less?

2. *Background.* If this person comes from a different racial, ethnic, or religious background, am I assuming that he or she is hostile to me? Am I allowing the prejudices of my family or friends to keep me from communicating with this person?

3. *Appearance.* Do I feel intimidated because this person is taller, more muscular, or better-dressed than I am? Or am I assuming that because my appearance is better, it is all right for me to behave impolitely?

4. *Language.* If a person's English is better than mine, am I embarrassed to open my mouth? If someone's English is worse, do I assume that he or she is too ignorant to understand me? How can I choose my language so that I communicate well with a specific person or group of people?

ACTIVITY

1. Think of a person you know well from school, your family, or your neighborhood. List things that a stranger might observe about this person. Include details of age, background, appearance, clothing, and speech. Decide whether a stranger would want to know or communicate with this person as a result of such observations. Then write down how you feel about and communicate with the person.

planning

How to Know Yourself as a Communicator

Each communication experience is slightly different from the others. Sometimes you feel at ease with people, as when you are talking to your family or friends. With other people, such as teachers and acquaintances, you feel less comfortable. The way you feel towards people will be reflected in your voice, posture, and language, as well as in the information you communicate.

Every day, in hundreds of different ways, we use words and gestures to show other people how we feel about them, and how we want them to feel about us. For example, when you say "Good morning" to a friend, you are not really giving that person useful information about the morning. Your words actually mean: "Because you're my friend, I'm glad to see you."

As a communicator, you have certain strengths and weaknesses. For example, your appearance and voice may cause people to pay attention to you. On the other hand, you may have nervous mannerisms which show others that you are uncomfortable when speaking. Such mannerisms can make you a less effective communicator. Before you begin to study speech and communication, evaluate both the strengths that can help you and the weaknesses that you can overcome.

Working with the Model

Read the following self-evaluation Susan wrote of her strengths and weaknesses as a communicator.

model

SELF-EVALUATION

Purpose: To identify my strong and weak points when I communicate with other people in conversation, so I can find ways of improving my communication skills.

Situations: Conversations with friends before and after school, between classes, on weekends; also, conversations with new acquaintances at friends' homes, at parties, or on Aerospace Club field trips.

Strong points: I dress neatly, and always try to keep a friendly smile and attitude. This seems to make people interested in talking to me. Since I seldom talk about myself, I don't think I'm likely to bore anyone. In conversation with strangers, I always ask questions about their work and hobbies.

Weak points: I feel fairly comfortable with my friends, but conversation with strangers, or people I know only slightly, can be painfully embarrassing to me. Even though I ask polite questions, many people don't seem eager to answer. I don't have any "small talk," casual remarks about the weather, fashions, entertainment, and so forth that help people feel at their ease.

Evaluation: After thinking about it, I believe that my conversation shows a lack of self-confidence. Because I don't feel that *I* and *my* interests are worth talking about, I spend too much time trying to "draw out" other people. Many of them naturally resent being questioned so much, and they must feel that I am making them do all the work in the conversation. Being informed and having good manners are points in my favor, but I must be more willing to talk about myself.

Suggestions for improvement: The next time I have a conversation with a new acquaintance, I'll try to spend as much time talking as he or she does. Of course, I'll ask the usual polite questions, but I also resolve to tell that person about the Aerospace Club, about the last book I read, and about my plans for college. I want to make myself sound interesting, but not egotistical. I'll try the new system for a month. Then I'll reread this evaluation, and see whether my conversation experience has changed in any way.

QUESTIONS

A. Think about the information Susan wrote under "Purpose," "Situations," "Strong Points," and "Weak Points."

1. What type of communication causes Susan the most trouble?

2. Which habits that Susan listed as "strong points" might actually be part of her problem? Explain your answer.

3. Among her "weak points" Susan listed her inability to make small talk. Name at least one way in which she might be able to develop this talent.

4. Imagine that you are having a conversation with Susan. Assuming that she has described her communication problems accurately, how do you think you would feel during the conversation? What would you do to make the experience more agreeable?

B. Think about the information Susan wrote under "Evaluation" and "Suggestions for Improvement."

1. Briefly summarize Susan's evaluation of her communication problem.

2. You have probably known at least one person who had as much difficulty in conversation as Susan has. How would you evaluate that person's communication problems?

3. Briefly summarize Susan's suggestions for improvement.

4. Name at least one suggestion that Susan could follow in order to become a better communicator.

Guidelines

In order to understand yourself better as a communicator, you should ask yourself the following questions:

Interests

What are my interests and enthusiasms?

What subjects do I know about that other people might be interested in?

How well do I convey information to others?

How successful am I in making other people share my enthusiasms?

Appearance and voice

How does my appearance either help or harm my ability to communicate?

How do people react to my posture, gestures, and way of speaking?

What effect does my voice have on people with whom I communicate?

Attitude towards myself

What is my attitude towards myself? Do I feel that I am an interesting person who is worth knowing?

What are my values? Do I believe in certain principles or goals? Are my values clear from what I say?

How consistent am I in what I believe and say to others? Do I change my ideas readily, or reluctantly?

Attitude towards others

How do I treat people whom I know well? Do I show loyalty and respect towards my friends?

How do I react to people I have just met? Do new acquaintances feel that I find *them* interesting?

How good are my manners? Would a new acquaintance describe me as basically rude, or basically polite?

By thinking about the answers to these questions, you can form an idea of the kind of communicator you are.

Preparing and Presenting _____

Although you will write your self-evaluation by your self, you will later discuss it with another student. To begin, reread Susan's self-evaluation in the Working with the Model section of this lesson. Then evaluate your own skills as a communicator, using the outline on the following page.

Purpose

Decide what type of communication causes you the greatest difficulties. Consider the following types of communication:

discussion with family members
conversation with friends
conversation with acquaintances
oral report before class or school organization
job interview

Situations

List each occasion on which you must take part in this type of communication. Remember to list situations in school and after school, at home, on the job, and in an organization.

Strong points

List all the qualities that help you communicate well. Include your appearance, voice, manners, and attitude; your background, interests, and enthusiasms; and your ability to make other people feel interested in you.

Weak points

List all the habits that keep you from communicating well. Include any problems you have with your appearance, voice, or manners; any difficulty in finding an interesting subject to talk about; any problems with attracting or holding other people's attention.

Evaluation

Decide what your principal problem as a communicator is, and what the causes of the problem are.

Suggestions for improvement

Identify at least one way in which you could change your habits or attitudes in order to become a better communicator. Describe a specific plan you could follow in order to improve your performance.

After you have written your self-evaluation, read it over and make any changes you think are necessary.

Evaluating

Exchange self-evaluations with another student. Read the other person's self-evaluation, then ask yourself the following questions:

1. How well has this person explained his or her communication problems? How could the explanation be made clearer?

2. How well do the lists of strong and weak points illustrate the problem? What information, if any, could be added to these lists to better illustrate the problem?

3. How accurate does this person's evaluation of his or her problem seem to be? In what ways, if any, could the evaluation be improved?

4. How well would the suggestions for improvement work? What other suggestions, if any, could this person follow to become a better communicator?

When both of you have thought about these questions, exchange self-evaluations again. Discuss your reactions to what you have read. Make any suggestions that would make the other person's self-evaluation more accurate or more helpful. Listen to the other person's suggestions, and change your self-evaluation accordingly.

Analyzing Your Career Interests

Whether you enter the job market now or later, you need to decide what career would best suit your abilities and interests, and which careers offer the best future. Answering the following questions can help you plan your career.

School
- Which subjects do I enjoy most? Which ones do I like least? Which ones inspire me to do work on my own?
- In which subjects do I get the best grades? Which require the most work? Which do I find easiest? Which are hardest?

Experience
- If I have had jobs, what did I like most and least about them?

Preferences
- What work activities interest me most?
- Do I prefer being indoors or outdoors?
- Do I prefer working with people, things, or ideas?
- Do I prefer working independently, or as part of a group?
- Do I prefer working in a highly structured environment, or under changeable conditions?
- Would I prefer to live in the city, in a town, or in the country?
- What kinds of activities or situations do I dislike most?
- How well do I respond to authority? Would I want to have authority over others, or want others to have authority over me?

Goals
- In what financial or social position will I be most happy?
- How much financial security do I need? Would I be willing to take risks in order to achieve my financial goals?

ACTIVITY

1. Answer each of the preceding questions. After thinking about your answers, write a brief summary of your talents, interests, and goals. Write down at least one possible career that would suit you.

1.2 Using Your Voice

Respecting Your Listeners

To communicate effectively with others, you must show that you respect their intelligence, feelings, and opinions. Whether you speak to a large group or a small one, remember these guidelines:

1. Be aware of your listeners' backgrounds, and the subjects on which they are likely to have strong opinions. Think of ways you can speak about such subjects without offending or antagonizing your listeners. At the same time, do not assume people have prejudices that they may not have (see Speaking Skills, lesson 1.1).

2. Try to look at controversial subjects from other peoples' points of view. When you speak, show that you know what their point of view is and that you understand it, even if you do not agree.

3. If at all possible, find ideas, topics, and opinions that you have in common with your listeners. As you speak, emphasize points of agreement rather than differences.

4. If you need to give your listeners basic information on some topic, do so without talking down to them. Make them feel that you and they are learning together, rather than that you are teaching them.

5. If you have to discuss sensitive subjects that will be either embarrassing or painful to some of your listeners, choose your language very carefully. As you speak, observe your listeners, and change your tone or choice of words if you see that your approach is not working.

ACTIVITY

1. Think of an incident in which a person was able to communicate successfully with other people whose background or opinions he or she did not share. Think of another incident in which a speaker showed no respect for his or her listeners. Describe these incidents briefly to the class. Ask other students to compare incidents they have reported with the ones you described.

attitude

14

How to Use Your Voice

To learn how to use your voice, you need to know where your voice comes from and why it sounds the way it does. There are three stages in the physical process of speaking:

1. The first stage (as you can see in the diagram on this page) takes place in your chest. Your *lungs* rest on a powerful curved muscle called the *diaphragm*. As you inhale, your diaphragm moves downward, drawing air into the lungs. At the same time, your rib cage expands to make room for the air. As you exhale, or when you speak, the diaphragm moves upward, forcing air out of the lungs.

   Most people have more than enough lung capacity to speak comfortably. Nevertheless, many people feel short of breath when they must speak in public. This feeling is caused by nervousness, and can be

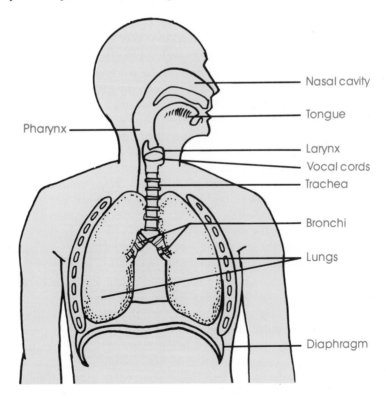

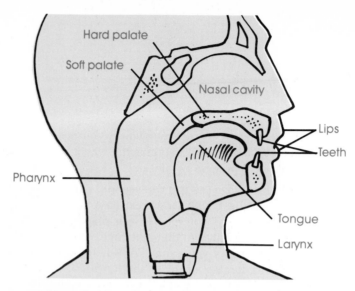

overcome. Instead of breathing rapidly and shallowly, practice breathing slowly and deeply. Use your abdominal muscles to steadily push out the air as you exhale. (This is the method singers use to produce a great volume of sound.) Be sure that the muscles of your chest, neck, and shoulders are relaxed, so that your rib cage can move easily and freely.

2. The second stage of speech takes place in the throat. Air moves up and out of your lungs through the *trachea,* or windpipe. At the top of the trachea, the air passes through the *larynx* (also called the voice box or Adam's apple). The *vocal cords* are a pair of muscular folds across the center of the larynx. When you breathe freely, these folds are relaxed. When you speak, however, the folds tighten and vibrate rapidly as the air flows past them. The more rapid the vibration, the higher the *pitch,* or frequency, of your voice.

    You can vary the pitch of your voice voluntarily, as singers do. Tension, however, can also tighten your vocal cords and make your voice squeaky, grating, or harsh. To control the pitch of your voice, you need to relax the muscles that control your larynx. Before speaking, warm up by gently stretching your neck muscles, breathing deeply and calmly, and humming or singing to yourself.

3. After the air has passed your vocal cords, it enters your throat and mouth. Before leaving your mouth, the air *resonates,* or echoes, in your *nasal cavity* and *pharynx* (see the diagram on this page). The shape of these parts of your mouth gives your voice its personal *coloration,* the quality that distinguishes it from any other person's voice. Too much nasal resonance can make you sound as though you have a cold. Tense throat muscles can make your voice guttural, thin, or strident. Many

unpleasant characteristics can be corrected by practice in relaxation and in reading aloud.

As you speak, you touch, or nearly touch, your tongue and other parts of your mouth together in order to form *consonants.* This list shows the parts of your mouth that produce each of these sounds:

lips only: b, m, p, w, wh

lips and teeth: f, v

tongue and hard palate: j, r, ch, sh, zh

tongue and soft palate: g, k, ng

tongue and gums: d, l, n, s, t, z

tongue and teeth: th

breath only: h

Unlike consonants, the *vowels* are produced by simply changing the shape of your mouth as you speak. The vowel sounds are represented by the letters *a, e, i, o,* and *u,* and by *diphthongs,* or pairs of letters, such as *au, oi,* and *ou.* American English has from thirteen to fifteen different vowel sounds. The way a person pronounces vowels shows which region of the country he or she comes from.

A speaker who has crisp, clear consonants and distinct vowels has good *articulation.* A speaker who pronounces words correctly, as well as clearly, has good *pronunciation.* Good articulation and pronunciation are characteristics of effective speakers. A good speaker also learns to vary the *pitch, loudness,* and *rate* (or speed) of his or her voice. Such vocal variety can make your speaking voice more attractive, and will keep your listeners from becoming bored or irritated by its sameness.

Working with the Model

Each of the following groups of words will give you practice in articulating specific sounds. The first thirteen groups will help you practice consonants, and the last thirteen will help you practice vowels. As you read the words aloud, try to make each sound clear and distinct.

model

b/p	k/g	d/t	f/v	h
battle	cot	dame	few	ail
paddle	got	tame	view	hail
beat	hock	nod	strife	edge
peat	hog	not	strive	hedge
rib	kale	medal	fan	owe
rip	gale	metal	van	hoe
browse	hackle	daughter	fender	Euston
prows	haggle	totter	vendor	Houston

j/ch	l/r	m/n	ng/nk	s/z
junk	lack	mail	sinker	noose
chunk	rack	nail	singer	news
jaw	light	moon	hanker	cease
chaw	right	noon	hangar	seize
Jill	liver	doom	thinks	spice
chill	river	dune	things	spies
Madge	kneeler	dumber	pinging	conduce
match	nearer	dunner	pinking	contuse

sh/zh	t/th	w/wh
assure	threat	wail
adjure	thread	whale
azure	death	weigh
insure	debt	whey
injure	other	witch
issue	utter	which
censor	both	wile
censure	boat	while

Exploring Careers in Communications

Careers in communications are not limited to public speaking and broadcasting. The following careers all require highly developed skills in speech communication.

Actor
Air traffic controller
Commercial artist
Counselor
Director of plays, films, or
   television
Editor of newspapers,
   magazines, or books
Executive
Executive secretary
Fund–raiser
Guide
Interpreter
Manager (any business)
Mediator
Newspaper reporter
   or freelance writer

Personnel director
Politician
Producer of films, plays, or
   television
Psychologist or psychiatrist
Public relations worker
Radio announcer
Receptionist
Salesperson
Teacher
Telecommunications worker
Television announcer
   or newscaster
Union organizer
   or representative

As you explore career possibilities, you should ask yourself how the ability to speak well and communicate effectively with other people can help you in your future jobs.

ACTIVITIES

1. Invite one or more people with occupations on the preceding list to speak to your class. Ask each speaker to describe the ways in which effective speech skills have helped him or her do the job and receive promotions.

2. Working with another student, research the ways in which speaking skills are used in one of the preceding occupations. Then select a situation that shows these skills in use. You might select a film director explaining a role to an actor, an editor telling a reporter how to write a story, or a guide showing your town to a group of tourists. Role-play this situation before the class.

career

2 Communicating with Others

Communication is a cycle, in which the speaker affects the audience and the audience affects the speaker. Good speakers learn to read their audiences. They know how their listeners are reacting to them, and they change their speech accordingly.

Lack of communication often leads to conflicts between people. If you understand the cause—whether prejudice, lack of information, or misunderstanding of others—you may be able to resolve the conflict through communication.

After working through this chapter, you should be able to

- understand the communication cycle
- know how to analyze your audience
- recognize the causes of conflicts
- communicate in order to resolve conflicts

The Speaking Skills lessons in this chapter will help you communicate with others. In these lessons, you will learn to

- communicate through posture and expression
- role play to understand communication problems

The Skills for Success lessons in this chapter will teach you how to communicate effectively in business and social situations. In these lessons, you will learn how to

- conduct a conversation with new acquaintances
- use the telephone effectively

2.1 Understanding Your Audience

Communicating through Posture and Expression

The way you use your face and body while speaking can help make the content of your speech more effective. Poor use of your face and body can distract your listeners. Remember these guidelines:

1. *Expression.* When you speak, your expression should be happy, alert, and confident. Your eyes should be open, and your expression cheerful (unless you are talking about a sad or solemn subject). As you practice a speech, observe your expressions in the mirror, until you feel you have complete control over them.

2. *Eye contact.* When you speak, look at individual members of your audience—not at your notes or at the ceiling. Look each person in the eye for a few seconds, then shift to another one. People with whom you have eye contact will almost always pay attention to your words.

3. *Posture.* Your posture should be upright, but not stiff. Stand with your head up and shoulders back. One hand can rest on the podium or hold your notes. The other hand can be free to gesture.

4. *Movement and gestures.* Move enough to show your audience that you are relaxed, but not so much as to distract them. Do not pace or sway from side to side. Use hand and arm gestures to emphasize important points. (See Speaking Skills, lesson 7.3.)

5. *Distance from your listeners.* In many speaking situations you will not be able to move closer to your audience. Sometimes, however, stepping out from behind the podium may help establish contact with your listeners. Leaning toward your listeners may help emphasize a point, but don't lean so close that you appear comic.

ACTIVITY

1. Observe a tape or film of a politician speaking at a convention or other meeting. Make notes on the speaker's posture, expressions, movements, and gestures, and his or her use of eye contact and distance from the audience. Also note how the speaker uses these techniques to emphasize specific parts of the speech. Report on your observations to the class.

movement

26

How to Understand
Your Audience

Whenever you communicate with other people, you have an *audience*. Often your audience is very small—for example, when you are having a conversation with one friend. Sometimes, however, you may have a large audience of dozens or even hundreds of people. Whatever the size of your audience, you need to understand how and why they are reacting to your speech. Your audience's reaction will affect the way you speak, your voice, gestures, and movements. It will affect the content of the speech you are delivering, and the form and content of future speeches.

Before you speak, you must think about *what* you are saying, *why* you are saying it, and *to whom* you are saying it. For example, you may be telling an anecdote, giving a campaign speech, or explaining a scientific theory. Your purpose may be to entertain, to persuade, or to inform. For each of these purposes, you would look for different qualities in your audience.

For example, suppose you were telling a humorous anecdote. You would want to be sure that your listeners would find the anecdote funny. They should be able to understand all the references you make to people and places without your having to explain them. They should share your ideas of what is humorous and what is not. You should also be sure that your listeners will not be offended by what you say. If all these conditions are favorable, your anecdote will probably be very effective.

You will often know a great deal about your audience in advance—for example, if you are speaking to friends or classmates. On other occasions, however, you must try to learn about your audience while you are speaking. As you speak, you will observe your listeners' reactions and modify what you say and the way you say it accordingly. Because the speaker reacts to the audience, as well as the audience to the speaker, the process of communication is a *cycle*.

Working with the Model

The cartoon on the following page helps illustrate the communication cycle. As you look at the picture and read the explanation, think about times when you have had to understand other people in order to communicate with them.

model

Speech Communication Cycle

1. The speaker has an idea that he or she wants to communicate to an audience.

2. The speaker puts this idea into words. At the same time, the speaker uses his or her posture, expression, and gestures to communicate with the audience.

3. The audience receives the speaker's words and gestures. At the same time, the audience is receiving information from other sources. This information may reinforce or contradict what the speaker is trying to say.

4. The audience forms its idea of what the speaker is communicating. This idea is affected by the speaker's words and gestures, and also by information from other sources.

5. The audience reacts to the speaker, with words, gestures, and expressions.

6. The speaker observes the audience's reaction, along with information from other sources. All this information causes the speaker to change what he or she is saying, and the way it is being said.

QUESTIONS

A. Study the Model illustration and the explanation that follows it. Then imagine yourself in the following situation: You want to invite your friend Vicki to go bike riding. However, when you finally find Vicki, she is standing with five of her teammates from the basketball team. Her teammates want her to spend the day practicing.

1. What might you say to Vicki in order to persuade her to go bike riding? What things would you specifically *not* say?

2. What other sources of information, besides your words, would probably affect the way Vicki reacts to your speech?

3. What would you observe in order to judge the way Vicki is reacting to your invitation?

4. What other sources of information, besides Vicki's reaction, might cause you to modify your speech?

5. Under what circumstances would Vicki be more likely to accept your invitation?

B. Imagine yourself in the following situation: A group of local business people is visiting your school. You have been asked to prepare and deliver a ten-minute speech on the goals and aspirations of the senior class to this group. You are speaking in a classroom, standing at the podium, while your audience of twenty-five is seated at the desks. The principal, the vice-principal, and your speech teacher are present.

1. What facts, opinions, or other information would you probably emphasize in your speech? What subjects would you either avoid or give little attention to?

2. What other sources of information, besides your speech, might influence the way the business people react to you?

3. What factors might prevent some members of your audience from understanding your speech completely?

4. How might the members of your audience show their reaction to your speech? In what ways might this reaction affect what you say?

5. What other sources of information, besides the reactions of the business people, would probably affect your speech?

Guidelines

In order to understand your audience and be an effective speaker, you should ask yourself the following questions:

Before Speaking

1. Who will be in the audience? How large will it be? In what setting will I be speaking? What will be my purpose in speaking?

2. How much does the audience already know about the subject of my speech? Are they likely to be interested in it? Do they have any prejudices on the subject that I will have to overcome?

3. What attitude will the audience have toward me? Will they have any prejudice for or against me? How can I dress and speak in a way that may make them like me?

While Speaking

4. How is the audience reacting to my words? If they appear puzzled, how can I make my meaning clearer? If they appear bored, how can I make my speech more interesting?

5. How is the audience reacting to my voice? Are my articulation and pronunciation clear enough that they can understand me? Is my voice loud enough to hear easily, but not loud enough to make people uncomfortable? Is my voice quality pleasant, and am I using enough vocal variety?

6. How is the audience reacting to my appearance, expressions, and gestures? In what ways, if any, can I improve these?

7. What sounds, sights, or other kinds of information are reaching the audience at the same time as my words? Is the audience being distracted? How is this information affecting their reaction to my speech?

8. How is the audience reacting to my speech? Is this the reaction I had expected? In what way can I change my words, voice, gestures, or manner of speaking to produce a more favorable reaction? In what ways should I make my future speeches different?

ACTIVITY

Look at the following cartoon, then answer the questions.

1. How many different people or groups of people are involved in this communication cycle?

2. What is wrong with this communication cycle? Do you think the ballplayer knows anything is wrong? Explain your answer.

3. This cartoon is funny because it shows a humorous failure of communication. Think of at least one other story, anecdote, or cartoon that also uses a failure of communication to make us laugh.

Preparing and Presenting

Work with three other students. Each student should find at least one example of imperfect communication—that is, communication that would have worked better if the speaker had understood his or her audience. Consider the following sources:

- events in history, either in the distant or the recent past
- problems of negotiation or diplomacy in current news stories
- movies or television dramas that show how a lack of understanding leads to conflict
- scenes from novels or short stories
- incidents in your own life or in the lives of your friends or family

Write your example as a short paragraph. Exchange examples with the other students in your group.

Evaluating

Read the different examples of unsatisfactory communication, then discuss ways in which each speaker might have better understood his or her audience. See if you can find one or more solutions for each example of imperfect communication.

Conducting a Conversation

The ability to conduct a conversation with people you have just met is an important skill, especially in business. Becoming a good conversationalist requires long practice, but certain guidelines will help you:

1. *Look for people who are interested in talking.* At a party, meeting, or convention, begin conversations with people who are standing alone or in a small group. Don't interrupt private conversations or arguments. If the people you want to talk to seem uninterested, excuse yourself politely and try elsewhere.

2. *Ease into a conversation.* Make a polite remark on your surroundings or a subject of interest to the other person. The remark should be easy to answer; for example: "Did you say you were from Chicago? I lived there until I was fifteen." Avoid criticism of your surroundings and personal remarks about others' clothes or appearance.

3. *Introduce yourself.* After you have exchanged a few remarks, tell the other person your name, and enough about your town, school, business, or background so that he or she can ask intelligent questions.

4. *Use the opportunity to learn.* Ask questions about other people's background and business, and show that you find them interesting. Don't bore people by talking endlessly about yourself.

5. *Be polite.* Never argue, and say nothing that could offend those you are conversing with. Avoid controversial subjects. Do not correct other people, even if you feel they are wrong or misguided.

6. *Be mobile.* Don't monopolize one or two people for hours. Circulate among those present, taking your new acquaintances with you: "You know, that looks like Coach Wolf over there. Shall we go and have a word with him?"

ACTIVITY

1. At a party, school meeting, or other gathering, pick a person with whom you are only slightly acquainted, and carry on a conversation with him or her. (If this person clearly does not want to talk with you, try someone else.) Try to converse for at least five minutes, and let the other person do most of the talking. Without using any names, report on your experience to the class.

2.2 Communicating to Resolve a Conflict

Role Playing to Understand Communication Problems

Role playing is a way of acting out situations or problems to understand them better. In a role-playing session, each person plays a part, such as job applicant, interviewer, customer, or store clerk. Each player acts the way he or she thinks the real person *would* act under the circumstances. Afterwards, the players often discuss what they have learned from the session. Here is an example of a role-playing session.

ROB: Can I help you, ma'am?

ETTA: I need a fan belt for my Volkswagen.

ROB: Let's see, is that a 'seventy?

ETTA: 'Sixty-eight!

ROB: All right, let me check. Hmm . . . we're out of 'sixty-eights.

ETTA: Don't you people ever have *anything* in stock?

ROB: However, this 'seventy belt should do just fine. Would you like one of our mechanics to install it?

ETTA: No! You people have enough of my money already!

ROB: I agree, it's always best to do it yourself. *(Ending the role-playing session.)* Well, Etta, how does it feel to be the customer for a change? Did you enjoy letting off steam?

ETTA: Yes, and I can understand why some of them get so angry.

ROB: How would you describe the way I handled it?

ETTA: No matter what I said, you were always polite.

ACTIVITY

1. Think of a problem that affects you at school, on a team, or on the job. Working with one or more other students, role-play the situation in front of the class. You may play either yourself or one of the other people involved. Discuss with the other students what the role-playing session has shown them about the problem and possible solutions.

problem solving

34

How to Communicate to Resolve a Conflict

Not every conversation is a pleasant or friendly experience. A conversation may end in an argument or conflict among the people involved. Or a conflict may grow over a period of days or weeks before it finally breaks out into an open disagreement. Most conflicts result from imperfect communication. They can often be resolved through communication as well.

The following six causes are probably the most common sources of conflict among friends and acquaintances:

1. *Prejudice.* A prejudiced person assumes that everyone having a particular age, background, appearance, or accent will think and act in the same way. Once prejudiced people make up their minds, they may not bother to find out the truth.

2. *Lack of information.* A conflict may develop because a person knows only part of the truth, but assumes that he or she knows everything. People who listen to rumors, for example, often act on inadequate information. They may misinterpret the actions of others because they did not check the facts.

3. *Verbal confusion.* Although it seems trivial, many people quarrel because they attach different meanings to the same word. For example, Gloria may tell Ron that his manners are extremely "gracious." Gloria means this as a compliment, but Ron, to whom "gracious" implies "phony," is offended.

4. *Different values.* Even when people share the same ideas of right and wrong, they may not perceive a problem in the same way. To one person, for example, conserving energy may be a serious principle of her life; to her friend, it may be a very minor concern. People who do not understand one another's values may find themselves in conflict when they did not expect it.

5. *Misplaced emotions.* Some people may quarrel, not with those who have made them unhappy, but with those who are most convenient. For example, a person with a headache may snap at a friend who asks him how he feels. Such an emotional reaction is unfair to the victim, and does not affect the barking dog which caused the headache in the first place.

6. *Desire to dominate.* Often, a conflict will continue because neither of the people involved will admit that he or she was wrong. Some people insist

on having the last word in an argument. Others always insist on giving orders, and will never take them. Many people feel that compromising means losing their dignity.

As you can see, most of the conflicts described could have been prevented if people were more willing to communicate their ideas, emotions, and interests to one another. Sometimes shyness keeps people from communicating, and at other times pride. The most important person in resolving a conflict is often a *mediator*—someone who knows both or all the people involved, and who can see both sides of the dispute. A mediator can encourage people to discuss their true feelings, and can separate the important issues from the trivial ones. However, even a skillful and sensitive mediator can do little unless the people involved are willing to resolve their conflict.

Working with the Model

The following scene shows a kind of conflict that you have probably encountered at school or in your neighborhood. As you read the scene, put yourself in the place of each of the characters, and try to understand the way he feels.

model

(*Scene: the school yard at lunchtime. Hugh is just finishing a sandwich as Ken and Ervin walk by.*)

KEN: Hi, Hugh!
HUGH: (*Mumbling*) H'lo, Ken. (*He walks away rapidly.*)
ERVIN: I know that guy, don't I?
KEN: Sure, that's Hugh Lonsdale, a good buddy of mine. You must have seen him at basketball practice.
ERVIN: Yeah, well, he didn't look too glad to see me.
KEN: Oh, I think he's not feeling too good; he hurt his knee in a game last semester—
ERVIN: I've seen that look around this school before. That's the old "You-transfer-guys-from-East-High-can-drop-dead" look.
KEN: Oh, no, Erv, I'm sure Hugh doesn't feel that way. I'll bet you two would really get along. You have a lot in common, you're going to be on the team—
ERVIN: Forget it.
KEN: (*Seeing Hugh*) There's Hugh . . . I'm going to get him over here. (*Shouting*) Hey, Hugh!
ERVIN: So long.
KEN: No, wait . . . (*Shouting*) Hey, Hugh! (*To Ervin*) Please wait, Erv, I just want to introduce you—
ERVIN: No way, man. I know where I'm not wanted. (*He goes.*)
HUGH: (*Coming up*) Well, your friend didn't last long, did he?

model

KEN: Listen, Hugh, I just wish you could get to know him—

HUGH: Him? You're nuts! I wouldn't even shake hands with that guy. I'd be afraid he'd steal my watch.

KEN: What do you mean?

HUGH: Those guys from East High are all thieves. They steal anything that isn't nailed down.

KEN: You don't know what you're talking about.

HUGH: Don't I? What about those thefts from the lockers last week? What about all the money that was taken?

KEN: Thefts? I only heard of one: Susan Spielman lost a book.

HUGH: I heard they took her purse with twenty dollars in it. I heard there were four or five other cases, but someone's hushing them up so we won't come down hard on those East High bums.

KEN: But Erv's no thief, he's a really nice guy—and he's never harmed you. Come on, Hugh, what's really eating you? Is your knee still giving you trouble?

model

HUGH: Yeah, it hurts whenever I play. Instead of being on the team, I'll be shooting baskets in the back yard.

KEN: I'm awfully sorry to hear that, Hugh. But that's no reason to be mad at Erv—just because he'll be on the team and you won't.

HUGH: It makes no difference. I just don't want to associate with people like that.

KEN: People like *what*, Hugh? If you could just get to know some of the students from East High ... Listen, Coach Wolf has been giving out passes to the Marauders game tomorrow night. Why don't you come? We could go have a pizza afterwards.

HUGH: Is that friend of yours going to be there?

KEN: Erv? Yes, but you don't have to sit next to him. Just be civil—

HUGH: Listen, if this Ervin and his bunch want to be accepted, they should make the first move. Let *them* come to *us*. It's our school, after all.

KEN: Hugh, we're talking about *people*—people who have their pride, too. How do you think they feel, being cold-shouldered like this?

HUGH: *(Going)* Let 'em come to us. That's all I say.

KEN: Will you go to the game?

HUGH: I don't know ... maybe. I'll think about it and give you a call.

KEN: You won't regret it.... See you later, Hugh.

QUESTIONS

A. Think about the different sources of conflict in this scene.
   1. Find two examples of prejudice on the part of different people.
   2. Find an example of a conflict caused by lack of information.
   3. Find an example of misplaced emotions.
   4. Find at least one example of a person who wants to dominate others or have the last word.

B. Think about the people involved in this scene.
   1. Which person does the most to cause the conflict? Which person does the least? Explain your answer.
   2. What steps does Ken take to try to resolve the conflict? How well do his actions seem to be based on his understanding of Ervin and Hugh? What actions, if any, seem to be miscalculated?
   3. In what way is this conflict caused by a failure in communication? How do you think the conflict could have been prevented in the first place?
   4. Do you think Ken's efforts to bring Ervin and Hugh together will be successful? Explain your answer.
   5. How do you think this conflict could be resolved?

Guidelines

The following steps are the most important ones in resolving a conflict:

1. *Establish communication.* Nothing can happen if people are not speaking to one another. They must be willing to talk about their differences without fighting. A mediator can persuade people to get together and talk in a pleasant, neutral setting.

2. *Exchange information.* Often, a conflict will exist because people have been misled by rumors or half-truths. A basic step toward resolution is to talk about the facts of the case. Sometimes a problem will disappear once the truth becomes known.

3. *Try to understand others.* People who want to resolve a conflict must understand one another's emotions and point of view. They must be willing to listen to another person's story. They should make an effort to be sympathetic.

4. *Define your terms.* When a conflict results from verbal confusion, it is important to people to explain exactly what they meant. In such cases, understanding why the words were misinterpreted will usually eliminate the problem.

5. *Define your values.* People cannot be reconciled unless each of them understands the other's principles, beliefs, and priorities. Explaining these may not always convert one person to the other's opinion. However, people who disagree on questions of values can still respect one another's integrity.

6. *Get to the root of the problem.* A conflict may arise because of a person's prejudice, an emotional problem, or a deep-seated resentment. Unless these causes come into the open, the conflict may continue unresolved.

7. *Find common ground.* When the people in a conflict have discussed their feelings, values, and points of view, they should be able to agree on important issues. If they belong to the same family, attend the same school, or work for the same company, they should have many goals, values, and problems in common. Agreement on these qualities can become the basis for resolving the conflict.

8. *Be willing to compromise.* If they truly want to resolve a conflict, both or all the parties must be willing to give up something they want. This does not necessarily mean compromising their principles. It does mean conceding that they may have been mistaken or misinformed, or that other points of view may also be worthwhile.

Preparing and Presenting

Work with two other students. Think about the conflict that was presented in the Model section of this lesson. Think about ways in which that conflict could be resolved through better communication. With the other students, write a script in which Ken, Ervin, and Hugh solve their differences. In your script, try to use as many of the rules for resolving conflicts as you can.

When the script is complete, rehearse it in a group, with each of you taking one of the three roles. As you rehearse the script, you may wish to rewrite it in order to make the characters and the conflict more convincing. When the script is finished, act it out before the class.

Evaluating

Ask the other students in your class to evaluate your script for resolving the conflict. They should discuss these two questions:

1. How likely is this resolution of the conflict, in light of the personalities of the characters involved?

2. How many different methods of resolving a conflict does this script illustrate?

If other groups of students have written scripts for resolving the conflict, listen to them and compare them with your own.

Using the Telephone Effectively

You should learn how to use the telephone to save yourself time and effort in making business contacts. You should also use it to make a good impression on the people you are dealing with. Remember these rules:

1. *Answer the phone politely.* Instead of simply saying, "Yes?", "Hello?", or "What is it?", answer with useful information:

   "Glenn's Gaskets. Can I help you?"
   "Glenn's Gaskets, Jill Thomas speaking."

2. *Identify yourself to the person you are calling.* Instead of "Is Jim Fernandez there?" or "Let me speak to Jim Fernandez," give your name and a polite request:

   "Good afternoon, this is Jill Thomas from Glenn's Gaskets. May I speak to Jim Fernandez, please?"

3. *State your business clearly.* Don't waste the other person's time on irrelevant conversation. Tell him or her as briefly as possible why you are calling, and exactly what you want. Give any information that will make it easier for the person to help you.

4. *Don't interrogate the person who answers the phone.* If you are told that a person is busy or in conference, don't try to find out what the person is really doing or with whom he or she is speaking.

5. *Leave clear messages.* Instead of saying, "I'll try later," leave your name and number, and some information that will help the person who has to call you back:

   "Please tell Jim that Jill Thomas called about the schedule for delivering the gaskets. My number is 555-6200."

ACTIVITY

1. Working with another student, role-play one of the following telephone conversations, or another conversation your teacher approves, before the class:

   Student inquiring about a job opening
   Garage owner placing an order for mufflers
   Retailer checking when catalogues will be delivered

   Ask the other students to evaluate the conversation and to suggest ways in which both speakers could have made more effective use of the telephone.

career

3 Active Listening

Communication involves listening just as much as it does speaking. A good listener is someone people enjoy talking to. Such a person shows his or her interest in what others are saying, and knows when and how to ask questions. Poor listening habits, on the other hand, can lead to confusion and conflict. An active listener avoids confusion by indicating when he or she understands what is being said, and when more information is needed.

After working through this chapter, you should be able to

- use the techniques of active listening
- provide feedback to the people you are talking with
- take part in an interesting, friendly conversation

The Speaking Skills lesson in this chapter will help you understand how you sound to others. In this lesson, you will learn

- how listeners interpret your words
- how to choose language that will not confuse your listeners

The Skills for Success lesson in this chapter will tell you about some of the ways hearing-impaired people communicate. In this lesson, you will learn

- what communication methods are used by the hearing impaired
- how hearing-impaired people use these methods to live normal, active lives

3.1 Listening to Communicate

Understanding How Listeners Interpret Your Words

Words are like money. You use words to communicate ideas, just as you use money to buy groceries. But what if your $10 bill was worth $5 at one store and $25 at another? Unfortunately, this can happen with words, since the same word can mean different things to different people.

Every word has its own history and associations for each listener. Words like *car* mean approximately the same thing to everyone. Other words, like *justice,* may mean something very different to different people. Some words, like *receiver,* may even have several different meanings (for example, "football receiver" and "stereo receiver") for most people.

When you plan a speech, avoid using words that may have multiple meanings for your audience, or meanings you didn't intend. When you give your speech, explain any meanings your words have for you that they may not have for your audience.

ACTIVITY

1. Sometimes the meanings of words are colored by recent events and experiences. *Camelot,* the legendary home of King Arthur and his Knights of the Round Table, took on a new shade of meaning with its application to the administration of J. F. Kennedy. At one time, *microwave* was a term used primarily by physicists. With the invention of the microwave oven, *microwave* acquired an additional meaning. When people say *microwave* today, they are usually referring to the oven, not to the wave itself. Make a list of other words whose meanings have been colored or have multiplied due to recent events or new products. After you have listed five words, discuss with another student how a speaker could make clear which of a word's meanings he or she intended.

language

How to Listen to Communicate

To really communicate with others, you must listen to them carefully and actively. In a conversation, speaker and listener share equally in the responsibility for achieving clear, harmonious communication. An inattentive or passive listener can do as much to cause a breakdown in communication as a speaker who isn't sure what he or she wants to say.

Think of some of the enjoyable conversations you've had, and of some of the difficult ones. How did the people in the enjoyable conversations let the speaker know that they understood (or didn't understand) what was being said? How did they show their interest in one another and in the topics being discussed? In the difficult conversations, what kinds of behavior seemed to lead to communication problems? Becoming aware of the kinds of behavior that lead to enjoyable or difficult conversations is the first step in learning to listen to communicate.

Working with the Model

A group of high-school seniors were talking after school one day, and their thoughts turned to what they were going to do after high school. As you read the following transcript of their conversation, look carefully at the listening skills each student displays.

model

SARA: My parents are really after me to make up my mind about next year. I'm just not sure.

INGRID: Me too. I really get it from home about my schedule and grades. Guess I'll have to do better.

MAURICE: I think Sara had something else in mind. Sara, didn't you mean you are being told to decide what college you're going to attend?

SARA: Right. I'm being pushed to go to Smith. Actually, I'd rather take the extra money that it would require and buy myself a new car. What are the rest of you going to do?

TOVA: Sara, I'm not sure I understood you right. Do you mean you don't care if you go to college?

SARA: Sure. Just because my parents want me to, doesn't mean I have to go to college. Do you do everything your parents want you to do?

model

JERRY: None of us does. But how can you get a decent-paying job without a college diploma? My counselor . . .

SARA: Oh, counselors don't know so much. My friend Wayman from Redmond didn't even finish high school, and he's already earned enough to buy a new sports car and a lot of fancy ski equipment.

MAURICE: What does your counselor say, Jerry?

JERRY: That if you finish college, you will earn 20 to 30 percent more than if you stop with high school.

SARA: Everyone can make up statistics to make a point.

MAURICE: Have any of you visited any of the state colleges?

INGRID: *(looking up from the school paper she has been reading)* What happened in French today?

JERRY: What's that got to do with what we're going to be doing next year?

INGRID: Huh?

QUESTIONS

A. Different students should take the parts of Sara, Ingrid, Maurice, Tova, and Jerry, and read this conversation aloud. This will help you get the feeling of the conversation, so you can complete the questions and activities that follow.

1. What comments in the conversation reveal that a person was actively listening to what was being said? What comments show that a listener was not paying attention?

2. As you watched the students read through the conversation in the model, what nonverbal cues showed that some members of the group were not giving their full attention to the conversation?

3. Extend the conversation by having the students role-play what they think will happen as the group keeps talking. For example, how will Jerry deal with Ingrid's response? As the role-playing continues, take notes on the various kinds of listening behavior the participants demonstrate.

4. List several examples from the model and from your notes on the role-playing of occasions when a member of the group didn't understand something that was said. What, if anything, did the listener do in each case to clarify the speaker's remarks? In each case, what else might the confused listener have done to understand the speaker's remarks?

5. Not all efforts to let a speaker know that you, the listener, don't understand a comment need come in the form of spoken remarks. What (if any) nonverbal cues were used by the students role-playing the extended conversation to indicate their reactions to what was being said? What other nonverbal cues might have been used?

B. Drawing from your observations of the role-playing and from your own listening experiences in conversations, make a list of suggestions of how people could improve their listening behavior. Then restate your suggestions as a list of guidelines for effective listening.

Guidelines

Follow these guidelines for being a good listener:

1. *Give active attention to what is being said.* When you are not speaking yourself, you should be alert and responsive to the remarks of others. Try to understand what is being said from the speaker's point of view. Be open-minded, and alert for new ideas and viewpoints.

2. *Provide feedback to let the speaker know whether he or she has been understood.* You can provide feedback by asking the speaker to repeat what was said or to expand on his or her comments by giving examples. Another way to provide feedback is to repeat what you heard and ask the speaker whether or not you have understood him or her.

3. *Work to clarify comments you don't understand.* Sometimes simply asking a question or paraphrasing a comment can clear up any confusion. Sometimes you may have to ask several questions before a speaker's remark is clear. In any case, never pass up an opportunity to clarify a speaker's remark because you're afraid that asking questions will make you look foolish.

4. *Be courteous.* When you disagree with the remarks of others, do so in a way that conveys your respect for them as persons. Focus your responses on the ideas expressed, not on the personality or shortcomings of the speaker.

Preparing and Presenting _____

The class should divide into groups of three or four. Each group should begin by listing five current events from your school, your community, and the nation. As you discuss these events, decide which of them is most interesting to all of you and which event is likely to have the greatest impact on your lives in the next five years. For example, you might talk about the championship football game being played this weekend, a fight at city hall over whether there is to be a curfew for those under 18, and the problems this country is having with the OPEC nations over oil prices. You may decide that the curfew issue is the most interesting, but that the cost of oil is likely to have the greatest impact on your life. After your group has reached agreement, select one member of your group to join representatives of other groups in the next round of activities.

The representatives of five to eight groups should form a small circle for discussion. Then chairs should be arranged for others in the class so that they can easily see and hear these representatives. While the rest of the students listen, the representatives should attempt to decide among themselves which of the events discussed in the original groups is most interesting and which will have the greatest long-term impact. The students listening to the representatives should take notes on the listening skills each representative displays. After five minutes, the representatives should stop their discussion. Each representative's listening skills should be rated aloud by three members of the audience, according to the guidelines presented in the Evaluating section.

After each of the representatives has been evaluated, a new representative should be selected from each of the original groups. This new group of representatives should continue the discussion for five minutes, and then each member's listening skills should be rated by three people from the audience. Continue this procedure until everyone in the class has had a chance to be a representative.

Evaluating _____

The listening skills of each representative should be rated aloud by three students from the audience, according to these four guidelines for good listening:

Good listeners . . .

- give active attention
- provide feedback
- seek to clarify
- are courteous

Being Aware of Communication Methods
Used by the Hearing-Impaired

About 14 million Americans have some hearing impairment, and about 2 million of these are deaf—that is, unable to hear or understand speech. Those with severe hearing impairments must rely on sight for communication.

Lip reading is used by many hearing-impaired people to understand what others are saying. Much information is lost, however, if speakers move their lips very little, or turn their heads so that their mouths are not visible. Hearing-impaired people also use two kinds of *manual communication*. One kind, the *manual alphabet*, uses the fingers to represent each letter of the alphabet. The other kind, *sign language* or *signing*, uses gestures of the hands and arms to represent words and ideas. Often, all three methods are used together. A person who is interpreting for hearing-impaired people will use signing to convey basic ideas. At the same time, the person will move his or her lips to reinforce the words, and spell out unusual words or names using the manual alphabet.

Interpreters using sign language often appear on television programs, especially news or public affairs shows. Recorded programs may be *captioned*. Some captions are printed subtitles that are seen by all viewers. Other programs are *closed captioned*, and must be decoded by special machines. Some hearing-impaired people also communicate by a machine called a *TTY*, which uses a telephone to type out and send messages.

ACTIVITY

1. Observe an interpreter "signing" a speech or news program on television. See how often you are able to understand the interpreter's gestures. Also compare the interpreter's speed with that of the speaker. If possible, invite an interpreter to speak to your class and explain the language and symbols he or she uses.

PART 2

Speaking to Inform

4. Interviewing

5. Expository Speaking

6. Listening to Understand

A Case Study

In January 1979, a fire on a Bay Area Rapid Transit train underneath San Francisco Bay claimed the life of a fireman and caused the tunnel to be shut down for safety reasons. BART officials learned that many passengers were confused by the wordy instructions they were given by the train operators. BART hired Dr. Elizabeth Loftus, a psychologist, to write a brief, clear evacuation message. Here is Dr. Loftus' 131-word announcement.

"May I have your attention, please? A fire has been reported on this train. BART Central would like you to leave the train for your own safety. Please leave the train now and walk slowly to the opposite tunnel. Follow these instructions for going to the opposite tunnel. The instructions to the opposite tunnel will be repeated while you are leaving the train.

"Open your own doors now. To get to the opposite tunnel, take the sidewalk to the nearest tunnel door. Then go through two tunnel doors, and you will be in the opposite tunnel. Once you are in the opposite tunnel, continue to walk along the sidewalk and tracks so that other people can come through the doors. As you leave the train, please help any people who need help."

THINK AND DISCUSS

Dr. Loftus believes that an emergency message must be simple, clear, and reassuring. How clear do you think her message is? What key phrase is repeated many times? Why do you think this phrase is repeated so often?

Do you think you would be reassured by this message? What ideas or sentences in the message are designed to prevent panic? What expressions might help reassure people that someone competent is in charge?

In Part Two, "Speaking to Inform," you will learn the most effective ways you can communicate information to other people. You will learn how to gather information by interviewing people, and how to take notes on a lecture or speech.

4 Interviewing

A good interview can tell you a great deal about a person's achievements, goals, life, and personality. Televised interviews can inform you about authors, scientists, business people, politicians, or celebrities. You can also use interviews to gather information on topics that may not be well covered in books or articles.

The interviews you conduct can inform others when you turn them into papers or articles. You will be interviewed yourself whenever you apply for a job. Whether you are interviewing or being interviewed, you should be prepared. The interviewer must know how to ask questions that will lead to good responses. The interviewee should be aware of likely questions and be prepared to answer them.

After working through this chapter, you should be able to

- prepare for interviews
- distinguish between good and poor questions
- prepare effective interview questions
- ask good follow-up questions
- conduct informative interviews

The Speaking Skills lessons in this chapter will help you prepare and conduct interviews. In these lessons, you will learn to

- locate information about the person you plan to interview
- record interview responses
- use appropriate language

The Skills for Success lessons will show how you can use your interviewing skills in your career and as a citizen. In the lessons in this chapter, you will learn to

- make an oral inquiry about a job
- interview candidates and public officials
- be interviewed for a job

4.1 Preparing
   for Interviews

Locating Information about
the Person You Will Interview

Before you interview a person, learn as much about him or her as possible. Having background information will save you time during the interview and enable you to ask questions that will lead to more interesting answers.

There are many sources of information you can use. If the person you are interviewing is well known, check the *Readers' Guide to Periodical Literature* for magazine articles about the interviewee. If the person is an author, he or she may have a biography in *Contemporary Authors*. You can find out about scientists in *American Men and Women of Science*. There are also reference books for people in sports, business, politics, religion, and other professions. Your reference librarian should be able to help you find these sources.

If the person you are interviewing is known only in your community, you may be able to find information by checking the index of your local newspaper, or by questioning people familiar with life in your city or town. You may wish to write or phone the interviewee and ask him or her to send you a brief biographical sketch to help you in preparing your questions.

ACTIVITIES

1. Think of a famous person whom you would like to interview. Using the *Readers' Guide* and other reference works available at your library, locate three sources of information about this person's life. These sources should contain information about the person's childhood, family, education, early career, and various achievements.

2. Using the sources of information you located for Activity 1, write ten questions you could ask the person in an interview. These questions should be based on information you found in the biographical sources, rather than on facts you already knew.

research

54

How to Prepare for Interviews

Good interviews do not happen by accident. They are the result of careful planning by interviewers who have researched their subjects and have foreseen the possible difficulties.

The first thing to think about is the *purpose* of your interview. You should make firm *arrangements* for the time, place, and setting of the interview. These should be convenient for both interviewer and interviewee. *Confirm* arrangements the day before the interview. Become informed on the *topic* of the interview. For example, learn any special vocabulary needed to talk about the topic. You should be sure you have the most current information on the subject, and should be aware of any controversies that exist. Examine your own *attitudes* toward the interviewee and the topic you will be speaking about.

You should plan your *opening remarks* in advance. These should include the purpose of the interview and your first question or questions. Finally, when you make an appointment for an interview, arrange your method of *recording* it.

Working with the Model

Kris is going to interview a columnist from a local newspaper. To prepare for the interview, she has completed the items on a pre-interview checklist.

PRE-INTERVIEW CHECKLIST

Person to be interviewed: Ed Rosenberg

Purpose of interview: To learn about his series of exposés of waste and inefficiency in city government

✓ **1. Confirm arrangements with interviewee.**
In response to my letter, Ed Rosenberg has agreed to be interviewed in his office at the *Times* on Saturday, July 5, from 11:00 A.M. until noon. If necessary, he says, we can continue over lunch. The day before the interview, I'm to confirm my appointment with his secretary.

✓ **2. Arrange interview setting.**
We can speak in Ed's office, and he will have his secretary hold calls so we will not be interrupted.

model

3. Become informed on interview topic.

Vocabulary: I've researched the city agencies Ed writes about: Public Works Board, Harbor Commission, Foothill Water District Board, and others. I've read his articles carefully for three months. I have also discussed Ed's series with my Civics teacher, who gave me useful information.

Current information: Ed's continuing exposé of the Water District is being covered in several newspapers, and I've read other articles as well as his columns.

Controversies: Editorials in the *Mirror* have called Ed irresponsible—get his reaction on this.

4. Examine own attitudes toward topic and person.

Ed Rosenberg is one of my heroes, so I'll have to make an effort to ask him tough questions about his use of evidence and about certain charges that sound flimsy.

5. Prepare opening remarks for interview.

After reminding Ed of the purpose of my interview, I'll ask him, "How did you first become aware of the problem of waste in the city government?"

6. Plan how to record interview.

Ed has given me permission to tape-record the interview. This will enable me to ask follow-up questions if Ed makes an interesting remark on a subject I had not covered in my prepared questions. Also, I will have a record of Ed's exact words—important when writing about such a complicated subject. (Memo: Buy new batteries, three 60-minute cassettes.)

QUESTIONS

A. Think about Kris' pre-interview checklist.

1. What is the purpose of the interview?

2. How will each item that Kris has checked off help her to achieve that purpose?

3. Name at least two other purposes for which Kris might have wanted to interview Ed Rosenberg.

4. Suppose that Kris had wanted to interview Ed Rosenberg about journalism careers for young people. Which parts of her checklist would she have had to change? Which parts would remain the same?

B. Read an interview in a newspaper or magazine, or listen to an interview on radio or television.

1. What was the purpose of the interview? If the purpose was not clear, do you think this was the interviewer's fault?

2. How well prepared was the interviewer? Find at least five things about the interview that show how much (or how little) preparation the interviewer had done.

57

Guidelines

Making a pre-interview checklist should enable you to arrive for an interview well-prepared. It should allow you to speak in comfortable surroundings, without interruption, for as long as is necessary. You should be able to ask intelligent questions, and record the interviewee's responses easily and accurately.

A pre-interview checklist should include the following items. It may not always be possible to do everything listed under each step. However, you should go through every step in order, to be sure you have not forgotten anything important.

PRE-INTERVIEW CHECKLIST

Person to be interviewed: _____

Purpose of interview: _____

Think about the different purposes you might have. You might want to obtain information about the person and topic in order to prepare an article or paper. You might want information that will help you make a major decision—for example, what courses to take in order to prepare for a career. Also consider the interviewee's purpose in speaking to you. The person may want to share important information about new developments in science, business, or government. Or the person may want to publicize a project, film, or book. Both of you should agree on what the purpose of the interview will be.

_____ **1. Confirm arrangements.**
Prepare a letter introducing yourself and giving the purpose of the interview. Specify the best time and place for you, but accept any arrangement the interviewee prefers.

_____ **2. Arrange interview setting.**
Decide what would be the ideal setting. Be sure that you will be free from interruptions and distractions. If the interviewee's home or office would not be suitable, be prepared to suggest an alternative setting.

_____ **3. Become informed.**
Decide what books and magazines you would read and what people you would talk to in order to learn about the topic and the interviewee. List special vocabulary words you should understand, and look up these words. Also list one or two sources of current information on the topic, and at least one controversy connected with it.

_____ **4. Examine attitudes.**

List both your positive and negative attitudes toward the person and the topic. List the difficulties these attitudes might create. Describe ways you could overcome these difficulties.

_____ **5. Prepare opening remarks.**

Write out opening remarks, including the first question or questions you will ask. Be sure to remind the person of the purpose of the interview.

_____ **6. Plan how to record interview.**

Decide whether you will write down or tape-record responses (see Speaking Skills, lesson 4.2). List materials you will need. Describe how you will get the interviewee's permission if you use a tape recorder.

Preparing and Presenting

Working with another student, select a celebrity, politician, scientist, author, or other well-known person you would both like to interview. Then, working independently, prepare pre-interview checklists. Follow the checklist form given in the Guidelines section of this lesson. Complete every step on the checklist that you can do without actually contacting the interviewee. Be sure to do research on the person and topic of your planned interview. (See Speaking Skills, lesson 4.1.) As you complete each step, check off that item on your list. Type your checklist, or write it neatly. Exchange checklists with the other student.

Evaluating

As you read each other's checklists, ask yourselves the following questions:

1. Is the purpose of the interview specific enough? How could it be made more clear?

2. Which steps, if any, are not closely related to the purpose of the interview? In what ways could each step do more to achieve the purpose of the interview?

3. How *practical* is each step in the checklist? Would a student have the time, influence, or sources of information to complete all the steps?

4. How *appropriate* is each step in the checklist for the interviewee? Considering what I have learned, would this person be willing to be interviewed under these conditions?

5. What steps did the other student follow in doing the items in the checklist that I did not follow?

6. What steps did I follow in doing the items in the checklist that the other student did not follow?

After evaluating each other's checklists, return each one to the person who wrote it. Discuss the ways in which each checklist could be improved.

Making an Oral Inquiry about a Job

Many of the job inquiries you make will be oral rather than written. You may phone about a job you have seen advertised, or you may speak in person to a personnel manager or job recruiter. Whether you make such inquiries by phone or in person, you should remember several points:

- Know the name and title of the person to whom you must speak.
- Have ready a list of questions about the job, including questions about qualifications, responsibilities, hours, pay, and benefits.
- Have pen and paper ready in order to take notes on your conversation.
- Identify yourself clearly at the beginning of the conversation. If necessary, add helpful information, such as "We talked at my high school's Career Day last week."
- Explain the reason for your inquiry. For example, are you interested in an interview, or do you just want information?
- Listen carefully to the other person, and be prepared to answer questions about your work experience and interests.
- Follow up your conversation with a letter or phone call confirming the arrangements made during the conversation, or simply thanking the person in case you have decided not to inquire further about the job.

ACTIVITIES

1. Read the help-wanted ads in your local newspaper. Select three ads for jobs in which you might be interested. Working with another student, take turns role-playing a telephone inquiry about each job. You can be asking for an interview, or simply requesting more information about the job.

2. Invite a personnel director or recruiter from a local company to speak to your class. Ask him or her about the problems young people have when inquiring about job openings. Ask why some job applicants are successful and others are not.

career

4.2 Preparing Interview Questions

Deciding How to Record Responses during an Interview

Two possible ways you can record a person's responses during an interview are (1) written notes and (2) tape recording. Each method has advantages and disadvantages.

Written notes are easy to refer to after the interview is over. You can rewrite and reorganize them before you turn the interview into a paper or article. A convenient way to take written notes is to write your interview questions in advance on separate index cards or separate pages of a notebook. As you ask each question, record the response underneath it. The disadvantage of written notes is that you must write down each response before you can ask the next question. This slows down the interview, and you may lose some information unless you write rapidly. If you take written notes, be sure to reread and clarify them while the interview is fresh in your mind. Once your notes are "cold," you may not be able to decipher them.

Tape recording is usually more convenient for the interviewer and the interviewee, and lets you record a person's exact words. Some people, however, are made nervous by tape recorders. Be sure to have the interviewee's permission before using one. Remember also to bring enough tape and spare batteries. The disadvantage of tape-recorded responses is that they must be transcribed, and it is difficult to find a specific question and response without advancing and re-winding the tape many times.

ACTIVITY

1. Working with another student, draw up a list of ten interview questions to ask a teacher or other person at your school. Then interview the person together, with one of you taking written notes and the other tape-recording the interview. Write up the written and recorded responses into brief articles. Compare your articles, and discuss with the class whether the written or tape-recorded notes produced more interesting or usable material.

research

How to Write
Effective Interview Questions

Writing effective questions is the most important part of preparing for an inteview. Good questions will help you obtain interesting, informative responses. Weak questions will lead to dull, confusing, uninformative responses. Try to avoid asking questions that can be simply answered *yes* or *no*. Ask for specific information in your questions. One way to get this information is by preparing questions that begin with *who, what, where, when, how,* or *why.*

You should be prepared to ask *follow-up questions.* One kind of follow-up question can be asked when the interviewee gives you an unexpected piece of information. You should follow up the person's response by asking for further information on the subject, even though it is not covered in your prepared questions.

A second kind of follow-up question should be asked when the interviewee has used a term or name with which you are not familiar. Ask for a brief explanation before you continue with your prepared questions.

When you have finished asking a series of related questions, summarize the interviewee's responses before you go on to the next group. Such a summary will enable the person to correct any misunderstanding you may have about his or her responses.

Working with the Model

Professional interviewer Larry Wilde conducted the following interview with Woody Allen in the late 1960s (this was before Allen's career as a movie director). As you read the interview, think about the interviewer's purpose and the way his questions help achieve that purpose.

WILDE: Woody, what made you stop writing for other comedians and become one yourself?

ALLEN: Writing for other comedians as a lifetime pursuit is a blind alley. I never had any intention of continuing writing for other comedians before I started performing. At that time, I was just writing for them to earn a living. And I was interested in writing for the theatre, which I'm still interested in doing. But then I got interested in performing. It occurred to me it might

model

be a good avenue of expression. So I decided to try it. But there is no future in being a TV writer. You can hack around from show to show and you're always worried—is the comedian you're writing for going to be dropped because of bad ratings? And if he is dropped you may find yourself moving three thousand miles to the other coast to write for a new comedian. It's a rough business.

WILDE: When you began creating material for your act, did you first decide what your image was and then begin to write?

ALLEN: No. There was never any sense of image. I still don't have any sense of that at all. I just wrote what I thought was funny and wanted to perform it. I found after a year or two of performing some sort of image formed itself. The critics and the people would come away and agree on certain images they had of me . . . certain aspects . . . I think the worst thing I could do would be to believe the images of me I read in the newspapers.

WILDE: Then you're simply doing what you feel is the right thing for you?

ALLEN: Yeah, whatever I feel is funny, I do, no matter what it is, without any regard to the subject matter, and if an image emerges, fine!

WILDE: Is it easier to write jokes for yourself than it was for the other comedians?

ALLEN: It has different problems. Other comedians are much less selective. I would write jokes for ten other comedians and they would use eight out of ten, finally, in putting together their acts . . . and it would work. I find I'm much more cowardly. I use like one out of ten jokes. I'm much more selective with my own material. I pamper myself more.

WILDE: You write ten jokes and only choose one. After a while what percentage of the jokes work for you?

ALLEN: What finally remains in my act is really a very, very small percentage of what I come up with. When I write a piece of material . . . something occurs to me at some point, an idea, a notion that I think would be funny or something that actually happened to me and I try and develop a long story on it with as many laughs coming as close together as possible. I find after I'm finished I have a lot of jokes, a lot of remarks to make—comments—and as I look at them I find ninety percent of them don't meet the standards I would like to present publicly to an audience. Then I condense what was a twenty-minute thing to six minutes and I go out and do it, and I find my judgment was wrong on part of it. The audience is not laughing at some parts where I thought they would laugh.

They're laughing at things I couldn't imagine they would laugh at, so I adjust it further and it comes down to four minutes, and gradually it's honed down. So in order to get a half hour act it takes me a long time, and I have to write a lot of material.

WILDE: How do you go about writing a piece of material for yourself?

ALLEN: There are two ways I have of working. One is spontaneously, where during my daily activities funny things occur to me. Ideas for jokes, premises. I write them down.

WILDE: Excuse me, what do you mean by a "premise"?

ALLEN: A premise would be like: If I was caught in an elevator during the blackout, trying to move a piano by myself. Now, that's not good for one joke. I found that that would lead me to a whole funny story of how I decided to move from one apartment to another in the same building ... why I decided to move, what was wrong with the first apartment, how I looked for the second apartment, why I didn't have moving men do it because I wanted to do it myself, and finally the hard work of doing it. Trying to lift the piano and getting into a little elevator with it ... trying to hold it up for the minute it takes to go up to the twentieth floor, and then the blackout comes and I'm stuck for six hours trying to hold the piano up. I find each step of the way should be told with as strong a joke as possible.

WILDE: Then by "premise" you mean a story that has a beginning, a middle, and an end?

ALLEN: Exactly. That idea which gives you a plot line to talk about for an extended length of time.

WILDE: And allows you to hang jokes or laughs on.

ALLEN: Right. As opposed to a single joke that would occur to me.

WILDE: I didn't mean to interrupt you. Then what do you do?

ALLEN: That's all right. So these premises or single jokes occur to me. I could be walking down the street or shaving, and I write them down on anything handy, like matchbooks or napkins, and I throw them in a drawer at home. Then when the time comes that I've got to get new material for appearances, I take them and lay them out in the room and I see which jokes are worth going for. I then combine those with the ones I write by mechanical process. That is, sitting down, without notes—just knowing that in three nights I'm going to appear ... and I've got to prefabricate a piece of material.

WILDE: Since it takes a certain amount of time to break in jokes or lines, or a premise, would you take a chance on a major TV program with material you had just written two or three days before?

model

ALLEN: I wouldn't want to and try to avoid it as much as possible. Sometimes it's unavoidable, and sometimes I have gone on television with things I have never edited or done anyplace before. I find it's not as good as things I've done before but that's because ... say a routine I want to do consists of twenty laughs, and if I do it in a club, I find there's really only sixteen laughs and finally four laughs are knocked out because they consistently don't work. The bit becomes tight and has a lot of punch ... but if I do that routine on television first and I discover there are four weak spots, it's been seen by everybody. It's too late, and those four weak spots considerably weaken the whole thing.

WILDE: Do you try out new jokes on friends or anybody who will listen, as some comedians do?

ALLEN: Not really, because I find it doesn't mean anything. It can only be discouraging.

WILDE: You wait until you get in front of an audience?

ALLEN: Yeah, that's really where it counts. And not these late second-show spots where a lot of performers feel they should try out a new piece of material because if it doesn't go over they won't get hurt very much. The best thing to do is to come right out and lead with your best. Your Saturday night full-house show is the perfect opportunity, because the conditions are right and the new material stands a better chance. You're asking for trouble by breaking in material under any conditions that are not the best. If you tell it to friends, it's very depressing. They'll say, "Yes, this joke is very funny, but that one doesn't thrill me too much." There's no point in hearing that from one or two people. It's better to do the joke before two hundred people. If someone says that joke isn't so great, I get very shaky and I might not try it on the floor.

WILDE: How do you go about creating a joke? The actual process?

ALLEN: That's very hard to answer. It depends on circumstances. When you do it, say when you're hired to write for Sid Caesar, there's a lot of different ways of doing it than you'd do it for yourself.

WILDE: How about just for yourself?

ALLEN: It's very, very intangible, really. Suppose I'm going to write the story about trying to move the piano. I try to take it right from the top. As far back as I can go. For instance, the first thought that occurs to you is getting stuck with the piano, and then I start retracing this backwards. Why am I moving myself? Because I don't want to spend the money on moving men. Why do I want to move? Because I don't like my apartment and I always have trouble with apartments. Why do I

model

always have trouble with them? What other apartments have I lived in? What was my apartment in Brooklyn like? Why was it poor? Because my parents couldn't afford very much rent. What did my parents do for a living? I find this can go back and back forever. So I might start with the business about the piano by saying my mother married my father because he was a cab-driver and finally through a lot of stories of how she met him and how they moved to Brooklyn and how they got their apartment and by a lot of circuitous talk, a lot of jokes hopefully, I finally get up to the part of the piano.

WILDE: Someone taking a course in journalism or creative writing or how to write a novel can learn certain basic methods and techniques. Are there also rules for creating jokes?

ALLEN: I don't think you can learn to write jokes. Not good ones. You can learn certain mechanical things — to create variations of other jokes written, even good variations, but it's nothing you can learn. It's purely inborn.

WILDE: Are there different kinds of jokes?

ALLEN: I don't know what you mean by that.

WILDE: Well, some jokes are two or three sentences, others last for five or six sentences. They have names.

ALLEN: There are names that drift around, like a "one-liner" or an "ad-lib," but that's no advantage or help to you when you're

model

writing material. . . . You can't learn how to write funny things . . . how to write individual jokes.

WILDE: Then it depends on the individual mind seeing a specific incident and seeing it humorously and expressing the humor he sees in words?

ALLEN: Yes. That's what is so tricky about it. Given an absolutely straight sentence, with no punch line to it whatsoever, you can have twenty people read the sentence, and Jonathan Winters reads it or W. C. Fields—it's just going to be funny without changing a word, for some intangible, built-in thing that's beyond reason. You see, it's not the jokes. . . . It isn't the jokes that do it, and the comedian has nothing to do with the jokes. It's the individual himself.

QUESTIONS

A. Think about the purpose of the interview you have just read.

1. How would you state the purpose of the interview?

2. Which questions show the purpose of the interview most clearly?

3. Write three other questions that could have been asked to help achieve the purpose of the interview.

4. Suppose Wilde had never interviewed a comedian before. What might the purpose of his interview have been? Which questions do you think he would have asked? What additional questions do you think he would have asked?

5. Suppose this interview had been conducted in 1981, after Allen had directed several successful movies. What do you think might have been the purpose of the interview then? Write at least three questions that would help achieve that purpose.

B. Think about the interviewer's questions.

1. Of the twenty questions the interviewer asked, how many appear to have been prepared in advance? How many are follow-up questions?

2. Identify two follow-up questions based on information that the interviewer had not expected to hear. Why do you think he asked each of these questions?

3. Identify two follow-up questions in which the interviewer is asking for clarification. At what other places in the interview do you think he might have asked for clarification?

4. Find the two places in the interview where Wilde says, "Excuse me" or apologizes. Why would it be a good idea to say such things while asking follow-up questions?

5. Write at least two further follow-up questions that might have been asked in this interview.

Guidelines

Good interview questions encourage good responses from the person you are speaking with. The following table shows seven differences between good questions and poor questions.

A good question . . .	A poor question . . .
• encourages an extended answer • is stated concisely	• can be answered "Yes" or "No" • takes so long that the interviewee loses track of the question.
• is based on a sound knowledge of the topic • encourages a specific, informative answer • makes the interviewee think before answering • shows an original or unusual perspective on the topic	• reveals the interviewer's lack of preparation • encourages a vague, rambling answer • permits a glib, unthinking answer • is obvious, and has probably been asked dozens of times by other interviewers
• builds on preceding responses	• is asked because it was next on the list, even if it is inappropriate

ACTIVITY

1. The following interview contains four poor questions. Read the interview, then decide which characteristic of good questions in the above table each question fails to meet.

SPORTSCASTER: Great game! Has the team ever played better?
COACH JONES: Nope.
SPORTSCASTER: I don't suppose you've had a season like this since you won the pennant in 1976. Do you feel as great this year as you did then?
COACH JONES: Well, actually . . . we lost the pennant in '76.
SPORTSCASTER: I think that must really be something, I mean, having players you can be so proud of . . . I wonder if Chuck Woodbridge will make it off the bench this season . . . And didn't Ed Murphy play well despite injuries? Aren't you proud, you know, a 14-2 season . . . ?

COACH JONES: I didn't get all of your questions ... Did you say Ed? Yeah, he played well, but who did you say I was keeping on the bench? Rick?

SPORTSCASTER: Chuck ... oh, never mind, I have a few more questions here ... um, do you think the team can go all the way to the pennant?

COACH JONES: Sure, why not?

Preparing and Presenting

Working with another student, decide on a person you would both like to interview. The person may be famous, such as a politician, entertainer, or sports figure. Or the person may be well known only within a given field, such as science or business. In either case, the person's achievements should be interesting enough to justify an interview. Research the person to gather material for an interview. (See Speaking Skills, lesson 4.1.) You should each decide on the purpose of your interview, and write down the purpose. Then write ten good interview questions that would lead to informative responses. Think about the information you have learned about the interviewee. Think of a subject area in which the person might give you unexpected information in his or her responses. Write at least two follow-up questions you could ask in response to this information. Think of a subject area in which the person might say something you would not understand. Write two follow-up questions you could ask so that the interviewee would clarify these remarks.

Evaluating

Exchange your list of questions with the other student. As you read each other's lists, ask yourselves the following questions:

1. How clear is the purpose of this interview? How appropriate is this purpose to the person who is being interviewed? In what ways, if any, could the purpose be made clearer or more appropriate?

2. How well does each of the prepared questions help to achieve this purpose? What other questions, if any, could also achieve this purpose?

3. Which questions, if any, do not follow the rules given in the Guidelines section? How could these questions be improved?

4. In what way is each follow-up question based on information the person might give in his or her responses? What other follow-up questions should an interviewer be prepared to ask?

5. What questions, if any, show a lack of preparation? What sources could the interviewer consult in order to write better questions?

6. What good questions did the other student write that I did not? What good questions did I write that the other student did not?

Interviewing Candidates and Public Officials

As a citizen, you should learn to question public officials effectively about their duties and responsibilities. As a voter, you should be able to question candidates about their platforms and qualifications. When interviewing a candidate or public official, remember these points:

- Have your questions written out beforehand.
- Write good interview questions that require clear, detailed responses. Avoid questions that can be easily evaded or answered "yes" or "no."
- Treat candidates and officials politely and respectfully, but don't be overawed by their titles.
- If a candidate or official answers in "officialese"—jargon that is difficult to understand—rephrase your question to obtain a clearer and more specific answer.

ACTIVITIES

1. Interview three candidates for student government (or members of student government) about their experience and qualifications, and the offices they are seeking (or currently occupy). Compare their responses on the following topics:
   - the importance of student government
   - the most significant problem confronting your school
   - their solutions for such a problem
   - their plans for the school's future
   - how student government can help you or your class
   - how you or your class can help student government

2. Interview a person in city or community government about his or her duties, responsibilities, and plans. You might question a supervisor, a member of the school board, an official in the assessor's office, a member of the police commission, or a candidate for one of these positions. Ask question on the following topics:
   - how the official is made accountable to the public
   - what laws or regulations require the official to share information with the public
   - the major problems in the official's job
   - the future scope and responsibility of the position the official holds

citizenship

4.3 Conducting Interviews

Using Language Appropriate to the Situation

Whether you are having a conversation, conducting an interview, or giving a formal speech, you should be careful to use language that is appropriate to the setting, the subject, and the other people present. Keep the following guidelines in mind:

- Your language should be neither too formal nor too informal for the situation.
- Be very cautious when using slang or colloquialisms. Some people may feel that colloquial language shows a lack of respect for them, or that it reflects ignorance on your part.
- Be sure that your language is not too technical for the people to whom you are speaking. If you must use specialized terms from the arts or sciences, define each term the first time you use it. If you are interviewing a person who works in a technical field, learn the basic vocabulary of the field while you prepare for the interview.
- Be alert to nonverbal cues from your listeners. If they seem confused or offended by the way you speak, adjust your language.

ACTIVITIES

1. Listen to people from one age group or background talking to people from a different age group or background. You might, for example, listen to a scientist talking to nonscientists, children talking to adults, or city tourists talking to people in the country. Make notes on the difficulties each group has in understanding the other, and in making itself understood. Discuss your findings with the class.

2. Think about the following list of people you might speak with or interview. Decide which kinds of language might be appropriate and inappropriate in each situation, and explain why.
   - a woman who just celebrated her one-hundredth birthday
   - a five-year-old just starting school
   - a famous rock singer (real or imaginary)

language

How to Conduct Interviews

After you have prepared for an interview and have written questions that will produce informative answers, the next step is to organize the interview so that it will go smoothly.

Organize your interview questions into three parts: introduction, body, and conclusion. In the *introduction,* remind the person being interviewed of the purpose of the interview. Ask the opening question you have prepared. Because your opening question should help put the interviewee at ease, it should not require too long or complex an answer.

In the *body* of the interview, ask your other prepared questions. You should be ready to change the order of your questions if it will help the conversation flow smoothly. For instance, if the interviewee brings up a topic at the beginning of the interview that you had planned to discuss later, you should ask your prepared questions at that point, rather than waiting. You should also be ready to ask follow-up questions about unexpected topics or topics that need clarification.

In the *conclusion* of the interview, ask your final questions. These should be more general questions about the person's life, work, or future plans. Then summarize the responses you have received throughout the interview, and ask the interviewee to clarify any points you have not understood. Obtain permission to use the interview material, and agree on the person's right of approval. (For example, if you are going to publish the interview, agree on whether the interviewee has the right to approve or revise the manuscript.) Thank the interviewee, and send him or her a letter of thanks the next day.

Working with the Model

Ross is interviewing Cathy Imamura, a young novelist, for a local newspaper. As you read the interview, notice the way the questions are organized.

model

ROSS: Cathy, at the age of twenty, you've just published your first novel—a science-fiction novel. I'm going to be asking you about your writing and your new career. But first, I think our readers would like to know about your background. Can you tell us something about your family, and how you got such an early start as a writer?

73

model

CATHY: Well, Ross, there's really very little extraordinary about my family. My parents run a small garage, and my mother also works as a bookkeeper. My older brother is a graduate student in physics, and my sister's in high school. None of them is a writer, but I've been writing ever since I was a kid.

ROSS: How long would that be?

CATHY: Oh, I started at a very early age—eight or ten, perhaps. I know I was writing stories by the time I was twelve—I still have some of them. Of course, they're pretty bad.

ROSS: How many other people read your stories?

CATHY: No one—I was too shy! It wasn't till I was in high school that I felt confident enough to let someone read my work. Fortunately, I received real encouragement.

ROSS: Who encouraged you?

CATHY: Miss Vollmer, my English teacher—I hope she's reading this, she's really a wonderful person! She read my stories—I had *reams* of them!—and urged me to polish the ones that showed promise.

ROSS: "Reams" of stories?

CATHY: At least twenty. Poor Miss Vollmer—she read them all! She helped me decide on four that I should try to publish.

ROSS: How successful were you in getting them published?

CATHY: Well, I had beginner's luck. The first story I submitted was "Old Ironsides"—a very short, humorous story about a robot. An editor liked it, bought it, and published it. I was absolutely amazed. I was paid fifty dollars, and I felt as though it were a million.

ROSS: What luck did you have with the other stories?

CATHY: Very little, at first. I had two rejections in a row, and I was very discouraged. It was a hard time, because I was just entering college, and I didn't know if I'd have enough time to write. But Miss Vollmer gave me pep talks, and my parents were very supportive. They told me they had a lot of faith in me, and they trusted me to make the right choices. As it turned out, I was able to write *and* go to school—if I disciplined myself. And then I had my second sale.

ROSS: "The Ravens of the Moon"? I read that when it came out last year, and I thought it was a wonderful story.

CATHY: Thank you, I really appreciate that, because it was so difficult to write. The story takes place in the distant future. It's about two children who discover they have telepathic powers and who have to escape from the authorities in order to avoid being killed. Most of the story describes the gradual discovery of these powers—and that is such a hard thing to write about! I went through four drafts, and I had to do more work

model

on the story after it was accepted. I'm still not entirely happy with it.

ROSS: And yet the story had a very favorable reception. How did that make you feel?

CATHY: Good, of course ... I was very pleased that others liked it. But, you know, a writer really has to please herself first. I'm my own severest critic.

ROSS: When did you begin work on your novel?

CATHY: Oh, I began *Footsteps on a Distant Star* when I was seventeen. But at first it was just an adventure story, and I lost interest in it after thirty or forty pages. Then, in my freshman year, I took it out of my desk and started work on it again. I realized that it could become a novel with ideas as well as adventures.

ROSS: How easy was it to complete *Footsteps*?

CATHY: Oh, terribly hard. As you know, the book is about a group of people who are exiled from Earth because of their political ideas. They believe in democracy, freedom of speech, and so forth at a time when it's not safe to do so. They're supposed to go to a prison planet in the Centaurus system, but there's

an accident with the space-warp drive—very convenient for the author!—and they wind up on an uninhabited world. And there they have to put their political ideas into effect, and they find it isn't so easy.

ROSS: Critics have praised your descriptions of these colonists trying to put democracy in action while struggling against a hostile environment. How difficult were those scenes to write?

CATHY: Not as difficult as you might think—that was what excited me about the novel, and I had plenty of ideas. Actually, the stardrive stuff gave me the most trouble. But my brother, who is in physics and is a real whiz, read those parts over and gave me some very good pointers. He said it was less important to make the physics accurate, since hyperspace is all fantasy, anyhow, than to make it *convincing*. And I think I succeeded.

ROSS: And that was just before you submitted the novel for publication?

CATHY: No, that was when I spent all summer rewriting it for the third time! Then I asked one of my magazine editors to recommend a book publisher with a science-fiction list. He recommended three, and the first one took *Footsteps* as a paperback original, after I'd made some changes.

ROSS: What were those changes?

CATHY: Mostly shortening the book by some 10,000 words. That was very painful, but I realize now that the novel is better for it.

ROSS: In general, how "painful" is writing for you?

CATHY: Quite painful, I'm afraid. "Old Ironsides" was a snap to write, but that was a fluke. The other stories and the novel involved a lot of drudgery, as well as the excitement of creating characters and new worlds.

ROSS: What science-fiction writers have influenced you?

CATHY: Well, Ursula Le Guin, of course. All the critics see her influence. There are other writers I admire greatly, but I don't think I could ever write like them. Philip K. Dick, for example: he writes such funny dialogue, and he has wonderful characters. That's really his private preserve, though, and I don't think I could ever poach on it.

ROSS: What are you working on now?

CATHY: I have a second novel. I'm almost halfway through the first draft, and I may finish it by the end of the year. But you have to remember that I'm a full-time student, and until I get my B.A., writing is only a sideline.

ROSS: How much time are you able to give to writing?

model

CATHY: One to two hours a day. That seems like very little time, but if you really *write* during that hour or two, you'd be amazed how much you can accomplish.

ROSS: How rapidly *do* you write—if you don't mind answering?

CATHY: Three pages a day, about twenty pages a week. That means that the first draft of a novel would take me six to ten months. Of course, professionals work much faster, but right now I'm more concerned with quality than quantity.

ROSS: Cathy, in this interview you've spoken a great deal about your luck and about the help you've received from others. I think most readers, though, would see you as a hard-working writer who has really earned her success. Drawing on your own experience, what advice would you give to other writers who are just starting out?

CATHY: In three words: Stick with it. Write, write, revise, and write some more. Finish what you begin, submit your best work, and don't become discouraged. It's possible you may never be successful, but unless you try—and I mean *really* try— you'll never know what you could have done.

QUESTIONS

A. Think about the introduction of the interview.
   1. What is the purpose of Ross' opening remarks?
   2. What is the subject of the first question? Why is this a good question with which to begin the interview?

B. Think about the body of the interview.
   1. In what order are the questions arranged?
   2. How many of these are follow-up questions?
   3. Write two other follow-up questions that Ross might have asked.
   4. One of Ross' remarks is a statement rather than a question. How could he have turned this into a question?

C. Think about the conclusion of the interview.
   1. How does Ross summarize the interview? In what other way could he have summarized it?
   2. What is the subject of the concluding question? Why is this an appropriate question to ask at the end of the interview?
   3. Write at least two other concluding questions that Ross could have asked Cathy Imamura.

D. Listen to an interview on radio or television. As you listen, take notes on the number and kinds of questions the interviewer asked in each part of the interview. As you look over your notes, see if you can identify the introduction, body, and conclusion of the interview. Think about how clear, interesting, or informative the interview was, and decide whether it was well organized, or whether it could have been better organized.

Guidelines

The following guidelines can help make an interview pleasant and informative:

1. *Maintain a friendly, interested attitude.* Make it clear that you are eager to learn about the person and the topic. Always be polite, even if the interviewee is irritable. If the conversation wanders from the subject, bring it back tactfully. Say, "I'd like to get back to this subject," rather than "You didn't answer my question." Don't badger a person who obviously does not want to answer a question. Polite, patient persistence will produce the best results.

2. *Be alert for nonverbal cues.* Observe the interviewee's facial expressions, posture, and gestures. If the person appears restless, he or she may feel that you don't understand the topic. If the person appears puzzled, you may have asked a confusing question that you should clarify. If the interviewee seems pleased by a particular line of questioning, you should ask follow-up questions on that topic.

3. *Make continual checks for understanding.* Ask follow-up questions whenever the interviewee talks about a person, book, or issue you do not understand. Summarize an especially long or complicated answer, and ask the interviewee if you have understood it correctly. At the end of the interview, briefly sum up the person's responses, and ask if he or she has anything to add.

ACTIVITY

1. Listen to an interview on radio or television. Note any places in the interview where the interviewee seems irritated, bored, or offended by the questions. Observe how the interviewer handles—or fails to handle—such reactions. Evaluate the interviewer's behavior. Decide in what ways the interviewer handled the interviewee's reactions well, and in what ways the interviewer should have acted differently.

Preparing and Presenting

Working with another student, decide on a person to interview. It can be one of the people you chose in lesson 4.1 or 4.2, or it can be another person. One of you will role-play the interviewer, and the other the interviewee. Each of you should research the person independently. The interviewer will gather material on questions to ask. The interviewer should also do all the steps in the pre-interview checklist that will help prepare good questions. The interviewee will gather material that he or she can use in answering possible questions. Although you should not rehearse the interview as you would a play, you should discuss the topic and possible questions to be sure that you are both prepared.

Role-play your interview before the class. Your prepared questions should take about ten minutes. Your follow-up questions may add three to five minutes to the length of the interview.

Evaluating

Ask your classmates to use the following checklists in evaluating your interview. Each item may be rated on a scale from 0 (very poor) to 10 (excellent). In the "Example" column, each student should write a specific example that shows why the interviewer or interviewee received that rating.

EVALUATIVE CHECKLIST: INTERVIEWER

Category	Rating	Example
1. Showed thorough knowledge of interview topic		
2. Understood vocabulary of interview topic		
3. Was aware of current information and controversies on topic		
4. Had good opening remarks which restated purpose of interview		
5. Asked clear questions that led to informative answers		
6. Organized interview into introduction, body, and conclusion		
7. Was sensitive to interviewee's responses and nonverbal clues		
8. Asked follow-up questions where appropriate		
9. Used summaries where appropriate		
10. Maintained polite, friendly, interested attitude		

EVALUATIVE CHECKLIST: INTERVIEWEE

Category	Rating	Example
1. Was polite and responsive to interviewer		
2. Answered questions fully and directly		
3. Showed thorough knowledge of interview topic		
4. Clarified answers in response to interviewer's follow-up questions		
5. Summarized responses whenever requested by interviewer		

After the class has evaluated your interview, read the evaluation forms. Decide which parts of the interview went well, and which parts could be improved. Make necessary changes in the questions and responses, then practice the interview by yourselves.

Being Interviewed for a Job

When you are interviewed for a job, you must present yourself as competent, confident, and likeable. Here are important guidelines to follow:

- Arrive a few minutes early for the interview.
- Dress neatly, even if good clothes are not required for the job.
- Bring an extra copy of your résumé, a list of references, your social security card, and a pen.
- Be prepared to answer questions about your education, experience, qualifications, and interests.
- Be confident and polite, but communicate your enthusiasm about the job.
- Don't slouch, smoke, mumble, or chew gum.
- Ask intelligent questions about the job and the company.
- Be alert to cues that the interview is over.
- Next day, write a letter thanking the interviewer for his or her time and interest.

ACTIVITIES

1. Invite a person who conducts interviews with prospective employees to speak to your class. Ask the interviewer to describe the qualities he or she looks for in an interviewee, and to list the things that a person being interviewed can do to improve his or her chances of being hired.

2. Research three or more jobs, making a list of qualifications, duties, hours, pay, and chances for promotion for each job. Working with another student, role-play an interview for one of these job positions. Let the class decide by ballot whether the person being interviewed should get the job, and ask them to discuss the reasons for their decision.

career

5 Expository Speaking

Much of what you have learned and of what you help others learn is communicated through expository speaking, the kind of communication people use to learn and to teach.

After working through this chapter, you should be able to

- explain a process
- arrange the information in an expository speech
- use notes to assist your speaking
- use visual aids to enhance communication
- adapt your speech to your audience
- improve your speaking through practice sessions
- respond to questions from your listeners
- prepare and present an analytical expository speech

The Speaking Skills lessons in this chapter will help you prepare and present expository speeches. In these lessons, you will learn to

- recognize the differences between written and spoken language
- use the steps in preparing an expository speech
- use transitions effectively
- use imagination in planning your presentations
- use an Audience Analysis Checklist
- deal with anxiety about speaking
- choose effective words

The Skills for Success lessons will show how you can use your expository speaking skills in your career and as a citizen. In these lessons, you will learn to

- explain a work process
- use visual aids to explain a work process
- introduce a speaker
- report an incident
- present an award
- give constructive criticism
- give testimony
- explain a document

5.1 Warming Up: Explaining a Familiar Process

Spoken and Written Language

Unlike written language, spoken language must be instantly understood. A listener cannot go back as a reader can and reread what has just been said. Spoken language is also more direct and personal than written language. Effective spoken language differs from good written language in these ways:

- Speakers use everyday language and familiar words more often than writers do.
- Speakers use shorter and simpler sentences than writers do.
- Speakers repeat key ideas more often than writers do.
- Speakers use transitional words and phrases more often than writers do.
- Speakers are able to select words and phrases to suit a particular audience more precisely than writers can, because writers often do not know who their readers will be.

ACTIVITIES

1. Keep a notebook in which you record spoken phrases you found effective; overworked expressions and trite phrases you found irritating; and new terms or phrases you think a speaker would find useful. At the end of two weeks, discuss your entries with other students.

2. Study several speeches recorded from television, reprinted in *Vital Speeches of the Day*, or collected in book form. For each speech, list all the examples of each of the characteristics of effective spoken language given above. Come to class prepared to point out these characteristics in the most effective of the three speeches you have chosen.

language

How to Explain a Familiar Process

You have undoubtedly explained a process—how to do something or how something works—many times in your life. You may not have realized it, but each time you explained something, you were giving a short expository speech. Many expository speeches are given to explain how to do something. The process the speaker explains to the audience may be some simple task, such as how to build a greenhouse, or it may be a more complex process, such as how a scientist reasons.

There are three steps to preparing a speech that explains a process. First, fix the specific purpose of the speech firmly in mind. In this case, the purpose is to inform the audience about a particular process. Usually, it is best to write your specific purpose—for example, "The purpose of this speech is to explain how to make woodblock prints to my speech class." Next, think through all the steps in the process, and the order in which they occur. These steps will be the main ideas in your speech. Finally, arrange the speech in a pattern that will help your listeners grasp the explanation of the process.

Working with the Model

Like baking a cake, reasoning scientifically is a process. Nearly a hundred years ago, British scientist and philosopher Thomas Huxley faced the task of explaining how a scientist reasons to an audience of the general public. A portion of that explanation follows. Study it carefully, and then answer the questions that follow it.

model

The method of scientific investigation is nothing but the expression of the necessary mode of working of the human mind. You will understand this better, perhaps, if I give you some familiar example. You have all heard it repeated, I dare say, that men of science work by means of induction and deduction. It is imagined by many that the operations of the common mind cannot be compared with these processes, and that they have to be acquired by a sort of special apprenticeship to the craft.

There is a well-known incident in one of Molière's plays, where the author makes the hero express unbounded delight on being told that he had been talking prose during the whole of his life. In the same way, I trust, you will be delighted with yourselves, on the discovery that

model

you have been acting on the principles of inductive and deductive philosophy during the same period. Probably there is no one here who has not in the course of the day had occasion to set in motion a complex train of reasoning of the very same kind as that which a scientific man goes through in tracing the causes of natural phenomena.

A very trivial circumstance will serve to exemplify this. Suppose you go into a fruiterer's shop, wanting an apple. You take up one, and, on biting it, you find it is sour. You look at it, and see that it is hard and green. You take up another one, and that too is hard, green, and sour. The shopman offers you a third. But before biting it you examine it, and find that it is hard and green, and you immediately say that you will not have it, as it must be sour, like those that you have already tried.

Nothing can be more simple than that, you think. But if you will take the trouble to analyze and trace out into its logical elements what has been done by the mind, you will be greatly surprised. In the first place, you have performed the operation of *induction*. You found that, in two experiences, hardness and greenness in apples went together with sourness. It was so in the first case, and it was confirmed by the second. True, it is a very small basis, but still it is enough to make an

model

induction from. You generalize the facts, and you expect to find sourness in apples where you get hardness and greenness. You found upon that a general law, that *all hard and green apples are sour;* and that, so far as it goes, is a perfect induction.

Well, having got your natural law in this way, when you are offered another apple which you find is hard and green, you say, "All hard and green apples are sour; this apple is hard and green, therefore this apple is sour." That train of reasoning is what logicians call a *syllogism.* And, by the help of further reasoning, you arrive at your final determination: "I will not have that apple." So that, you see, you have, in the first place, established a law by *induction,* and upon that you have founded a *deduction,* and reasoned out the special conclusion of the particular case.

Well now, suppose, having got your law, that at some time afterwards you are discussing the qualities of apples with a friend. You will say to him, "It is a very curious thing, but I find that all hard and green apples are sour!" Your friend says to you, "But how do you know that?" You at once reply, "Oh, because I have tried them over and over again, and have always found them to be so."

Well, if we were talking science instead of common sense, we should call that an *experimental verification.* And, if still opposed, you go further, and say, "I have heard from the people in Somersetshire and Devonshire, where a large number of apples are grown, that they have observed the same thing. It is also found to be the case in Normandy, and in North America. In short, I find it to be the universal experience of mankind wherever attention has been directed to the subject." Whereupon, your friend, unless he is a very unreasonable man, agrees with you, and is convinced that you are quite right in the conclusion you have drawn. He believes, although perhaps he does not know he believes it, that the more frequently experiments have been made, and results of the same kind arrived at, the more certain is the ultimate conclusion, and he disputes the question no further. He sees that the experiment has been tried under all sorts of conditions, as to time, place, and people, with the same result. He says with you, therefore, that the law you have laid down must be a good one, and he must believe it.

In science we do the same thing. The philosopher exercises precisely the same faculties, though in a much more delicate manner. In scientific inquiry, it becomes a matter of duty to expose a supposed law to every possible kind of verification. We take care, moreover, that this is done intentionally, and not left to a mere accident, as in the case of the apples. And in science, as in common life, our confidence in a law is in exact proportion to the absence of variation in the result of our experiments.

QUESTIONS

A. Look carefully for any unusual words or terms and for the main ideas in Huxley's explanation.

   1. Make a list of any words or terms Huxley used that you do not understand. Some of the terms in the model, such as *fruiterer's shop* (fruit store), are probably not familiar to you. Discuss with other students the words on your lists, until you are all certain you understand every sentence in the model. Consult a dictionary if necessary.

   2. What main ideas was Huxley trying to explain as he described the processes of induction and deduction?

B. Consider the fact that Huxley's lecture was given in the nineteenth century.

   1. How much of Huxley's explanations of induction and deduction made sense to you? Explain why you were confused by whatever didn't make sense to you.

   2. Rewrite Huxley's explanations of these methods of thinking in your own words. First, write a definition of inductive thinking and a definition of deductive thinking. Then think of an example to illustrate each kind of thinking. Finally, tell your complete explanation to a friend. You can tell how effective your explanation is by asking your friend whether he or she understood it.

Guidelines

In the model, only a portion of Huxley's speech was reprinted. A complete expository speech must be arranged in an introduction, body, and conclusion. The following outline is one example of how such a speech can be arranged.

I. Introduction

   A. Direct your audience's attention to the topic, not to yourself.

   B. State your specific purpose clearly.

   C. Preview your speech by briefly mentioning each of your main ideas.

II. Body

   A. State a main idea, keeping it clearly related to your purpose. (Limit your explanation to two to four main ideas.)

      1. ⎫
      2. ⎭ State and develop supporting ideas, using examples and illustrations. (You can have from two to four supporting ideas.)

   B. State a second main idea, keeping it clearly related to your purpose.

      1. ⎫
      2. ⎭ State and develop supporting ideas, using examples and illustrations.

C. State a third main idea, keeping it clearly related to your purpose.
    1.⎱ State and develop supporting ideas, using examples and illus-
    2.⎰ trations.

III. Conclusion

  A. Restate your main ideas.
  B. Emphasize any fact or example that you feel strongly illustrates your purpose.

Sometimes this organization is described by the rule "tell your listeners what you are going to tell them, tell them, and then tell your listeners what you have told them."

ACTIVITIES

1. Use the preceding outline format to outline the model. Find each main idea and its supporting ideas, and fit them into the outline format. What part or parts of a complete expository speech, as represented by the outline format, are missing from the Huxley selection?
2. Write an outline of a short speech, using the explanation you prepared of inductive and deductive reasoning as the body of the speech.

Preparing and Presenting _____

Prepare a three-minute expository speech on how to do something. Choose your own topic or use one of these:

- how to make potato salad
- how to eat a pomegranate
- how to warm up before jogging
- how to keep your Boston fern (or other plant) alive
- how to hook up your new speakers to your old receiver
- how to replace the plug on an electrical appliance
- how to throw a curve ball
- how to get a part-time job
- how to operate a video cassette recorder
- how to give a large dog a bath

Work through the following steps to prepare your speech:

1. Write your specific purpose. Your purpose is to inform or explain; your specific purpose is to explain the process you have chosen to the class.
2. Make sure you know the major steps (main ideas) involved in the process, and the order in which they are performed.
3. Prepare an outline of your speech, including an introduction, body, and conclusion.
4. Practice your speech by giving it to a partner. Have your partner write down anything that is unclear. After your practice session, adjust your speech so that the main ideas are clear.

Give your speech to the class.

Evaluating _____

Have your classmates answer these questions about your speech:

1. What was the speaker's specific purpose?
2. How did the speaker present a clear statement of the process to be explained? In what part of the speech did this statement occur?
3. What were the main ideas?
4. What main ideas were left out of the summary?
5. If the speech was too long, how could the speaker get it closer to the assigned length?
6. What (if anything) is still unclear to you about the process the speaker explained? How could the speaker make this part of the speech more clear?

Explaining a Work Process

Both at school and at work, you will often have to explain a process to another person. The process may be as simple as the routine for punching a time card, or it may be as complicated as the rules for using a computer terminal.

Whatever the process is, your explanation should have three parts. In the *introduction,* explain to the other person why the process is important, and what steps you will be describing. In the *body,* explain the steps one at a time, demonstrating or illustrating each of them. As you speak, observe your listener, to be sure he or she understands what you are saying. After each step, ask whether the person understands what you have said. In the *conclusion,* briefly go over the steps again, and remind your listener of any important rules or warnings.

ACTIVITIES

1. Pretend that a member of your class is a new student at your school. Explain to this student a process that takes place at your school; for example:
   - how to prepare a class schedule
   - how to register for a class
   - how to have a teacher sponsor your organization
   - how to find and check out a library book

2. Pretend that a member of your class is a co-worker in a business or office. Explain a work process to this student; for example:
   - how to use a cash register
   - how to prepare a fast-food lunch
   - how to take a customer order on the phone
   - how to find an item in the stock room

career

5.2 Organizing the Information in an Expository Speech

Preparing an Expository Speech

Here are the steps in preparing and presenting an expository speech. Sometimes you can complete a step quickly; nevertheless, be sure to check your work against all the steps on this list when you are preparing an expository speech.

1. Select your topic.
2. Do enough research to become familiar with your topic.
3. Analyze your audience.
4. Narrow your topic.
5. Write the specific purpose of your speech.
6. Complete your research, using several sources.
7. Decide what pattern—chronological, spatial, or topical—you will use to organize your information. You may decide instead to organize your speech in terms of causes and their effects, or problems and their solutions.
8. Write an outline of the main ideas of your speech. State your main ideas as sentences.
9. Add supporting ideas and examples under each main idea in your outline. State your supporting ideas and examples as sentences or phrases.
10. Decide what visual aids, if any, will enhance your speech.
11. Prepare the introduction of your speech.
12. Prepare your speaking notes.
13. Give your speech for a friend or classmate.
14. Revise your speech, based on your listener's suggestions after the practice session.
15. Deliver your speech to your audience.
16. Ask your listeners what they thought of your speech. Following their suggestions will make your future speeches even better.

planning

How to Organize the Information in an Expository Speech

Arranging your information in patterns helps your listeners understand what you have to say. A *chronological pattern* presents the parts of a speaker's information in the order in which they occurred. For example, you would tell your audience how to prepare a car for a new paint job by describing each of the steps in chronological order. *Spatial patterns* present the information in terms of physical spaces that are familiar to the audience. If you give a speech about the cheeses of France by explaining which cheeses come from each region of France, you are using spatial organization.

A *topical pattern* presents subdivisions of the subject of the speech, discussing the significant people, ideas, and events associated with each subdivision. If you organized your talk about French cheeses in terms of the three major categories of cheese—soft, semisoft, and hard—you would be using a topical pattern.

There are two other patterns, but speakers use them less often than these first three. Speakers sometimes organize their information in terms of *causes and their effects,* and sometimes in terms of *problems and their solutions.*

Begin planning your expository speech by choosing a topic and narrowing it to workable proportions. Suppose you choose genetic engineering as your topic. You could narrow this topic to the research applications of genetic engineering or to the industrial applications of genetic engineering. If you decide to talk about the industrial applications of genetic engineering, you could narrow your topic even further, and talk about the development of a bacterium that ingests oil spills.

At this stage, you should write your specific purpose. In any expository speech, your general purpose is to transmit information. In this expository speech, your specific purpose is to tell the class about the development of a bacterium that ingests oil spills.

The next step is to decide which pattern will do the most to make your information easy to understand. You are then ready to begin outlining your speech.

In outlining a speech, it is acceptable to write supporting items as phrases. You will condense your outline even further when you prepare your speaking notes.

Working with the Model

In 1964, President Lyndon Johnson gave a speech to the graduating class of the University of Michigan. In this section of his speech, the President tells his audience how Americans can build the Great Society.

model

I have come today from the turmoil of your Capitol to the tranquility of your campus to speak about the future of our country. The purpose of protecting the life of our Nation and preserving the liberty of our citizens is to pursue the happiness of our people. Our success in that pursuit is the test of our success as a nation. For a century we labored to settle and to subdue a continent. For half a century, we called upon unbounded invention and untiring industry to create an order of plenty for all our people. The challenge of the next half century is whether we have the wisdom to use that wealth to enrich and elevate our national life, and to advance the quality of our American civilization.

Your imagination, your initiative, and your indignation will determine whether we build a society where progress is the servant of our needs, or a society where old values and new visions are buried under unbridled growth. For in your time we have the opportunity to move not only toward the rich society and the powerful society, but upward to the Great Society. The Great Society rests on abundance and liberty for all. It demands an end to poverty and racial injustice, to which we are totally committed in our time. But that is just the beginning. The Great Society is a place where every child can find knowledge to enrich his mind and to enlarge his talents. It is a place where leisure is a

welcome chance to build and reflect, not a feared cause of boredom and restlessness. It is a place where the city of man serves not only the needs of the body and the demands of commerce, but the desire for beauty and the hunger for community.

It is a place where man can renew contact with nature. It is a place which honors creation for its own sake and for what it adds to the understanding of the race. It is a place where men are more concerned with the quality of their goals than the quantity of their goods. But most of all, the Great Society is not a safe harbor, a resting place, a final objective, a finished work. It is a challenge constantly renewed, beckoning us toward a destiny where the meaning of our lives matches the marvelous products of our labor.

So I want to talk to you today about three places where we begin to build the Great Society—in our cities, in our countryside, and in our classrooms. Many of you will live to see the day, perhaps 50 years from now, when there will be 400 million Americans; four-fifths of them in urban areas. In the remainder of this century urban population will double, city land will double, and we will have to build homes, highways and facilities equal to all those built since this country was first settled. So in the next 40 years we must rebuild the entire urban United States.

Aristotle said, "Men come together in cities in order to live, but they remain together in order to live the good life."

It is harder and harder to live the good life in American cities today. The catalogue of ills is long: There is the decay of the centers and the despoiling of the suburbs. There is not enough housing for our people or transportation for our traffic. Open land is vanishing and old landmarks are violated. Worst of all, expansion is eroding the precious and time-honored values of community with neighbors and communion with nature. The loss of these values breeds loneliness and boredom and indifference. Our society will never be great until our cities are great. Today the frontier of imagination and innovation is inside those cities, and not beyond their borders. New experiments are already going on. It will be the task of your generation to make the American city a place where future generations will come, not only to live but to live the good life. . . .

A second place where we begin to build the Great Society is in our countryside. We have always prided ourselves on being not only America the strong and America the free, but America the beautiful. Today that beauty is in danger. The water we drink, the food we eat, the very air that we breathe, are threatened with pollution. Our parks are overcrowded. Our seashores overburdened. Green fields and dense forests are disappearing.

model

A few years ago we were greatly concerned about the Ugly American. Today we must act to prevent an Ugly America.

For once the battle is lost, once our natural splendor is destroyed, it can never be recaptured. And once man can no longer walk with beauty or wonder at nature, his spirit will wither and his sustenance be wasted.

A third place to build the Great Society is in the classrooms of America. There your children's lives will be shaped. Our society will not be great until every young mind is set free to scan the farthest reaches of thought and imagination. We are still far from that goal. Today, eight million adult Americans, more than the entire population of Michigan, have not finished five years of school. Nearly 20 million have not finished 8 years of school. Nearly 54 million, more than one-quarter of all America, have not even finished high school.

Each year more than 100,000 high school graduates, with proved ability, do not enter college because they cannot afford it. And if we cannot educate today's youth, what will we do in 1970 when elementary school enrollment will be 5 million greater than 1960? And high school enrollment will rise by 5 million. College enrollment will increase by more than three million. In many places, classrooms are overcrowded and curricula are outdated. Most of our qualified teachers are underpaid, any many of our paid teachers are unqualified. So we must give every child a place to sit and a teacher to learn from. Poverty must not be a bar to learning, and learning must offer an escape from poverty.

But more classrooms and more teachers are not enough. We must seek an educational system which grows in excellence as it grows in size. This means better training for our teachers. It means preparing youth to enjoy their hours of leisure as well as their hours of labor. It means exploring new techniques of teaching, to find new ways to stimulate the love of learning and the capacity for creation.

These are three of the central issues of the Great Society. While our government has many programs directed at those issues, I do not pretend that we have the full answer to those problems. But I do promise this: We are going to assemble the best thought and the broadest knowledge from all over the world to find those answers for America. . . .

QUESTIONS

A. Think about how President Johnson structured his speech.

1. The purpose of this speech is to inform the listeners. How does President Johnson state the specific purpose of his speech? In what part of his speech does he tell the audience his specific purpose?

2. What are the three "central issues of the Great Society"? How does knowing that the speech is organized around three issues help you identify what pattern of organization is being used? What pattern has President Johnson used to organize his information?

3. If President Johnson had traced the evolution of the major problems in America from 1960 up until the time of the speech in 1964, what kind of pattern would he have been using? What kind of pattern would involve discussing the problems of the West, then the Midwest, the South, and the East?

B. Think about the speaker, the listeners, and the occasion.

1. Why is it particularly appropriate to speak to a group of graduating seniors about "the future of our country," "the challenge of the next half century," and "the opportunity to move . . . upward to the Great Society"? What challenge is the President presenting when he says, "Your imagination, your initiative, and your indignation will determine whether we build a society where progress is the servant of our needs, or a society where old values and new visions are buried under unbridled growth"?

2. Why do you think President Johnson chose the pattern of organization he did? What makes his pattern more appropriate than a chronological pattern for presenting the problems of the nation?

3. Suppose the President had been addressing the mayors of the nation's ten largest cities on ways to reduce the problem of violent crime. What pattern of organization might he have used?

Guidelines

Once you have chosen and narrowed a topic, written a specific purpose, and arranged the main ideas necessary to accomplish that purpose in a definite pattern, your next task is to develop your main ideas. Main ideas may be developed in six different ways:

1. Use *definitions* to explain the meaning of an idea. In the third paragraph of his speech, President Johnson spends several sentences defining his concept of the Great Society.

2. Use *examples* to demonstrate an idea. When President Johnson says, "We must seek an educational system which grows in excellence as it grows in size," he gives "better training for our teachers" as one example of how this can be done.

3. *Comparison* or *contrast* may be used to develop main ideas. President Johnson contrasts the traditional concept of "America the beautiful" with the reality of pollution, to develop his idea that the countryside must be reclaimed.

4. *Narratives,* brief anecdotes, can be used to develop main ideas. For example, President Johnson could have developed his idea of the gravity of the pollution problem by telling the story of a family who returns to their favorite lakeside campsite, a place of unspoiled beauty, only to find the lake polluted and the fish dead.

5. *Testimony* or *quotations from experts* can be used to develop main ideas. In his speech, President Johnson quotes Aristotle to reinforce his idea that cities should be places where people can live well, not just survive.

6. *Statistics* are a useful means of developing main ideas. President Johnson states that in 1964 nearly 54 million adult Americans, nearly one-quarter of the population at that time, had not even finished high school. This statistic develops the main idea that America is still far from its goal of adequately educating its youth.

ACTIVITY

1. List the main ideas in President Johnson's speech and the method or methods he used to develop each one. Why are statistics a better method than quotation of an expert to develop his idea about the need to improve education in America? Why did President Johnson use a quotation instead of statistics to develop his idea about the quality of life in the cities? Discuss these questions with other students in your class.

Preparing and Presenting

Prepare an outline for a five-minute expository speech on one of the following topics, or on a topic of your choice:

- fitness
- the natural resources of your state
- the location of the major oil fields in America

Use these steps to prepare your outline:

1. Select your topic.
2. Do enough research to become familiar with your topic.
3. Narrow your topic.
4. Write the specific purpose of your speech.
5. Complete your research, using several sources.
6. Decide what pattern to use to organize your information—topical, spatial, or chronological—or whether to organize it in terms of causes and their effects, or problems and their solutions.
7. Write an outline of the main points of your speech; state your main points as sentences.
8. Add supporting ideas and examples for each main point; state supporting items as sentences or phrases.

Share your completed outline with another student. Explain why you chose the kind of pattern you did to organize your information. Modify any part of your outline that the other student finds unclear.

Evaluating

1. To what extent have you narrowed your topic? If you have not narrowed your topic enough so that it can be adequately presented in five minutes, narrow it further and modify your outline.
2. Where do you state your specific purpose? If you do not state your specific purpose clearly in your introduction, modify your outline.
3. What pattern did you use to organize your information? If another pattern would make your speech easier to understand, modify your outline.
4. How much detail is needed to make each main idea clear to your audience? Modify your outline if your main ideas need to be developed more fully (see the Guidelines section for help).
5. If you have forgotten to include an introduction or a conclusion, modify your outline to add it now.

Introducing a Speaker

Remembering these points will help you introduce a speaker with grace and poise:

1. Become familiar with the background and accomplishments of the person you will introduce.
2. Focus your introduction on the speaker's qualifications to speak on his or her subject to this particular audience.
3. Praise the speaker, but don't embarrass him or her by making extravagant predictions that will be impossible to live up to.
4. Deliver your introduction in the form of a good expository speech.
5. Deliver your introduction with warmth and enthusiasm.
6. Be brief; don't steal attention from the speaker.

ACTIVITIES

1. Prepare and deliver a speech of introduction for one of the following people or for another person of your choice. The person you introduce can be someone now living, a person from history, or a character from a novel or film.
   - Captain Ahab
   - your next-door neighbor
   - Queen Elizabeth I of England
   - one of your classmates

2. Do research on the background of a state or local politician, and prepare a speech of introduction to present this person to your class. You might choose one of the following people:
   - a school board member
   - a member of the city council
   - a county commissioner
   - your mayor or city manager
   - a state legislator
   - a district attorney

5.3 Preparing and Using Speaking Notes

speaking skills

Using Transitions

Transitions are words or phrases that connect the ideas in a sentence or paragraph with the ideas in the next sentence or paragraph. They help your listeners grasp the direction in which your speech is headed, and help remind them of the ground you have already covered. Transitions are particularly important for speakers, because they keep listeners from losing the train of thought during a speech.

Words and phrases which serve as transitions include the following:

first	in addition	by way of contrast
second	on the other hand	moreover
third	furthermore	therefore
next	in conclusion	however
finally	another point	now let's consider another point

Voice and bodily action can also serve as transitions. For example:

- a pause can indicate the end of a thought
- a gesture may be used to signal or emphasize main points
- a change in loudness may indicate a shift in thought

Speakers should avoid trite transitions such as "last but not least." Speakers should also avoid false transitions, such as saying "in conclusion" when there is actually another major point to be made.

ACTIVITY

1. Listen to a cassette or recording of a well-known speech, from real life or from literature. (If no recorded speech is available, use a published speech from *Vital Speeches* or from a book of collected speeches.) List all the transitional words or phrases the speaker uses, and all the points at which you felt the speaker should have used a transition. Then read the speech to the class, omitting all the transitional words and phrases. Have your classmates tell you what parts of the speech they found confusing. Ask them to suggest appropriate transitional words or phrases, and compare their suggestions with the transitions the author actually used.

language

How to Prepare and Use Speaking Notes

Once you have completed your outline, you can begin thinking about delivering your speech. You can make your speech livelier and more spontaneous by maintaining good eye contact with your listeners, so that they feel you are really talking to them. To maintain contact with your listeners and observe how they are responding to your speech, you must keep from looking down at your speaking notes too often.

Properly prepared notecards free you from the necessity of reading your speech word-for-word. Once you have completed your outline, list the main ideas of your speech on 3" x 5" notecards. Under each main idea, write a word or phrase that will remind you of its supporting ideas and examples. Suppose that one of your main ideas is that many writers have used their experiences in other jobs as material for their books. Your supporting idea might be that several physicians have used their medical knowledge in novels and stories, and your examples might be the doctor-writers Michael Crichton, A. J. Cronin, and J. G. Ballard. Your notecard for this main idea would look like this:

```
II. Many writers use experiences in other jobs as
    material
    A. Doctor-writers
       1. Crichton
       2. Cronin
       3. Ballard
```

Such notecards remove any fear of forgetting your speech, and let you give your listeners the attention they deserve.

Oral reports are one expository speaking situation in which carefully prepared notecards are especially helpful. Sometimes your teacher will already have chosen and named a topic for you, and sometimes you will choose the topic yourself. In both cases, the key to giving a good oral report is understanding the assignment. Be sure that the written purpose of your speech fulfills the assignment.

Working with the Model

After their biology class had completed a study module on how plants respond to their environment, Lauren Smith and Jason Martinson were asked to prepare short oral reports. Here is the assignment they were given:

model

Using at least three sources, prepare an oral report to give to the class during the first week of October. Your report should be from ten to fifteen minutes long. It should explore in detail one of the relationships that we have studied between plants and their environment. Be sure to include at least two examples for each main idea in your report. If you use a chart or other visual aid, be sure that the lettering is large enough to be read from the back of the room. End your report by giving two sources where your listeners can read more about your topic.

Lauren and Jason both decided to do reports on the relationship between water supply in the environment and plant life. Read the notecards each of them prepared:

Jason's Notecards

> purpose: to explain relationship between water ①
> supply and plant life to my biology class
> intro.: we all know too little water will cause
> plants to die, but the relationship between
> water supply and plant life is more
> complex than that: plants adapt not only to
> amount of water, but to frequency of water
> supply

model

②

main ideas:
plants adapt to <u>amount</u> of water
A. cactus
  1. leaves modified into spines to prevent
    water loss
  2. barrel cactus—storage tissue
    (SHOW DRAWING OF CROSS-SECTION OF
    BARREL CACTUS)
B. mesquite: extra long roots

plants adapt to <u>frequency</u> of water
A. In areas w/dry seasons, trees are seasonal
  too—that is, deciduous (lose their leaves)
B. In Sahara, some herbs complete entire life
  cycle in 2-wk. wet season

③

conc.:
1. plants adapt to both <u>amount</u> & <u>frequency</u>
  of water supply
2. water supply is probably the most impt.
  environmental factor in determining a plant's
  characteristics
3. for more info: Rost et al., <u>Botany</u>; Raven &
  Curtis, <u>Biology of Plants</u>

Lauren's Notecards

Water is important in the life of plants
  You can see one kind of adaptation to water
  supply when you look at cactus
Plants also adapt to the frequency of water supply

model

> Deciduous trees have a life cycle adapted to a
> seasonal water supply
>   see Rost, <u>Botany</u>
> The next time you water your houseplants,
> remember that water supply is probably the most
> important thing in a plant's environment!

QUESTIONS

A. Imagine that you were given the same assignment as Jason and Lauren.

1. When are you expected to give your report?

2. What directions have you been given about structuring your report?

3. For how long are you to speak?

4. What guidelines has the teacher provided about the use of visual aids?

5. How many sources are you to use in preparing your report?

6. What specific information are you to give your listeners?

7. Why has the teacher given this assignment—to review material you covered previously, to introduce a new topic, or to study in depth something the class already has some knowledge about?

B. Read carefully the notecards prepared by Lauren and Jason.

1. Which report will fulfill the assignment most accurately? Reread the assignment, and discuss how each student's notecards fulfill or fail to fulfill it.

2. Which set of notes will help the audience grasp the purpose of the speech? Why?

3. Review the outline of an expository speech given in the Guidelines section of lesson 5.1. Which set of notes most resembles the outline? How do you think writing notes in this format will help the speaker? How will it help the audience?

4. Which set of notes will best help the audience grasp the speaker's main points? What does that set of notes remind the speaker to do to help the audience remember the main points?

5. Which set of notes contains a reference to a visual aid? What may happen to a speaker who plans to use a visual aid, but includes no reference to it in his or her notecards?

6. What definition has been included in the notecards? How might this help the listeners during the speech?

7. Jason has numbered his notecards. How might numbering the notecards help a speaker?

Guidelines

Follow these suggestions in preparing your speaking notes:

1. Your speaking notes should be small enough so that they do not distract your listeners. Three-by-five-inch notecards are an ideal size and are stiff enough to be held easily.
2. Print the information on your cards large enough so it can be read at a glance from arm's length.
3. Arrange your notes so that the main ideas can be picked up at a glance. Underline major thoughts, capitalize items so you can spot them easily, and use color coding for any point you want to emphasize.
4. Write information on only one side of each card.
5. Number your cards. Don't experience the panic of dropping your cards just before the speech and being unable to get them back in order.
6. Limit the total number of cards to as few as possible while still retaining a comfortable number of reminders of your main points.
7. In deciding what to include on your cards, you may want to select specific quotations that you want to state accurately, facts or figures that are complicated or difficult to remember, phonetic spellings of hard-to-pronounce words, and precise definitions of confusing terms.

Preparing and Presenting

Read carefully the outline you prepared in lesson 5.2. Imagine yourself giving your speech, and think about what words or phrases most vividly bring your main ideas to mind. Then turn your outline into notecards. Your main ideas, stated in complete sentences in your outline, may become abbreviated sentences or phrases in your notecards. Your supporting ideas and examples may become single words.

When you have finished, look carefully through your outline again. Does your speech contain any information—statistics or quotations—that you must cite exactly? If so, write this information into your cards in full, exactly as you will deliver it. Do you use any terms which may need to be defined for your audience? Add such definitions now, along with any notes on when to use visual aids. Check that your cards are easy to read, and number them.

Now give your speech for a friend or classmate. As you deliver your speech, look at your notes as little as possible. The purpose of this practice session is to see how well your notecards work. Although it is important to keep your speaking notes as brief as possible, they must effectively remind you of everything you want to say and contain any numbers or passages you want to quote verbatim.

Evaluating

Discuss your speech with your listener, and answer these questions about it together:

1. What parts of the speech were unclear to the listener? What additional information or change in organization would make this part of the speech clearer? Make any necessary changes in your cards.

2. To what extent (if at all) did your listener find the way you held or looked at the notecards distracting? Make a mental note to change any habits of physical delivery that took your listener's attention away from the speech.

3. What parts of the speech did you find awkward to deliver? Discuss with your listener ways to smooth over these rough spots. You might add more information to your cards, quote a source completely and precisely, or change the arrangement of information on the cards, so that each card ends at a natural division in the speech.

Reporting an Incident

One of the most important skills in giving an accurate report of an incident to the police, insurance investigators, or other authorities is the ability to understand and communicate cause-and-effect relationships. To begin with, the person giving the report must be able to distinguish causes from effects. Moreover, this person must also be aware that

- causes precede effects
- not all the events that preceded an incident helped cause it
- more than one cause can contribute to an effect
- if there are several causes, they may not contribute equally to an effect

The best way to arrive at correct cause-and-effect explanations is to intelligently and persistently question yourself and others who witnessed the incident.

ACTIVITIES

1. A person involved in a traffic accident often is called upon to explain why the accident occurred. As a citizen you may be concerned with other kinds of incidents, such as vandalism or arson, in which the authorities must search for a cause or explanation. Make a list of the types of incidents in which citizens may be asked to provide cause-and-effect explanations. Search newspapers and magazines to find one example of each of the kinds of incidents on your list. Bring your examples to class, and discuss the possible cause-and-effect explanation of each incident. If the newspaper or magazine article reveals the cause of the incident, discuss the consequences for the people involved if this cause is reported inaccurately to the authorities or insurance investigators.

2. Talk with a police officer about traffic accidents. For each accident you discuss, ask the officer to distinguish causes (speeding, negligence, drunk driving) from effects (injured drivers, damaged vehicles).

3. Search the newspapers for examples of faulty reasoning from cause to effect (for example: "Coach Pinson wore the same shirt for ten days while the Mariners were on their winning streak"). Bring in three examples to discuss with the class.

citizenship

5.4 Using Visual Aids

Using Your Imagination

Some people believe that all our thinking is done in terms of pictures or images, since we tend to associate images with abstractions and concepts. Creative thinking that draws on these images is what we call "imagination." Here are some ways to tap your imagination:

- *Engage in some sort of play.* If you set aside a problem to play a game of checkers or chess, you'll often find that the solution occurs to you spontaneously.

- *Give yourself time for fantasy and reflection.* Fantasy and reflection are moods that encourage the association of images, presenting us with relationships between ideas that we may not have thought of before.

- *Use intuition, feeling, and qualitative judgments in solving problems.* Sometimes your intuition or feelings about a problem can lead you to the solution faster than rational analysis.

- *Avoid stereotyping.* Stereotyping leads you to give your listeners exactly what they expected. As a result, they are usually bored.

- *Use all the senses when you are observing something.* Observing something by using a sense you would not usually use to examine it (such as feeling an unfamiliar object instead of just looking at it) can lead you to fresh insights.

- *Put yourself in someone else's place, and look at a problem from that person's point of view.* This technique will deepen your understanding of any problem, and is especially valuable in listening.

ACTIVITY

1. Tap your imagination by putting yourself in someone else's place:
   - retell a traditional children's story in terms of contemporary life; then retell a newspaper item as a traditional children's story.
   - ask a friend to give you a situation that represents a solution, and make up a problem to fit it

planning

110

How to Use Visual Aids

Since people receive information through their eyes as well as their ears, a visual aid will often increase your ability to communicate information in a speech. To decide whether you could improve your speech by using a visual aid, read carefully through your outline, looking for kinds of information that are best communicated visually as well as verbally. Here are some kinds of information to look for:

- the main ideas and examples in your speech, to help your listeners follow them more easily (see the chart on the left below)
- technical or unusual terms (see the chart on the right below)

Traditional Energy Sources	Natural Gas Industry: Important Terms

I. Oil
  A. Location of Established Fields
  B. New Fields
    1. Alaska
    2. North Sea
    3. Alberta, Canada
  C. Role of OPEC
 	
II. Natural Gas
  A. Present Resources
  B. Exploring for Natural Gas
  C. Storing Natural Gas
	• Acetylene
	• Butane
	• Propane
	• Ethane
	• Ethylene
	• Methane
	• Hydrocarbon
	• Petrochemicals

- information that you want your audience to compare with previous information in your speech (Visual aids help communication whenever you ask your audience to consider two things at once, since words restrict you to presenting pieces of information one at a time.)
- information that is difficult to visualize, such as the structure of an intricate piece of machinery

- information about something unlike anything your audience has ever seen (such as the exotic fish found in very deep water)
- information that is usually accompanied by a visual reference (For example, newspaper stories about archeological discoveries almost always contain maps.)

There are several types of visual aids you can use to illustrate your information. Three-dimensional *models* (in materials such as cardboard, wood, cloth, plaster, or plastic) can be used to explain structure: the structure of an ancient Roman villa, the human skeleton, the earliest ice skates, or DNA. *Maps* are useful in speeches on history, politics, exploration, or ecology. *Charts* can be used to show the organizational structure of a company or a government agency. Pie charts, bar charts, and graphs are particularly useful when you want your audience to compare two or more pieces of information. (Notice the effect of presenting the same information—the number of flu cases between December and April—in the two graphs below. The line graph emphasizes the progress of the flu epidemic. The bar chart emphasizes the difference in the number of cases each month.)

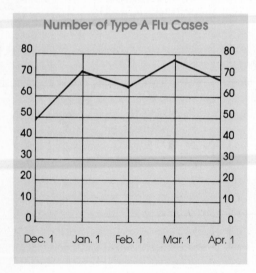

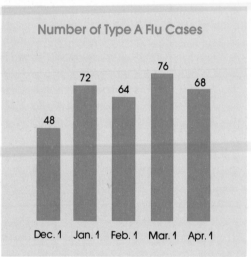

Diagrams help your audience understand the relative size and position of the parts of something, such as the parts of an engine or of the heart. *Photographs* or *color slides* let your audience see something totally unfamiliar to them, such as a snow leopard. After you have decided which ideas in your speech to supplement with visual aids, think carefully about what kind of visual aid will most help your audience understand each idea.

When you prepare a chart or diagram, be sure that it is orderly and attractive, and that any lettering is large enough to be read from the back of the room. If you will be using special equipment such as a slide projector, be sure that it is in working order and that you understand its operation. Indicate in our notecards where in your speech you will use each aid, and practice using the aids when you practice your speech. When you give your speech, remember not to block your listeners' view of each aid, and not to look at it continuously as you talk.

Working with the Model

Here is the visual aid Jason Martinson used during his speech on water supply and plants:

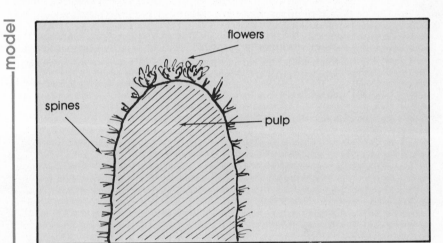

QUESTIONS

A. Reread Jason's notecards in the Working with the Model section of lesson 5.2.

1. What piece of information has Jason decided to supplement with a visual aid? Why did he choose to use a visual aid with this particular item?

2. Where else in his speech might Jason have used a visual aid? What terms in the speech might be new to the audience, or what information might be difficult to remember?

B. Think about the type of visual aid Jason decided to use.

1. What type of visual aid did Jason choose?

2. Why do you think Jason used this visual aid instead of color slides of a barrel cactus?

3. Jason's father offered to buy him a cross-section of a real barrel cactus. What would be the advantages and disadvantages of Jason's using a real barrel cactus, instead of the visual aid he prepared?

4. When Jason explained that the leaves of cactus have become spines to prevent water loss through evaporation, he passed several different kinds of cactus spines around the room for the class to see. What are the advantages and disadvantages of using a visual aid in this way? How else might Jason have shown the class what the spines of several different types of cactus look like?

C. Borrow from your audiovisual department and bring to class an example or a picture of each of the following visual aids: slides and 35-millimeter projector; transparency and overhead projector; film and 8- or 16-millimeter projector; videotape cassette; videotape recorder and monitor; flipchart and stand; poster; chalkboard; working model (as in the photo below); map; handout. Discuss with your teacher and other students the advantages and disadvantages of each of these visual aids, in terms of cost, ease and scope of use, preparation time, and effectiveness with different audiences. What other visual aids can you identify?

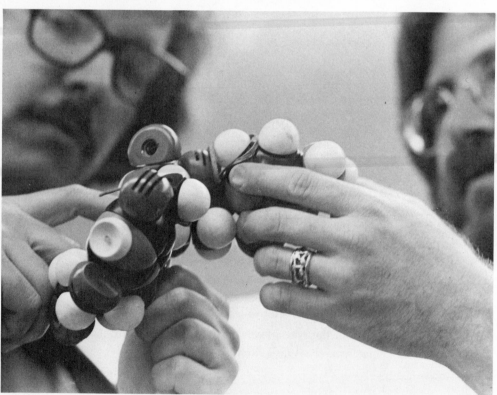

Guidelines

A few simple rules will help you use visual aids effectively:

1. Be sure the aid is large enough so that the smallest detail you want your audience to see is visible from every point in the room.
2. Stand so that you are not blocking your audience's view of the aid.
3. If the aid requires the use of special equipment, such as a slide projector or a videotape recorder, make sure you can operate the equipment. Just before your speech, check to make sure that the equipment is working properly.
4. Make the aid neat and attractive.
5. Do not look at the aid continuously as you talk. Point out each major feature in the aid briefly, but keep your eyes on the audience to see whether they are understanding your speech.
6. Be cautious about distributing materials to be looked at by listeners. Such activity will probably distract them from your speech instead of aiding communication. (You may, however, wish to distribute such materials immediately after your speech.)

Preparing and Presenting

Read carefully through the outline you prepared in lesson 5.2, looking for ideas or examples that could be communicated more effectively with the help of a visual aid. Make a list of these ideas and examples.

Next, think carefully about what kind of visual aid will best help your listeners understand each idea or example on your list. For example, if one of your main ideas is the location of oil fields in America, you will want to use a map like the one shown here, rather than color slides. Write the

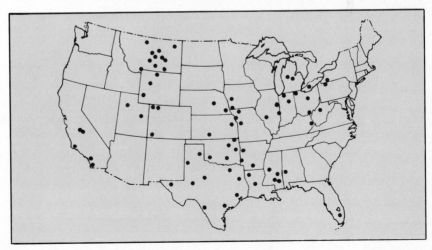

115

visual aid for each idea opposite it on your list. On the notecards you prepared for lesson 5.3, indicate at what point in your speech you will use each visual aid.

Now prepare your visual aids. Be sure that all parts of each aid, including all lettering, will be visible to everyone in the class. (Notice the size of the lettering on the pie chart and picture graph below.) When you practice your speech, include the use of your visual aids as part of your practice.

Give your speech to the class. Look at your listeners as you use each visual aid—remember that you are communicating with them, not it.

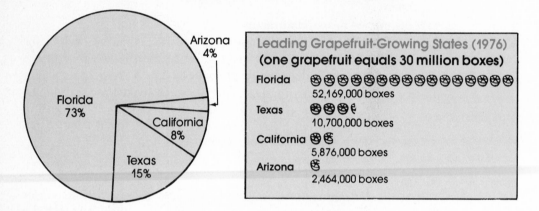

Evaluating

Ask your classmates to answer these questions about your speech:

1. What was the purpose of the speech? What pattern did the speaker use to organize his or her information?
2. What visual aid or aids did the speaker use? What idea or example did each aid supplement? How did each visual aid make an idea or example easier to understand?
3. What other kind of visual aid (if any) would have been more effective in communicating one of the speaker's ideas? Why?
4. What information in the speech would have been easier to understand with the help of a visual aid? Why? What visual aid would you have used?
5. What did you find distracting in the speaker's use of notes or aids? How can the speaker overcome this problem?

Using Visual Aids
to Explain a Work Process

On-the-job explanations often require the use of visual aids. When you explain how to use a piece of machinery, the machine itself is your "visual aid." If this is the case, be sure your demonstration is complete and absolutely accurate, to protect the safety of the worker you are training.

If your explanation of a work process involves a chart, flow diagram, or other visual aid, the guidelines you've learned in this lesson hold true. Make the aid neat and attractive. If your explanation will be given to a group of workers, be sure the aid is large enough so all its lettering and details can be seen by everyone in the group. Remember that the purpose of the aid is to assist your explanation; don't fiddle with it or look at it continuously as you talk.

ACTIVITIES

1. Using a chalkboard, an overhead projector transparency, or a large piece of poster board, draw a diagram showing the main steps in a work process you are familiar with. Use this diagram to explain the work process to your class or to a group of friends.

2. Use a visual aid to help communicate one of the work processes you explained in Skills for Success, lesson 5.1.

3. Obtain a small piece of machinery or a working model of a piece of machinery. In a presentation to your class, demonstrate how it works.

4. Demonstrate to the class how to play a musical instrument or how to use a piece of sports equipment. Use the instrument or piece of sports equipment as a visual aid.

5.5 Adapting a Speech to Your Audience

Using an Audience Analysis Checklist

Part of preparing a speech is adapting it to your audience. Whether you write out the answers or merely think them through, consider the following questions carefully as you plan your speech. They will help you see it from your listeners' point of view.

Knowledge. What do the people in the audience know about you and the subject of your speech?

Attitudes. What feelings do the people in the audience have towards you and the subject of your speech?

Interests. What are the main interests of the people in your audience? What relationships exist between these interests and your topic?

Events. What recent events have strongly influenced the people in your audience?

Purpose. Why will the people in the audience be present?

Competition. Will other activities occurring at the same time as your speech or in the immediate future compete with your efforts to get the audience's attention?

ACTIVITY

1. Find a detailed article on how to grow a vegetable garden (or on some other reasonably complicated process), and distribute a copy of the article to everyone in the class. After everyone has read the article, explain how you would adapt a speech on how to grow a vegetable garden to the following audiences, in terms of each of the items in the Audience Analysis Checklist:

   • a ten-year-old who is interested in gardening

   • a group of people your own age who aren't interested in gardening

   • a gardening club for adults

   After you have finished your explanation, ask your classmates for their comments and suggestions.

planning

How to Adapt a Speech to Your Audience

Imagine that you are an experienced mechanic, and that you've been invited to give a short talk to your uncle's senior citizen group. You have decided to talk about your hobby: restoring vintage cars. You feel you have prepared a good speech—your information on how to restore a Duesenberg engine is clearly organized in a chronological pattern, and you even have photos of each step in the process.

As you deliver your speech, you notice that people don't seem to be paying much attention. Your audience is easily distracted, and not overly sympathetic. Later your uncle explains their reaction: most of your listeners didn't know enough about cars to understand your explanation. Moreover, most of them expected a talk on how to save money by doing minor repairs themselves; naturally, they were disappointed and bored by your speech.

A successful speaker takes the audience's knowledge, needs, and interests into account.

Working with the Model

The following speech was given by Thomas J. Watson, Jr., the son of the founder of IBM, to the graduating class of Brown University in 1964. As you read it, be particularly aware of the speaker, the listeners, and the occasion. Try to find all the ways in which Watson, a successful executive with one of the nation's largest corporations, has adapted his speech to this group of inexperienced college seniors.

model

Twenty-seven years ago I sat where you now sit in the graduating class of 1937 at Brown University. I'm sure I seem several generations away from you in age, but these twenty-seven years have gone so quickly that it's not at all hard for me to remember that vivid day of my own graduation. Strangely enough, the one thing about that day that I cannot remember is what the commencement speaker had to say. My thoughts, like yours, were targeted upon my family and my friends and my plans for the summer. But of one thing I'm sure: If the speaker made a short speech, I know I blessed him.

Therefore, I surmise, there is only one sure way to earn a place in your memory and that is to be brief. I will.

My subject today is in the general area of self-protection. I want to spend a few moments contrasting the drive for physical protection in and out of college with the great difficulty all of us have through life in protecting the non-physical parts of our being.

In college sports, one is constantly protecting one's body with all kinds of devices, from shoulder pads to shin guards. Even in later life, we continue this drive for physical safety with such things as padded dashboards and shatter-proof windshields. All these things help to keep one's body safe and unmarked, and they are good things.

However, all of you graduating today possess something much more important to you than your body. I am speaking to you of your mind, your spirit, your ability to think and speak independently, and your ability at this point as college seniors to stand up and be counted with a clear and firm position on nearly any of the issues which affect your life or the life of the nation.

The fundamental convictions and principles which help you to form your firm, clear position are your most precious possession. Paradoxically, all the wonderful equipment available for shielding the body is worthless for protecting the spirit and the mind.

What then can you do to protect these priceless personal assets? You can't hide them; you can't smother them; you can't rely on some kind of padding. On the contrary, you can protect them only by exposing them to danger, only by defending your personal beliefs regardless of opposition and, like tempered steel, toughening your convictions by the hot shock of conflict.

model

If you succeed in preserving your principles in the years ahead, without becoming so radical that nobody will listen or follow your example, you will become a part of that elite group in the world which Crawford Greenwalt, Chairman of the DuPont Company, calls the "uncommon man." ...

It may seem fantastic to you that you could lose this outspoken ability you have been developing throughout your scholastic career. Yet it's a fact that the mass world in which we live tends to etch away the tough hard bumps of conviction and belief. I venture to predict that not one of you will be at work very many years before you will have to look into your heart and answer some very difficult questions. Your answers will, in a very real sense, begin to determine whether your parents, this institution, and the world in which you have lived have produced a common or uncommon human being.

You will have to choose between the safe, conservative silent position and the choice of speaking your mind, of stating your true position and thereby earning yourself some enemies.

Will you develop the reputation of being outspoken, sometimes uncooperative but always honest in supporting what your beliefs indicate is right?

Or will you be a steadfast, reliable ... [person] who can always be counted on to cooperate? ...

All the great ... [people] of history have had to answer the same critical questions. Each had to choose between the safe protection of the crowd and the risk of standing up and being counted. And you can find no truly great ... [individuals] who took the easy way.

For their courage some suffered abuse, imprisonment, and even death. Others lived to win the acclaim of their ... [contemporaries]. But all achieved greatness.

Through history, examples are abundant:

- Columbus
- Charles Darwin
- Galileo, who confirmed the theory that the earth traveled about the sun, and who for his affirmation became a prisoner of the Inquisition.
- Socrates, who told his judges at his trial: "Men of Athens, I honor and love you; but I shall obey God rather than you, and while I have life and strength, I shall never cease from the practice and teaching of philosophy."

If we turn to our own times, we can all of us recall other ... [people] of other lands who refused to take the easy way out, who stood up against the current for what they believed right and just. Nehru in India, de Gaulle in France, Churchill in England.

model

And in our own country, it wasn't easy in 1956 when the British, French and Israeli forces invaded Egypt—in the midst of an American presidential election—for the President of the United States, Dwight D. Eisenhower, to condemn the use of force and to call upon the aggressors to get out. But he did it—and the electorate overwhelmingly upheld his courage.

And it wasn't easy for another American President of a different political party—John F. Kennedy—to take an unequivocal stand on civil rights, when that stand might have cost him votes of the South, which in the 1960 election gave him his tiny margin of victory. But he did it and thereby added a post-publication chapter to *Profiles in Courage*....

All these ... [people], despite their great variety, had something in common. Every single one of them put principle first, safety second; individuality first, adjustment second; courage first, cost second....

We need more such ... [people], more than ever before, living at this hour. The issues are the biggest in history—the need for courageous dialogue greater than ever....

Now suppose you try, in your own manner, to follow this course. What will happen to you?

Well, Nicholas Murray Butler, the great President of Columbia University at the beginning of this century, said that the world is made up of three groups of people.

A small elite group who make things happen.

A somewhat larger group who watch things happen.

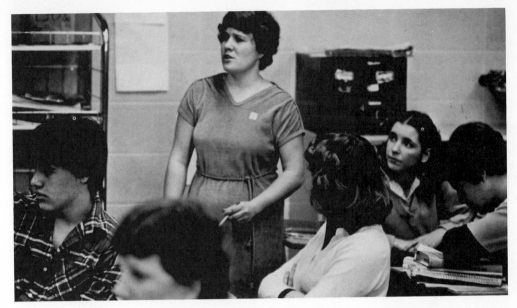

And the great multitude who don't know what happens.
This means that the leaders, the makers of opinion in the world, are a very limited group of people.

So as you stand and are counted you will first run into the group who equate newness with wrongness. If it's a new idea, it's uncomfortable and they won't like it. These are the conventionalists.

Second, you're sure to meet cynics, people who believe anyone who sticks his neck out is a fool. I am sure all of you have heard of measures which passed the Congress in a breeze on a voice vote, and later go down to crashing defeat where some Congressman insists that every vote be recorded in the *Congressional Record.*

Third, you'll run into the group of people who believe that there are certain taboo questions that should not be debated. These suppressors of dissent think that once a stand has been taken it is forever settled. Disarmament, the admission of Red China to the U.N., a change in policy toward Castro or Vietnam—all such touchy subjects, these people warn, should be left alone.

If you stand up and are counted, from time to time you may get yourself knocked down. But remember this: . . . [Someone] flattened by an opponent can get up again. . . . [Someone] flattened by conformity stays down for good. . . .

Follow the path of the unsafe, independent thinker. Expose your ideas to the dangers of controversy. Speak your mind and fear less the label of "crackpot" than the stigma of conformity. And on issues that seem important to you, stand up and be counted at any cost.

QUESTIONS

A. Think about how Watson has taken the audience's knowledge, needs, and interests into account.

  1. What is the purpose of Watson's speech? Why is this purpose well adapted to his audience?

  2. How does Watson capture the audience's interest by letting them know that he knows how they feel? Where in his speech does he do this?

  3. What experiences familiar to his audience does Watson use to illustrate his main ideas?

  4. What authorities familiar to his audience does Watson quote to support his main ideas? How does he give his audience information about authorities with whom they may be unfamiliar?

B. Think about the speaker, the listeners, and the occasion.

  1. This speech was given on a college campus by an important executive of a major American corporation. Discuss how Watson would have had to change his speech to present it to a philanthropic organization like the Elks, many of whose members are themselves in business. How might Watson have modified the purpose of his speech? What examples (both experiences and authorities) might he change?

  2. Imagine that Watson was asked to speak to the PTA. How might he modify the purpose of his speech? Which experiences and examples in his speech might he have to change? For example, how well do you think his metaphor of "shoulder pads and shin guards" would work with an audience of PTA members?

Guidelines

You should let your audience know that you are aware of their knowledge and interests from the very beginning of your speech. A good introduction has the following characteristics:

  • it directs the attention of the audience to the topic of the speech
  • it makes the purpose of the speech clear
  • it ties the speech to the knowledge and interests of the audience
  • it uses humor or other attention-getting techniques to further the purpose of the speech, rather than merely to entertain
  • it includes a linkage or bridge to the body of the speech; often this bridge is a preview of the main ideas of the speech.

Preparing and Presenting

Prepare an outline of a five- to ten-minute speech in which you define a concept for your audience. You may choose a concept from the biological or physical sciences, from sports, from the arts, or from politics and the social sciences. Your speech will answer the question "What is ..." (for example, "What is genetic engineering?"). It should contain a definition of the concept, plus a brief explanation of how the concept works.

Your definition should tell the class what sport, science, art, or social science your concept belongs to, what class within that area your concept belongs to, and what characteristics set it apart from other similar concepts. For example, the term *general anesthesia* belongs to medicine, specifically to the class of anesthesia, denoting the loss of sensation. Unlike the similar concept *local anesthesia,* general anesthesia involves the entire body, and results in loss of consciousness as well as loss of sensation. Be sure not to use any technical words your audience may not know in your definition.

In the rest of your speech, explain how the concept works. First, use a metaphor or simile to help explain how your concept works (review how Watson used the metaphor of padding to explain the concept of self-protection of the mind and spirit). Then, give one or more examples of how your concept works. Use one of the following concepts or a concept of your own (with your teacher's approval):

The Arts	*Science*
montage	solar energy
collage	photosynthesis
opera	immunization
a cappella singing	gravitation
Expressionism	"greenhouse effect"

Social Science/Politics	*Sports*
buffer state	blocking
laissez-faire	power play
superego	birdie
behaviorism	dressage
colonialism	dunk shot

To begin your preparation, analyze your audience by completing the Audience Analysis Checklist in Speaking Skills, lesson 5.5. Share your analysis with two other students. Discuss the differences and similarities in your analysis of the class. In particular, see whether you agree on the class's probable knowledge of and interest in each of the concepts the three of you have chosen.

As you complete work on your speech, be sure that your introduction reflects the knowledge about your audience you gained in completing the Audience Analysis Checklist. Share your introduction with the other two students.

Evaluating

1. How many of the differences between your completed analysis form and those of the other students were due to differences in your knowledge of the audience?

2. How many of the differences were due to differences in your topics?

3. What details about the audience's opinions and beliefs were in either of the other forms, but not in yours? How might knowing these details affect the success of your speech?

4. How interesting and effective do the other students feel your introduction will be with this audience? What changes can they suggest to make your introduction more effective?

Presenting an Award

When you are asked to present an award, you will be expected to "say a few words" about the award and its recipient. The important thing to remember is to be brief, and to focus attention on the receiver of the award, not yourself.

Plan to deliver your speech extemporaneously—reading a speech tends to make you seem unenthusiastic or even insincere. Tell the audience about the history and significance of the award, and describe the qualifications and achievements of the recipient. Praise the recipient warmly and sincerely, but not to such lengths as to embarrass him or her. Finish by expressing your congratulations and best wishes.

ACTIVITY

1. Prepare and deliver a presentation speech for one of the following awards (or for an award of your choice):
   - a trophy for the varsity football team's most valuable player
   - a book for the winner of a short-story contest for high-school students
   - a certificate for first prize in your school's science fair
   - an "Oscar" for the best performer in your school's play
   - a plaque for the student with the most creative shop project
   - an award for the student who put in the most volunteer hours at the local hospital
   - an award for the most unselfish student in the school

5.6 Using Practice Sessions to Improve Your Speech

speaking skills

Overcoming Your Fear of Speaking

Most speakers know what it's like to face an audience with damp palms, shaking knees, and a lump in the throat. Try the following suggestions to relieve these symptoms of anxiety:

1. *Understand your fears and put them in their place.* Even the most experienced speakers sometimes feel nervous. In fact, many of our greatest performers say that a certain amount of anxiety helps them do better. Moreover, don't forget that most audiences are friendly—they want you to succeed. To them, you will not seem as nervous as you feel.

2. *Proper preparation overcomes much of the fear of speaking.* If you become thoroughly familiar with your topic and prepare and practice your speech carefully, you are more likely to approach the speaking situation with confidence.

3. *Control your fears as you present your speech.* Establish a routine which leaves your body relaxed and permits you to breathe naturally while you are delivering your speech.

4. *Successful experience increases confidence.* As you appear before more audiences and give more speeches, you will find your anxiety diminishing.

ACTIVITY

1. Practice this relaxation routine. Pretend you are about to give a speech. Take a deep breath and then swallow. Yawn several times. Press your fingertips together. Walk at a normal pace to the location of your speech. Pause. Arrange your notes and thoughts. Make sure your weight is evenly distributed on both feet, and press the balls of your feet against the floor. Then look up at your audience. You are now ready to begin speaking.

attitude

How to Use Practice Sessions to Improve Your Speech

You may have heard stories of how Abraham Lincoln would jot down ideas on the back of an envelope as he sat listening to another speaker, and then give a polished performance when it was his turn to speak. There is some evidence that Lincoln did jot down ideas on the backs of envelopes. There is much more evidence that Lincoln was a successful speaker because of long hours of practice, during which he sought the critical assistance of others to help him perfect the content and delivery of his speeches.

Holding a practice session gives you a listener's reaction to your speech before you have to face your audience. This listener's ability to give you valid criticism is an important advantage of the practice session; if you've been doing something wrong, practicing by yourself will just strengthen this mistake you've been making.

Before you schedule a practice session, review your speech to be sure that you have already completed these steps:

- Link the topic of your speech to subjects that are familiar to your listeners.
- Organize your information in a pattern: chronological, spatial, topical, by cause and effect, or by problem and solution.
- Use metaphors and other figures of speech to make your explanations more vivid.
- Use audio and visual aids to increase your listeners' interest and comprehension.

Working with the Model

To complete the Preparing and Presenting section of lesson 5.5, Missy decided to define and explain the concept of mutualism. Before they gave their speeches, the students in Missy's class were required to hand in a speech outline and a practice record of at least one practice session. Read Missy's outline carefully to find its strengths and weaknesses. Then read the practice record George completed when he, Jane, and Sherry listened to Missy practice her speech.

model

Specific purpose: To explain the biological concept of mutualism to my speech class

I. Introduction

  A. *To gain audience's attention:* Most of us think of friendship as a relationship that is mutually beneficial. Friends depend on each other, and each one benefits from the relationship. But did you know that this sort of relationship also exists in nature? When two species depend on each other and each one benefits from the relationship, biologists call this relationship *mutualism.*

  B. Today I'm going to answer the question "What is mutualism?"

II. Body

  A. Mutualism is a relationship between two species, from which both benefit.

    1. The concept is from biology.

    2. Mutualism is a kind of symbiosis (symbiosis: interdependence of two species).

      a. mutualism differs from *commensalism,* a kind of symbiosis in which one member benefits and the other is unaffected

      b. mutualism differs from *parasitism,* in which one member benefits at the cost of the other

  B. Mutualism is like the friendship between two neighboring families with tight budgets.

    1. If Mrs. Smith teaches the Gomez children to ice skate and Mr. Gomez teaches the Smith children to draw, both families have benefited from the relationship.

    2. Both families live better because of the relationship, because without it the families would have to pay for ice skating and art lessons.

  C. There are many examples of mutualism in nature.

    1. *Rhizobium* bacteria live on the root nodules of legumes like peas and peanuts. The plants benefit because the bacteria change the nitrogen in the soil into a form the plants can use.

    2. Certain small birds obtain food by eating the insect parasites from the backs of African Cape elk. The elk benefit from removal of the parasites.

    3. Certain protozoa find a protected home in the intestinal tract of termites. The termites benefit because the protozoa digest the cellulose in the wood the termites eat.

III. Conclusion

  A. Mutualism is a relationship between two species that benefits both of them.

  B. You can think of mutualism as nature's "good neighbor policy."

George's Practice Record

PRACTICE RECORD

Person(s) Listening _Jane_   _George_   _Sherry_

When _12/8/82_   Where _Jane's house_ Length of speech _10 minutes_

Specific Purpose (as heard by listener) _To explain the concept of mutualism._

Main Ideas (as heard by listener) _1) Mutualism is a biological partnership from which both parties benefit; 2) Mutualism is like friendship; 3) Mutualism occurs only at the microscopic level._

Audience Adaptation	poor			good		Comments
To their knowledge	①	2	3	4	5	_What exactly is a "species"? You don't define "symbiosis."_
To their interests and feelings	1	2	3	④	5	_I'm not interested in biology, but I can understand the benefits of friendship._
Language and Examples						
Concrete	1	②	3	4	5	_You should have given examples of commensalism and parasitism._
Vivid	1	2	③	4	5	
Appropriate	1	2	3	4	⑤	_Your explanation in terms of neighbor families was good!_
Voice						
Loudness	1	2	3	④	5	_It's easy to hear you._
Variety	1	②	3	4	5	_You tend to speak in a monotone._
Pronunciation	1	2	3	4	⑤	_You're able to pronounce all the scientific terms._
Articulation	1	2	3	4	⑤	
Bodily Action						
Movement	1	2	3	④	5	_Your movements look relaxed and natural._
Eye Contact	1	②	3	4	5	_Not enough! It seems you don't know we're there._

Suggestions

1. Define "symbiosis."

2. A visual aid listing each type of symbiosis would help, especially if you used arrows to indicate the dependent relationships. Using a visual aid might help you develop better eye contact, too.

QUESTIONS

A. Reread the Preparing and Presenting assignment in lesson 5.5, and think about how Missy's outline fulfills that assignment.

1. What is the specific purpose of Missy's speech?

2. How does Missy's speech fulfill the assignment given her class?

3. How does Missy link her topic to something familiar to her audience? Where in her speech does she do this? Why do you think she does it in this portion of her speech?

4. How does Missy define mutualism for her audience? Where in the speech does she do this?

5. What metaphor or simile does Missy use to help her audience understand the concept of mutualism? Where in the speech does she do this?

6. What examples of mutualism does Missy give her audience? How effective do you think these examples are? Explain why you find them (or don't find them) effective.

7. Which of the patterns for organizing information that you studied in lesson 5.2 does Missy's outline most resemble? Why (or why not) is the pattern she used effective?

B. Read George's practice record carefully.

1. George's practice record shows that he thinks mutualism occurs only at the microscopic level, even though this is not the case. Why has George received this false impression? How can Missy change her speech to avoid giving her listeners this false impression?

2. What two reasons does George give for suggesting that Missy use visual aids?

3. What visual aids to you think would most help you understand Missy's main ideas?

4. What problems does George have with the language in Missy's speech? How can she solve these problems?

C. Suppose that you are Missy, and that you have just reviewed the practice record completed by George.

1. George thinks that you didn't define *symbiosis*, but you know from your outline that you intended to, and you're almost certain that you did. How can you use the practice records completed by Jane and Sherry to see whether you really did define symbiosis in your speech?

2. What aspects of your speech and your delivery would you feel were successful?

3. What aspects of your speech and delivery need more work? How would you go about improving each of them?

D. After reading the practice record completed by George, what information will you particularly look for in the practice records completed by Jane and Sherry?

Guidelines

Keep the following points in mind as you practice your speaking:

- Work with someone in whom you have confidence, someone with whom you are comfortable.
- Agree beforehand with your listeners which items should be stressed during the practice session. Use the practice record form in this lesson. Make sure that you all agree on the meaning of the terms in the practice record before the practice session takes place. You may want your listeners to concentrate on evaluating one or two aspects of your speech, such as its organization or your use of gestures.
- Practice your speech as if you were actually giving it. Don't sit in a chair and mutter your speech. Stand up and deliver it as if you were in front of your final audience.

- Work to avoid being overly sensitive to constructive criticism. Listen carefully and give fair consideration to each of your listeners' suggestions.
- When helping others, seek to be constructive in your remarks. Make sure to remark on things the speaker is doing well, as well as noting things which should be corrected.
- Take advantage of practice sessions to try out new ideas. If they don't work, drop them and try others—that is what practice is for.

Preparing and Presenting

Arrange a practice session to practice the speech you prepared in lesson 5.5. (Before you schedule the session, you may want to check your outline against Missy's outline in this lesson, to be sure you have fulfilled all the requirements of the assignment.) Prepare any audio or visual aids that will make your presentation more vivid, and prepare your speaking notes.

Arrange to meet three classmates at a specified place and time to hold the practice session. At the beginning of the session, distribute blank practice forms (like the one in this lesson) to your classmates. Mention any aspects of your speech or delivery you would like them to pay special attention to. Then present your speech to your classmates.

Evaluating

Carefully read the practice records completed by your three classmates, then complete each of the following steps:

1. Ask your three classmates to explain anything in their practice records that you don't understand.
2. Ask your classmates to describe in detail the things they felt you did especially well in your speech.
3. Ask your classmates to discuss their suggestions for how you can improve your speech. Pay particular attention to how well they feel you accomplished your specific purpose—this is the best measure of the effectiveness of your speech.
4. At the end of your outline, write a brief summary of the strengths and weaknesses of your speech, as reflected in the three practice records. Then write a list of the steps you will take to improve your speech. Turn your outline and the three practice records in to your teacher.
5. Revise your speech, based on the suggestions you received during the practice session

Giving Constructive Criticism

Sometimes it may be part of your job to provide constructive criticism to a new worker or to someone working under your supervision. You can conduct such communication with tact and clarity by following these suggestions:

1. Be sure that the words you use have the same meaning for your listener that they have for you.

2. Limit your criticism to a particular aspect of the job or to a particular assignment.

3. Keep the purpose of your criticism uppermost in your mind. Your purpose is to give the worker information that will help him or her do a better job, not to tell everything you think about him or her. Focus on the behavior, not the personality, of the person whose work you are criticizing. It's more constructive to say "Please proofread your typing" than "You're a lousy secretary."

4. In addition to providing constructive criticism, make a point of telling the worker what aspects of the job he or she does well.

ACTIVITIES

1. With a partner, watch a person being interviewed on television. (A person being interviewed on a newscast or a sports star being interviewed after a big game would be a good choice.) As you listen to the interview, take notes on how the interviewer could improve his or her speaking. Then compare notes with your partner, and decide what the two of you would say to this person if he or she came to you for constructive criticism.

2. Interview a school counselor, or ask a counselor to talk with your class. Ask the counselor to discuss ways in which a person can provide constructive, helpful feedback to another person who has requested it.

3. Interview a foreman or the manager of a small business. Ask this person how he or she provides criticism to improve job performance. Also ask about the problems involved in providing such criticism, and how they can be overcome.

speaking skills

Using the Right Word

Every speech you give is a series of words. Using words that are accurate and specific will help your listeners understand your speech. Follow these suggestions to improve your choice of words:

1. Use a familiar word rather than an unusual one.
2. Use a concrete word rather than an abstract one.
3. Use verbs that express action rather than verbs that only express existence (such as *is* or *are*).
4. Use adjectives sparingly.
5. Whenever possible, use one word instead of a phrase.
6. Whenever possible, use short words instead of jargon or officialese.

ACTIVITIES

1. Study this *Shoe* cartoon, and discuss the point it makes about over-complicated language. Then look for examples of statements by government officials or agencies that do not follow the guidelines above. Explain to the class how each of your examples obscures meaning instead of communicating.

2. Study the Gettysburg Address or a speech by Winston Churchill. Then study a contemporary speech (or part of a speech) printed in a newspaper or magazine. Come to class prepared to explain how the Gettysburg Address or Churchill speech follows the six guidelines for using the right word. Also be prepared to explain how the contemporary speech does or does not follow the guidelines.

language

How to Respond to Questions from Your Listeners

Expository speeches are often followed by a question period. How well you answer your listeners' questions will strongly influence their opinion of your speech as a whole.

The best way to prepare for answering questions is to become thoroughly familiar with your topic. Once you know your topic in depth, you will be able to use several other techniques for answering questions effectively. For example, you can ask a questioner to clarify his or her question; that is, to make it more clear. You can repeat a question, to be sure that everyone in the room knows what question you are about to answer. If a listener asks several questions at once, you can answer them one at a time, repeating each question before you answer it.

Working with the Model

When Missy finished her speech on the concept of mutualism, the students in her biology class asked her some questions. Read this transcript of the question period:

MISSY: *(concluding her speech)* ... and so you can see that mutualism is a relationship between two species that benefits them both. You can think of mutualism as nature's good neighbor policy! Do any of you have questions?

BRENDA: Isn't the lichen an example of mutualism? But how can one plant be an example of a relationship that involves two different species?

MISSY: Let me answer those questions one at a time. Yes, you're right; the lichen is an example of mutualism. Now, what was your other question?

BRENDA: How can a single plant be an example of mutualism, if mutualism always involves two different species?

MISSY: That's a tricky one. You see, what we call a lichen really is two plants: an alga living in a mutualistic relationship with a fungus.

TOM: Can you explain how that works?

MISSY: I'm afraid I don't remember the exact nature of the relationship between the plants.

LARRY: I remember. Lichens grow in cool, dry environments. The

model

alga, which has chlorophyll, manufactures food for itself and for the fungus, which can't manufacture it's own food because it has no chlorophyll. The fungus captures and stores water for both plants.

MISSY: Thanks, Larry. Are there any other questions?

MAURICE: Are there other examples of mutualism on the non-microscopic level?

MISSY: Oh yes—there are lots of them.

TOM: Lots of what?

MISSY: I'm sorry, Tom. I should have repeated the question. Maurice asked whether there were other examples of mutualism on the non-microscopic level, and I said that there were lots of them. The first one that comes to mind is the mutualistic relationship that exists between certain fish that live in the waters around coral reefs and the shrimp that inhabit those waters. A shrimp stands on the coral and waves its antennae to attract the fish. The shrimp then eat the parasites clinging to the fish. You can see that this relationship benefits both the shrimp and the fish. Any more questions?

JANINE: My biology teacher last semester said that lichens were an example of symbiosis.

MISSY: I'm not sure I understand your question.

JANINE: Well, my teacher said that lichens were an example of symbiosis, but you say that they're an example of mutualism.

MISSY: Oh, I understand you now. In a way, your teacher and I are both right. You see, although some people use the term *symbiosis* to describe what I've been calling *mutualism,* others use *symbiosis* to describe any kind of interdependence between species, beneficial or not. Since *symbiosis* is used in these two different ways, many people prefer to use *mutualism* to make it clear that they are describing a mutually beneficial relationship between species.

QUESTIONS

A. Think about the techniques Missy used in answering the questions from her audience.

1. Brenda asks Missy two questions at the same time. How does Missy answer Brenda? What does Missy do to make sure that the audience remembers the second question before she answers it?

2. What might have happened if Missy had pretended to know the answer to Tom's question, and bluffed a response? How might Larry and the others who did not know the answer have reacted? What effect might Missy's discovered bluff have had on her listeners' attitude toward the rest of her speech?

3. What technique did Missy use to make sure that everyone in the class knew what question Maurice had asked?

4. Janine did not really ask a question at first. How did Missy get Janine to put her statement into question form before she attempted to answer it? What techniques did Missy use to clarify the question in a tactful manner? How did this help to reduce any tension that might have been caused by Janine's seeming to challenge the information in Missy's speech?

5. Tom seems very interested in Missy's speech. What might have happened to Missy's hold on her audience's attention if Tom had kept on asking questions, without giving the others a chance to participate? What techniques do you think a speaker can use to keep an individual from monopolizing the question period?

B. Build your skill in answering questions by working with three other students in a question-answering group. Each member of the group will pick a topic and spend five minutes answering questions about it. Pick your topic, and then answer questions from the other three students. Answer each question as completely and accurately as you can. Don't try to answer questions beyond your knowledge; just admit that you do not know the answer. Ask the others to clarify questions when necessary, and repeat any particularly long or complicated question before answering it, so that everyone in the group will know what question you are answering. (When you are answering questions before a group of ten or more people, it's a good idea to repeat every question before answering it.) After you have answered questions for five minutes, ask the other group members which of your answers were unclear or incomplete. Rephrase these answers to make them as clear and specific as possible.

Guidelines

Follow these guidelines when you answer questions from your listeners:

1. Be sure you understand a question before you attempt to answer it. If you aren't sure what a question means, ask your questioner to clarify it.

2. Be sure your audience knows what question you are answering. Unless you are speaking to a very small group, repeat each question before answering it.

3. If you are asked several questions at once, answer them one at a time. If your first answer is very long, ask your listener to repeat his or her other questions.

4. Make your answers direct and understandable. Limit your answer to the question you have been asked. Use specific examples in your answer. Use concrete language, and adapt your language to your audience.

5. Watch your listeners to be sure they understand your answers. If they look confused, you may not have understood the question in the first place, or they may not have understood your answer. If this happens, ask that the question be repeated, and repeat your answer as well.

6. If you don't know the answer to a question, don't bluff.

7. Treat the people who ask you questions with respect, even if they don't all treat you that way.

Preparing and Presenting

Prepare to present the speech you outlined in lesson 5.5 and practiced in lesson 5.6.

First, review your notecards and your Audience Analysis Checklist. Then make a list of the questions you think your audience is likely to ask at the end of your speech. Do any additional research necessary to make yourself feel thoroughly prepared to answer their questions.

Next, review the question-answering techniques Missy used in the Working with the Model section of this lesson. Give your list of questions to a friend, and have him or her ask them in a way that lets you practice your question-answering techniques. For example, have your friend ask you several questions at once, a question that must be clarified, and a question that seems to challenge the information presented in your report.

Finally, give your speech defining a concept to the class.

Evaluating

After you have given your speech and answered questions, ask the class to answer these questions about the speech:

1. What was the speaker's specific purpose?
2. Do you feel the speaker achieved this specific purpose? Explain why or why not.
3. How did the speaker's introduction capture your attention and direct it to the topic? How could the introduction be improved?
4. What pattern was used to develop the body of the speech? What other pattern (if any) would have been more effective?
5. What additional information or details (if any) would have made the speech more understandable?
6. Which question-answering techniques did the speaker use? What other techniques (if any) would have helped him or her do a better job of answering questions?

Giving Testimony

At some point in your life you may be required to testify under oath in the course of a trial or before an investigating committee or commission. The purpose of testimony is to present facts and evidence which other people (a judge, a jury, or committee members) will use to draw conclusions. A witness should follow these rules:

1. Listen carefully to the entire question. Do not interrupt the questioner or anticipate what he or she is going to say.
2. Answer only what was asked in the question.
3. If you do not understand a question, ask for clarification.
4. State your answer in terms of facts—things you have seen, heard, and done.
5. Do not give your opinion unless you are asked. If asked for your opinion (for example, "Which person was the aggressor?"), be prepared to cite facts in order to explain it.
6. Take your time answering questions. Do not allow yourself to be rushed.
7. Remain calm. Do not lose your temper, even if you feel you are being baited, made fun of, or attacked.
8. Do not evade the question or conceal any facts that should be part of the answer. Remember, your oath included a promise to tell "the whole truth."

ACTIVITY

1. Observe a committee investigation on television or in person. Learn the purpose of the investigation and the reasons why particular witnesses were called. As you listen to the questioning of witnesses, observe whether or not the questioning is relevant to the purpose of the investigation. Observe also whether the witnesses' testimony seems likely to help the purpose of the investigation, or whether committee members are using the testimony to gain publicity for themselves. Report on your findings to the class.

citizenship

5.8 Giving an Analytical Expository Speech

Finding Authoritative Sources of Information

It is often important to support your facts by citing the opinions and findings of authorities. Before citing information as evidence, however, you must be sure that it is truly authoritative. In evaluating information, follow these guidelines:

- The authority should be speaking or writing about a topic on which he or she is qualified and unbiased.
- Some authorities are much more qualified than others in the same field. Reference books can tell you about an authority's education, experience, publications, and honors.
- Be sure you know what the authority actually said. Secondhand or hearsay information is usually inaccurate. Even books and articles can be misleading unless the authors understand the subject and have checked the authority's exact words. Whenever possible, check the earliest published source of information.
- Because authorities often disagree with each other, evaluate each person's arguments, evidence, and credentials. You may have to cite both sides of the argument in order to show your knowledge of the subject.
- You should be prepared to question an "authoritative" statement if it contradicts your own experience.

ACTIVITY

1. Imagine you must prepare a report on international energy policy. Rank the following authorities in order from the most reliable to least reliable. (There is no single "right" answer.) Discuss your ranking with the other students, and see if they agree or disagree.

   The U.S. Secretary of Energy
   The head of your city's Department of Power
   A representative of OPEC
   A local service-station operator
   The president of a large oil company
   A local conservationist

research

How to Give an
Analytical Expository Speech

Now that you have given several expository speeches, you are ready to work on a speech that requires more preparation. Often you will be asked to give an oral report analyzing a topic from an area you have been studying. This kind of speech is called an *analytical expository speech.* In it you may analyze a speech, a poem, a novel, an advertisement, a song, or a short story for your audience.

As you analyze something for your audience, you will answer one or more of the following questions:

- *What does it mean?* What are the literal meanings in your selection? What implicit or suggested meanings does it contain?

- *How does it convey meaning?* How does the sequence of ideas in your selection help convey its meaning? What other devices (such as rhyme or alliteration in a poem) help to convey its meaning? How are these elements organized?

- *Why was it created?* If you are analyzing a work of literature, you will deepen your audience's understanding of it by explaining why it was created, especially if its author created it in response to a particular event.

- *What is its value?* Is your selection good or poor, compared with the best-known examples of its kind? In what ways is it different from other poems, plays, or stories?

There are several steps to preparing an analytical expository speech. First, *analyze your audience.* Will they be familiar with the novel, play, poem, or story you are analyzing? If not, give them enough background information so that they will be familiar with the examples you use in your analysis. This may mean summarizing the plot of a novel before you present your analysis of one of its chapters, or it may mean explaining the circumstances that led a poet to write the poem you are analyzing.

Second, *read expert analyses of your selection.* Even if your own analysis differs considerably from those you read, the opinions of experts can add to your audience's understanding of your selection. If you decide to quote a literary critic or other authority in your speech, be prepared to rephrase or expand his or her remarks, to help your listeners understand them. Also be prepared to define any unusual or technical terms in the expert's remarks.

Be careful to keep your analysis distinct from that of the experts, and to separate fact from opinion. One way to do this is to clearly *identify all expert sources* you use in your speech. Give the audience enough information about the authorities you cite to make it clear that they are knowledgeable sources.

The third step is to *prepare your speech* so it will be easily understood by your audience. Use your audience analysis checklist to find some link between your audience's interests or opinions and the topic of your speech. Then use this link in your introduction to capture your audience's attention and direct it to your topic. Present your analysis in a pattern that makes it easy for your audience to understand. Remember that you are asking them to understand in a few minutes an analysis that may have taken you several weeks to prepare. Use language appropriate to your audience, and explain any technical terms in your speech.

Working with the Model

The students in Jewel's class were asked to analyze a poem, play, speech, or short story for the class. Jewel decided to analyze a poem by Stevie Smith, a modern English poet. Before beginning her analysis, Jewel passed out copies of the poem, and asked her classmates to read it. Read the poem carefully, and then read Jewel's analysis.

model

Not Waving but Drowning

Nobody heard him, the dead man,
But still he lay moaning:
I was much further out than you thought
And not waving but drowning.

Poor chap, he always loved larking
And now he's dead
It must have been too cold for him his heart gave way
They said.

Oh no no no, it was too cold always
(Still the dead one lay moaning)
I was much too far out all my life
And not waving but drowning.

—Stevie Smith

Jewel's Analysis

Have you ever tried to communicate your feelings to someone, but found that you just weren't getting through to that person? I think most of us have that experience at one time or another. Stevie Smith's poem "Not Waving but Drowning" is about that kind of failure in communication. It sounds like a very simple poem at first, but—as I am going to show you—there's a great deal of meaning in it.

Stevie Smith, who died in 1971, was really named Florence Margaret Smith. She didn't make her living as a poet, but as a secretary. For many years, people did not take her poems very seriously. They sounded almost like nursery rhymes, and Stevie Smith illustrated them with cartoon-like drawings. In fact, this poem is effective just *because* it is so short and easy to read. It has only twelve lines, and not one word is wasted.

First, let's look at the poem's *literal* meaning, the basic meaning of the words. There are two voices speaking in the poem. One speaker is a man who has just drowned. The other voice belongs to his friends on the beach. They saw him waving his arms, trying to get help. However, they thought he was "larking"—that is, clowning around, having a good time. Now that the man is dead, they blame his death on the coldness of the water. The dead man, however, knows differently. He says, "It was too cold always / . . . I was much too far out all my life, / And not waving but drowning."

Now, when we read the last stanza, we realize that the poem is about much more than a man who has drowned in the ocean. Dead men, after all, cannot speak. Yet it is very important in this poem that we should know what the dead man is saying, what he knows that the others do not. The clue is in the line "I was much too far out all my life." If you think about it, you understand that he has been "drowning" for years. Even while he was alive, he was asking people for help. But throughout his life, nobody understood him.

In this poem, then, the ocean is not just a literal, real ocean. It is a *symbol*—that is, it stands for something else. I think you can see that the ocean stands for human life. In fact, we often speak of life as an ocean. We talk about "embarking on a new career" or being "overwhelmed by difficulties."

Now let's see how this symbol helps us understand the poem. In the first stanza we find out that a man has "drowned." This may mean that the man is actually dead, but it might also mean that he's been overwhelmed by problems. Why didn't people help him? Unfortunately, they couldn't tell he was in danger. He says, "I was much farther out than you thought"—but, of course, no one hears him when he says this.

In the second stanza, we hear from the other people. They're mildly sorry for him, but not very sympathetic. They say, "Poor chap"—that doesn't show very great emotion. Listen to the seventh line of the poem: "It must have been too cold for him his heart gave way." I think that line is meant to be read very rapidly, without any expression. This line is a *cliché*. It shows how little people understood about the drowned man.

In the last stanza, we hear from the dead man again. "It was too cold always," he says. What he means, I think, is that he was always treated coldly, without any affection or interest. In the same way, he was "too far out"—that is, too far away from people. In a sense, the people on the shore are right when they say, "His heart gave way." The man's heart broke because he did not have the love or friendship of other people.

The line "And not waving but drowning" appears twice in the poem. It is also used in the title. Maybe you can understand this line better if you think about some person you know who is always doing things to attract attention. Perhaps the person wears strange clothes, or talks too much, or behaves wildly. We usually say, "Oh, he's just having a good time"—in other words, "he always loved larking." We think a person like that is always "waving"; that is, trying to show us how

model

much he's enjoying himself. But suppose the person is actually "drowning," suffering from loneliness and the feeling that people are cold toward him. Perhaps the things he does to attract our attention are really a plea for our love and understanding. After reading this poem, maybe you'll think about that person again. Ask yourself whether he or she is "not waving but drowning."

You can see, then, that this little poem is about one of the most important problems in people's lives: understanding when other people need our help. Yet because the poem is so simple, its meaning strikes us almost immediately. Only a very fine poet could speak to us so well in so few words. Stevie Smith, too, must have felt such a lack of communication in her own life. As the English poet Philip Larkin wrote, "For all the freaks and sports of her fancy, . . . Miss Smith's poems speak with the authority of sadness."

QUESTIONS

A. Think about the four questions you should answer in an analytical expository speech, and how they apply to the poem.

1. Find the part of her speech where Jewel answers the question "What does it mean?" How does Jewel organize the answer to this question?

2. Find the part of her speech where Jewel answers the question "How does it convey meaning?" What aspects of the poem does Jewel point to in answering this question?

3. How does Jewel deal with the question "Why was it created?" Find the part of her speech where she suggests an answer.

4. How does Jewel answer the question "What is its value?"

B. Think about the way Jewel's speech illustrates her knowledge of her audience.

1. How does Jewel connect the knowledge and interests of her audience to the topic of her speech? At what places in her speech does she do this?

2. What background information does Jewel give her audience to help them understand the poem?

C. Think about the way Jewel organized her speech.

1. What does Jewel do to attract her audience's interest?

2. What aspect of the poem does she discuss first?

3. What aspect of the poem does she discuss next?

4. What point does Jewel make in her conclusion?

5. Do you think Jewel's conclusion would have been more effective if she had summarized her main points? Explain why or why not.

Guidelines

When you are preparing an analytical expository speech, be careful not to confuse your opinions about the object of your analysis with facts about that object. For example, critics' *opinions* about the merit of Dickens' novels have varied greatly since the time they were written. However, it is a *fact* that almost all of them were great popular successes when they first appeared.

As you present your opinions, make it clear that they are your own. When you present the analytical opinions of others, be sure to give your source, and enough background about the source to make it clear that he or she is an acknowledged expert.

An analysis usually presents one perspective, or viewpoint, on a subject on which several points of view are possible. When you are preparing an analytical expository speech, concentrate on *explaining* your point of view, rather than on convincing others that it is the right one. Do not be sarcastic toward your subject. Even if you dislike a poem or story, it is not necessary to belittle the work or its author in order to present an intelligent, informative analysis.

Preparing and Presenting

Prepare an analytical expository speech that will take about ten minutes to present. Choose the topic of your speech from one of these four groups. Ask your teacher to approve your topic before you begin work.

Television production:	Select a dramatic special or series.
Film:	Select a recent or older movie.
Literary work:	Select a short story, speech, novel, poem, or play.
Live concert:	Select a concert you attended recently or will attend before the date of your speech.

Once you have selected a topic from one of these groups, follow these steps in preparing your speech:

1. Familiarize yourself thoroughly with the topic of your speech.
2. If they are available, read informed analyses of your topic by acknowledged experts.
3. Analyze your audience's knowledge of and opinions about the topic of your speech.
4. Narrow your topic.
5. Write the specific purpose of your speech.
6. Prepare an outline of your speech.
7. Prepare an introduction that will get your listeners' attention by linking your topic with their interests and opinions.
8. Prepare your speaking notes.
9. Practice your speech.

Present your speech to the class. After you have finished your speech, answer questions from your listeners.

Evaluating

Ask the members of your class to answer these questions about your speech:

1. What was the speaker's topic?
2. What was the speaker's specific purpose?
3. How did the speaker use the audience's interests and opinions to establish a link between his or her topic and the audience?
4. What were the speaker's main points?
5. If the speaker previewed the main points, how effective and accurate was the preview? If the speaker did not preview the main points, how could he or she have done this?

6. Which of the following questions were answered in the speaker's analysis: *What does it mean? How does it convey meaning? Why was it created? What is its value?* Were these questions answered to your satisfaction? Explain why or why not.
7. What examples did the speaker use to support the main points?
8. What background information about the topic did the speaker give the audience?
9. What information did the speaker give the audience about experts cited in the speech?
10. What unusual or technical terms did the speaker define for the audience? What terms should have been defined, but were not?
11. What pattern did the speaker use to organize the information in the speech?

Explaining a Historical Document

As a citizen and future voter, you should understand the documents that express the ideas on which this country was founded. Imagine that you have to explain this paragraph from the Declaration of Independence:

We hold these truths to be self-evident, that all men are created equal, that they are endowed by their Creator with certain unalienable Rights, that among these are Life, Liberty and the pursuit of Happiness.

You would want to explain what the ideas in this passage meant to the authors, and what words had a different meaning when the passage was written. You would also explain the purpose of the Declaration, and its meaning for us today. You might explain the passage as follows:

"The authors of the Declaration were taking a serious and dangerous step—breaking the colonies' ties with Great Britain. They wanted to explain their actions, so the entire world would sympathize with them. They announce that three principles, or 'truths,' are 'self-evident'—that is, these principles cannot be proved logically, but every human recognizes them as true.

"The first 'truth' is that 'all men are created equal.' 'Men,' in the eighteenth century, meant both men and women—that is, every human being on earth. By 'equal,' the authors of the Declaration meant 'entitled to equal rights and treatment.' The second 'truth' is that people are born with certain God-given rights ('endowed by their Creator'). These rights are 'unalienable'—that is, they cannot be taken away by the actions of kings or governments. This means that human rights are more basic and important than any government.

"These rights are (1) 'Life'—that is, the right to live in safety and to protect one's life; (2) 'Liberty'—freedom of thought, speech, and religion, and also freedom to choose one's government; and (3) 'the pursuit of Happiness'—the right to live as one thinks best (without threatening the rights of others) and to own property."

ACTIVITY

1. Explain a passage from the Constitution or the Bill of Rights. Be sure to check words which may have changed their meaning in an unabridged dictionary. Deliver your analysis to the class.

citizenship

6 Listening to Understand

When you listen to a speech or a lecture, you are usually interested in information. You want to learn facts, ideas, and opinions from the speaker. You also need to remember what you have learned. For these reasons, you should take accurate notes on the speech. Good notes are based on good listening habits. They include all essential information, and are easy to read and study afterwards.

After working through this chapter, you should be able to

- recognize a speaker's signposts
- take notes using outline format
- record the essential information in a speech or lecture

The Speaking Skills lesson in this chapter will help you use outlines. You will learn to

- use the informal outline format
- record topics and subtopics in your notes

The Skills for Success lesson in this chapter will help you take notes on the job. You will learn to

- take notes on a training lecture
- test the accuracy of your notes

6.1 Listening and Taking Notes

Using Outlines

Making effective outlines is a useful skill for listeners as well as for speakers. Because formal outlines (using letters and numbers) are difficult to make while listening to a speech, you will probably prefer to make informal outlines. The informal outline has only two levels of information: main topics and subtopics. Here is an example of an informal outline:

Categories of Auto Insurance

Personal Injury Liability
—has per-person limit
—most expensive coverage
—required by law in many states

Property Damage Liability
—has per-occurrence limit
—more expensive for young, single people
  (as is personal injury coverage)

Medical Payment
—for driver, passengers
—generally low dollar limit
—paid regardless of fault

Comprehensive
—loss due to theft, fire, disasters
—owner pays deductible
—usually not worth having on older cars

ACTIVITY

1. Working with a partner, select a short chapter or section of a chapter from one of your textbooks. Make an outline of the material you have selected, listing only major topics and subtopics. Compare your outline with your partner's. Discuss whether either outline contains sufficient information (or unnecessary information). Then discuss which outline more accurately reflects the content you chose.

listening

How to Listen and Take Notes

You are probably used to taking notes when you do library research for a paper or a report. Taking notes on a speech or lecture, however, is different from taking notes on a book. You usually cannot ask a speaker to slow down so that you can take better notes. You cannot ask a speaker to repeat an earlier section of his or her speech. Furthermore, you will probably not have an outline of the entire speech in front of you as you write. When taking notes on a speech, you will record only the important points, and you will use a very simple outline form.

Effective note taking is based on effective listening. Listen for *signposts*—the words or phrases the speaker uses to tell you what part of the speech you are hearing; for example:

"To begin with ..."   "On the other hand ..."

"My first point ..."   "In conclusion ..."

"Secondly ..."

Also listen for signposts that emphasize the ideas the speaker thinks are most important; for example:

"First and foremost ..."   "Above all ..."

"Let me remind you ..."   "I repeat ..."

"I cannot emphasize too strongly ..."

The points that the speaker emphasizes should all go into your notes.

A speaker may outline a speech for the audience in advance (for example, a teacher may write the main points of a lecture on the board). Usually, however, you will be able to recognize only the speaker's main topics and the subtopics or supporting details. An *informal outline* format is best for recording a speech when you do not know in advance how it will be organized:

- First main topic
  —first subtopic
  —second subtopic
- Second main topic
  —first subtopic
  —second subtopic (and so forth)

When you take notes using the informal outline format, pay close attention to the relationships between the speaker's ideas. If you are not certain whether an idea is a main topic or a supporting detail, write it in whichever position is easier at the moment. When you review your notes afterward, you should be able to decide where the idea belongs.

Take your notes in the most concise form possible. Use phrases instead of sentences, and single words instead of phrases, whenever you can. Use abbreviations, initials, and symbols rather than complete names. Later, reread your notes to be sure that all abbreviations and shortened expressions are understandable.

Working with the Model

Ronald Reagan delivered his inaugural address on January 20, 1981. Read the following passage from the beginning of the speech, then read the notes that Vincent took while watching the speech on television. As you read the notes, notice which ideas Vincent chose to record.

The Inaugural Address

These United States are confronted with an economic affliction of great proportions.

We suffer from the longest and one of the worst sustained inflations in our national history. It distorts our economic decisions, penalizes thrift, and crushes the struggling young and the fixed-income elderly alike. It threatens to shatter the lives of millions of our people.

Idle industries have cast workers into unemployment, human misery, and personal indignity.

Those who do work are denied a fair return for their labor by a tax system which penalizes successful achievement and keeps us from maintaining full productivity.

But great as our tax burden is, it has not kept pace with public spending. For decades we have piled deficit upon deficit, mortgaging our future and our children's future for the temporary convenience of the present.

To continue this long trend is to guarantee tremendous social, cultural, political, and economic upheavals.

You and I, as individuals, can, by borrowing, live beyond our means, but for only a limited period of time. Why, then, should we think that collectively, as a nation, we're not bound by that same limitation?

We must act today in order to preserve tomorrow. And let there be no misunderstanding—we are going to begin to act, beginning today.

The economic ills we suffer have come upon us over several decades.

model

They will not go away in days, weeks, or months, but they will go away. They will go away because we as Americans have the capacity now, as we have had in the past, to do whatever needs to be done to preserve this last and greatest bastion of freedom.

Vincent's Notes

- U.S. confronted by great "economic affliction"

    --inflation harms econ., citizens

    --idle indust.→unemployment

    --tax system penalizes achievemt, prod'ty.

    --high pub. spending "mortgaging future"

    --→soc., econ. upheaval

    --nation living beyond means

- "Must act today in order to preserve tomorrow"

    --we (admin.) will

    --econ. ills came & will go slowly

    --Amer. have capacity to succeed

QUESTIONS

A. Think about the points made in Reagan's speech.
   1. What are the main topics of this passage?
   2. What are the subtopics and supporting details of this passage?
   3. What signpost words or phrases, if any, has Reagan used in this passage? Why do you think he has not used more signposts?

B. Think about Vincent's notes.
   1. What ideas or topics has Vincent included in his notes?
   2. What subtopics and details has Vincent omitted from his notes? Why do you think he omitted them?
   3. What abbreviations and symbols has Vincent used? Do you think they would be easy or difficult to understand? What other abbreviations do you think he might have used?
   4. What expressions has Vincent quoted directly from the speech? How has he indicated that these are exact quotes? Why do you think he did not record more direct quotations?

C. Some listeners prefer to take notes using a paragraph format. They write the main topic as the first sentence of a paragraph, and underline it. Then they write the subtopics and details as sentences in the paragraph. Rewrite Vincent's notes using the paragraph format.

Guidelines

In order to take good notes, you need to have good listening habits. Try to practice the following habits while listening to a speech or lecture:

1. Have all your note-taking materials ready *before* the speech begins. Have a pen that writes well, a notebook with enough blank pages, and a firm surface on which to write.
2. When the speaker begins, concentrate entirely on what he or she is saying. Don't think about the people next to you, your other classes, or your plans for the weekend.
3. Identify the *purpose* of the speech as soon as you can, and include it in your notes.
4. Listen for signpost words and phrases that identify the important points in the speech. Use underlining or symbols in your notes to make these points stand out.
5. Indent subtopics and supporting details to show their relation to the main topics. Include only the most important supporting details. Don't try to write down everything.
6. Use as many abbreviations, symbols, and initials as possible, but be sure that you will be able to understand them when you reread your notes.

7. As you listen, try to understand the speech rather than evaluating it. Listen carefully to the speaker's actual words, instead of anticipating what he or she will say.

8. If you have failed to record a piece of information correctly in your notes, wait until the speech is over before you go back to insert it. Polishing your notes during the speech will cause you to miss more important information.

9. Pay special attention to unfamiliar vocabulary and new concepts. Be sure to record and define these correctly.

10. After the speaker has finished, ask questions (if possible) to clarify any information you are uncertain about.

11. Review your notes while the speech is fresh in your memory. Make sure they are both legible and understandable. Rewrite any passages that you think might be difficult to understand a few weeks or months from now. Note any topics on which you need additional information.

ACTIVITY

Listen to a recording of a speech by a politician or other public figure. As you listen, take notes on a section of the speech lasting two to three minutes. Several days later, reread your notes, and try to write out that section of the speech as it was originally delivered. Then listen again to the recording. See how many of the important points you wrote down in your notes, and how many you missed. Think about ways in which you could have listened more carefully and taken better notes.

Preparing and Presenting

Work with a partner. Choose a lecture, speech, or program on which you can both take notes. Listen carefully to the speech, paying particular attention to signpost words and phrases. Take notes in the informal outline format, making the main points and subtopics clear.

Reread your notes, and rewrite any information that you think might be difficult to understand. If necessary, recopy your notes. Exchange the notes with your partner. Compare the information contained in your notes with the information in your partner's notes.

Evaluating

Think about the following questions on your listening habits and note taking:

1. What main topics did I record that my partner did not? What main topics did my partner record that I did not?

2. What subtopics and supporting details did I record that my partner did not? What subtopics and details did my partner record that I did not?

3. What information did I record as a main topic that my partner recorded as a subtopic, and vice-versa? Why did each of us record the information this way?

4. What abbreviations and symbols did each of us use? How easy is it for the other person to understand these abbreviations and symbols?

5. Which set of notes more accurately reflects the content and meaning of the speech?

When you have compared the notes and thought about these questions, discuss the notes with your partner. Try to decide which items should have been recorded as main topics and which as subtopics. Discuss which set of notes is easier to understand, and which one is more accurate.

Taking Notes on a Training Lecture

When you start a new job or learn a new skill, you will need to take accurate, useful notes on the oral instructions you are given. Follow these guidelines for taking notes on a training lecture:

- Listen carefully for the major steps in the procedure being taught, and be sure to record the steps in the right sequence.
- Be precise in recording figures and other technical information (measurements, times, sizes, numbers, colors, and so forth). Your notes should be clear and accurate enough that anyone could use them as a guide.
- Don't hesitate to ask the instructor to repeat or clarify information.
- Check the accuracy of your notes by going over them with the instructor (if possible) and by doing the procedure yourself.

ACTIVITIES

1. Ask another student to explain a task or procedure to you while you take notes on it. Then, using your notes as a guide, explain the procedure to the student who lectured you. Compare the accuracy of your notes, and find ways in which they might be improved.

2. With other members of your class, arrange to visit a business (such as a garage, a printing plant, or a fast-food restaurant) or one of the shops in your school. Ask a supervisor to explain a procedure to your group while you take notes. Then compare your notes with the other students'. Decide whose notes would be the best guide to carrying out the procedure, and explain why.

career

PART 3
Speaking
to Persuade

7. Group Discussion

8. Parliamentary Discussion

9. Persuasive Speaking

10. Debates

11. Critical Listening

A Case Study

In 1980, two speech professors, using computers and market research techniques, developed a "perfect" campaign speech on foreign policy. The speech was designed to appeal to everybody and to offend nobody. The ideas of the speech were vague and not specific. The language of the speech made listeners feel good, but meant very little. Here are some excerpts from that speech.

America requires a President who is experienced in diplomacy and capable of managing world stability. The international scene demands a chief executive who carries out a coherent and consistent foreign policy that can be understood and respected by allies and adversaries alike.

Today's international scene is one in which the major powers have reached military parity. What we must do is manage and stabilize our relationships with each other and maintain the balance of power.

The U.S. will continue to meet its responsibilities to its allies. However, to maintain world order, we will continue to seek and negotiate stable relationships with all nations.

The U.S. needs a President with a moral vision of promoting the welfare of mankind. America requires a leader who treats other nations with mutual respect; who promotes and encourages increased human rights and fundamental freedoms; who responds consistently in a calm, cool and reasoned manner.

THINK AND DISCUSS

Find five groups of words that you think were chosen for their reassuring effect. Tell why you think each phrase is reassuring.

Choose one sentence that states in a vague way something that this country should do. Then list at least two specific ways that thing could be done.

In Part Three, "Speaking to Persuade," you will think about some of the issues raised in this Case Study. You will learn ways of persuading people to agree with you wherever you are speaking.

7 Group Discussion

A group discussion can help you and other students or co-workers find a solution for a specific problem. In order to work well, a group discussion requires preparation, understanding, and consideration for others. If you want to participate effectively in such a discussion, you need to have information available with which to argue your position. You should understand the ways different members of a group contribute to the discussion. All the group members should listen to each other thoughtfully and with open minds.

After working through this chapter, you should be able to

- make a prediscussion outline for a group discussion
- understand the different roles of group members
- work effectively in small groups

The Speaking Skills lessons in this chapter will help you solve problems in group discussions. You will learn to

- use a problem-solving sequence
- evaluate sources of evidence
- use gestures to communicate

The Skills for Success lessons in this chapter will help you solve problems at work and in public organizations. You will learn to

- solve a community problem
- work with others to solve a problem
- develop agreement within a political organization

7.1 Making a Prediscussion Outline

Learning a Problem-Solving Sequence

The following sequence of steps and questions can be used in solving problems. You can work through this sequence by yourself when solving a personal problem. You can also work through it with others, when an entire group is faced with a problem. Be sure to answer the questions in each step before you go on to the the next step.

Step 1. Define and understand the problem.
- What are the symptoms—the signs that a problem exists?
- How many people are affected by the problem?
- What are the causes of the problem?

Step 2. Determine the standards for evaluating possible solutions.
- What should a solution to the problem accomplish?
- What standards will guarantee that a solution to the problem will not create new problems?

Step 3. Identify possible solutions.
- What possible solutions are available?
- What would have to be done to put each solution into effect?

Step 4. Evaluate the possible solutions and select the best one.
- How well does each solution satisfy the standards established in Step 2?
- Which solution or combination of solutions best satisfies the standards?

ACTIVITY

1. Select a personal problem that you are willing to discuss with others. Work through the possible solutions, making a written outline of each step. You might choose one of the following problems:
   - what kind of summer job to apply for
   - which classes to take next semester
   - which colleges or other schools to apply to
   - whether or not to buy an automobile

problem solving

How to Make a Prediscussion Outline

Conducting a group discussion can be a particularly effective means of exploring a specific problem and arriving at a solution to it. Working together, group members share their ideas and build on one another's contributions to solve the problem.

Members of a successful problem-solving discussion group must understand and use the four steps in the problem-solving process. These are the steps:

1. Begin by describing and understanding the problem. This step may involve defining the symptoms, scope, and causes of the problem.
2. Next, identify specific criteria, or standards, by which all the possible solutions to the problem can be judged. Notice that these criteria are established before the possible solutions are explored.
3. Then, identify and define all the possible solutions to the problem. It is especially important to keep an open mind during this step in the problem-solving process, so that all possible solutions may be considered by the group.
4. Finally, evaluate each possible solution according to the criteria you have established. On the basis of these evaluations, select the best solution to the problem.

The members of a problem-solving discussion group should keep these four steps in mind while preparing for the discussion. The first step in preparing for the discussion is to do research. Each group member should gather facts, statistics, and opinions about the problem, the possible solutions to the problem, and the criteria by which those solutions might be judged. To do so, each member should read books and magazines, listen to relevant programs on television and radio, and conduct interviews.

While doing research, each discussion group member should take notes on his or her findings and should then organize those notes into a prediscussion outline. In preparing and using their outlines, the group members must understand that each person's outline is a summary of the information he or she has gathered during research. It is not a specific outline showing how the discussion will be conducted. During the actual group discussion, each group member will refer to his or her own outline. However, each group member should also be prepared to consider new facts and ideas contributed by the other group members.

Working with the Model

Edrill and the other members of her group chose to consider this problem: What special provisions should be made for the education of physically disabled children? Edrill did research on the problem. Then she prepared the following prediscussion outline. Study Edrill's outline, thinking about how she collected facts and opinions and how she organized those facts and opinions in her outline.

Discussion problem: What special provisions should be made for the education of physically disabled children?

I. What is the problem?

A. Public Law 94-142 (Education for All Handicapped Children Act) requires "free and appropriate public education" for all school-aged disabled children (*Newsweek,* Sept. 4, 1978).

B. How to determine what an "appropriate" education is and how to provide it is the responsibility of individual school districts.

C. Scope of the problem: There are more than eight million disabled children in the U.S. (Donahue, *America,* April 14, 1979); "roughly one-tenth of all children are handicapped" (Gliedman and Roth, *The Unexpected Minority*).

II. What criteria should be used to evaluate possible solutions?

A. Solution should have positive psychological and educational effect on disabled children.

B. Solution should have at least no negative psychological or educational effect on nondisabled students whom it involves.

C. Solution should not cost any more than any other, equally effective solution.

D. Solution should meet the requirements of federal law.

III. What are the possible solutions?

A. No special provisions should be made. Disabled children who are able to take advantage of regular classroom facilities should do so; others should be the responsibilities of their own parents (Interview, local taxpayer).

B. Disabled children should be assisted in participating in regular classes as much as possible. Additional educational and support services should be offered according to each child's needs (Donahue). Further, nondisabled children should be educated to understand physical disabilities (Leishman, *McCall's,* April 1978). This approach is usually called "mainstreaming."

C. Disabled children should be grouped together and taught in special classrooms. The unusual needs caused by their physical

model

disabilities should be directly met by specially trained teachers (Interview, parent of 8-year-old girl with cerebral palsy).

IV. How well does each solution meet the established criteria?

    A. No special provisions should be made.

        1. This would have positive psychological and educational effect only for slightly disabled children, who can adjust readily to a regular classroom; its effect for most disabled children would be negative, since they would feel excluded from "normal" activity and would not receive public education (Interview, elementary school principal).

        2. Since it would not significantly change the make-up of regular classrooms, it would not have much effect on nondisabled students.

        3. This approach would actually lower current spending for education (Interview, elementary school principal).

        4. This approach does not meet legal requirements for free public education for all disabled children.

    B. Disabled children should be "mainstreamed" into regular classrooms.

        1. Positive psychological and educational effects include increased pride, enthusiasm, self-confidence, ability to deal with other people, and motivation to learn (Bernstein, *Today's Education,* Feb./Mar. 1980). Negative effects, however, may include too much competition with standards physically disabled children are not prepared to meet and decreased opportunity "of mixing with other children who have similar

model

disabilities (which can be helpful in assisting the child to assess the effects of his or her disability upon his or her achievement)" (Bowe, *Handicapping America*).

2. The effect on nondisabled children who are taught to understand disabilities and to learn and work with physically disabled children is usually positive (Daley, *Better Homes and Gardens,* Sept. 1979). However, some people express concern that the educational needs of nondisabled children may be neglected by teachers who give too much attention to the physically disabled students in the classroom (*Newsweek,* Sept. 4, 1978).

3. Congress has allotted funds to assist school districts, but providing full educational facilities and support systems for disabled children will necessitate additional spending by most school districts. It may even require some cutbacks in their regular educational programs (*Newsweek,* Sept. 4, 1978).

4. This approach meets legal requirements by providing "free and appropriate public education" for disabled children.

C. Disabled children should be grouped together and taught in special classrooms.

1. Smaller class size and specially trained teachers may provide educational benefits; however, negative effects include decreased opportunity for mixing with nondisabled children and increased probability of "labeling and stigma" (Bowe, *Handicapping America*).

2. Nondisabled children face no risk of disruption or decreased attention in the classroom. However, the lack of consistent, positive experiences with disabled children may be considered a negative effect.

3. Because of the small class size and special facilities required, special education classes are more expensive than regular classes. Establishing such special classes, however, is usually less expensive than is providing special assistance to students throughout the school district, as required in mainstreaming (Interview, elementary school principal).

4. This approach meets legal requirements by providing "free and appropriate public education" for disabled children.

QUESTIONS

A. Think about the prediscussion outline Edrill prepared.

1. What specific sources did she consult in doing her research? What notes about her sources did she include in her prediscussion outline?

How might she use those notes about her sources when she participates in the group discussion?

2. How did Edrill organize the information in her outline? How will the organization of her outline help her participate in the group discussion?

3. When Edrill participates in the group discussion, she should be ready to help the group members agree on the definitions of several key terms. One of those terms is *physically disabled children.* What other terms used in her prediscussion outline should Edrill be prepared to help define?

4. How did Edrill evaluate each of the possible solutions she included in her outline? How did she use each of the criteria she established?

5. Edrill might have included a final note in section IV of her outline. That note would have indicated which solution she considers best. Based on the information in her outline, which solution do you think Edrill would have chosen? Why do you think she would have chosen that solution?

Guidelines

Think about the following guidelines as you prepare to participate in a problem-solving group discussion:

1. There are four steps in the problem-solving process:
   a. Describe and understand the problem.
   b. Identify specific criteria for evaluating possible solutions to the problem.
   c. Identify and define possible solutions to the problem.
   d. Evaluate each possible solution according to the established criteria.
2. Each member of the group should research the problem, gathering relevant facts and opinions.
3. Each member of the group should prepare a prediscussion outline. In that outline, each member organizes and records the information he or she gathered in research. The information should be organized in the order of the four steps of the problem-solving process.

Preparing and Presenting

Join four to seven other students in forming a discussion group. With the other members of your group, select an issue to consider in a problem-solving discussion. If you wish, you may choose one of the following problems:

- What should the federal government do to improve care for the aged?

- What should citizens do to decrease violence in their neighborhoods?
- What programs (if any) should be provided to prepare high-school students for parenthood?
- What part should competitive sports play in the high-school curriculum?
- What specific requirements for high-school graduation should be imposed on all students?

Once you have selected a problem, work independently to gather information and opinions on it. Use a variety of sources in your research. Read at least one book chapter, two magazine articles, and one reference book article. Also, watch one radio or television program on the problem. If possible, interview at least two people who have knowledge or experience that relates to the problem. Take particular care in recording your sources, so you can quickly refer to them if other group members have questions about your information.

After you have completed your research, write an outline that will help you participate in a discussion of the problem. Your outline should have four main sections, corresponding to the four steps in the problem-solving process. Prepare your outline using only the left half of each page, so you will be able to use the right half for taking notes during the discussion.

Evaluating

Compare your prediscussion outline with the outlines written by the other members of your group. After reading the other students' outlines, ask yourself the following questions:

1. What technical or unusual terms should I define in my outline?
2. How can I make the description of the problem in my outline more clear and more specific?
3. What criteria for evaluating solutions should I add to the second section of my outline?
4. What possible solutions should I add to the third section of my outline?
5. If I feel that one of these solutions is definitely the best, have I indicated this in my outline?
6. How can I make the evaluations in the final section of my outline more comprehensive?
7. Have I identified all the sources of my information?
8. What further research should I do to prepare myself for the discussion?

If necessary, do more research, and make improvements in your prediscussion outline.

Solving a Community Problem

To solve a problem that faces your community, follow these general rules:

1. *Define the problem.* What exactly is wrong? How many people does the problem affect? Is it limited to a few families on one block, or does it involve an entire neighborhood? Can the problem be solved? Is it the responsibility of a single person or agency, or will I have to do research to find someone who will help solve it?

2. *Contact people who can help you.* Enlist friends, neighbors, and other members of your community on your side. Explain the seriousness of the problem, and why you should all be concerned about it.

3. *Define possible solutions.* Follow the problem-solving sequence (see Speaking Skills, lesson 7.1). Select only the most workable solutions, and be sure that they will eliminate the causes of the problem.

4. *Decide whether you need official help.* Many community problems can be solved if the people involved cooperate with one another. Other problems, however, may require the help of the city council, the public works department, or other government agencies. In most cases, you will get the fastest help if you go directly to the person with the most power: the mayor, the council member for your district, or the highest-placed person on a board or agency. (See Skills for Success, lesson 9.1.)

5. *Keep track of the problem and its solutions.* Don't simply drop the problem on an official's desk. Watch to see how well it is solved.

ACTIVITY

1. Working with three other students, define a problem that affects your community. It can involve conflicts between neighbors, or it can be a public problem such as vandalism. Discuss the different people you could enlist to help you solve the problem, and the different suggestions they might have. Then role-play a problem-solving session before the class. During the session, try to find at least three possible solutions and identify three people or agencies that might help you. Ask the class to suggest further solutions.

citizenship

7.2 Understanding the Roles of Group Members

Evaluating Sources of Evidence

When you research an issue in preparation for a speech or interview, you need to evaluate the accuracy of your sources. Ask yourself the following questions about each source:

- Is it up-to-date? Check the date of publication of a periodical, the copyright date of a book, and the dates of books or events mentioned in the text to be sure that your information is current.
- Is it thorough? Consider whether the source treats a subject in depth or merely provides pictures and vague generalizations.
- Is it unbiased? Read carefully to detect any political, social, or economic bias in the source.
- Is it authoritative? Most reliable sources have footnotes or bibliographies that refer you to other, more detailed treatments of the subject. Periodical and encyclopedia articles by qualified authors are usually signed.
- Is it consistent with what you know? Compare the facts in each source with the facts in other books, articles, and encyclopedias.
- Do other experts consider it a reliable source? Teachers, authors, and librarians can tell you which sources, in their areas of special knowledge, are most accurate and complete.

ACTIVITIES

1. Invite the school librarian to speak to your class about the best sources of information in a particular area of knowledge (for example, science, business, history, or current events). Ask him or her to describe how librarians learn about reference works and other sources in areas with which they are unfamiliar.

2. Working with several other students, select an issue of current interest. Investigate the subject, with each student using one source of information. When you have each done your research, compare the results, and discuss the differences among the sources in terms of accuracy, completeness, and bias.

research

How to Understand the Roles of Group Members

During a problem-solving discussion, group members may relate to other group members in many different ways. One person, the group leader, is committed to a formal role. The other members assume informal roles, either positive or negative.

Each problem-solving discussion group should have one leader. The leader accepts specific responsibilities toward the other group members. First, he or she must make any necessary arrangements for the group's meeting. Then, during the discussion, the group leader is responsible for keeping the discussion directed toward its goal, the exploration and solution of a specific problem. Usually, this involves encouraging group members to participate, keeping group members from discussing unrelated issues, and tactfully resolving any conflicts that may arise between group members. The discussion group leader should concentrate on guiding the other group members and must be especially careful to avoid giving too much attention to his or her own ideas.

The informal roles that discussion group members most often assume are listed in the chart on the following page. During a discussion, each group member usually plays at least several of these informal roles. Group members who know and understand the informal roles that may be played during a group discussion can evaluate and improve their own participation. They can also respond constructively to the participation of other group members.

INFORMAL ROLES PLAYED BY GROUP DISCUSSION MEMBERS

Positive Roles

Information Seeker	One who asks questions to elicit information
Information Giver	One who gives the group facts and data
Opinion Seeker	One who asks the opinion of others
Opinion Giver	One who gives the group his or her opinions
Summarizer	One who recalls and briefly restates contributions made by various group members
Builder	One who listens thoughtfully and adds to the contributions of others
Procedural Technician	One who reminds other members of the routines and processes necessary to successful group functioning
Vision Builder	One who sees possibilities ahead
Reality Tester	One who seeks to verify the accuracy of information contributed by others
Boundary Tester	One who tries to stretch the group's thinking
Mediator	One who helps resolve conflicts and helps maintain harmony
Expediter	One who keeps the group moving toward the accomplishment of its purpose

Negative Roles

Dominator	One who tries to talk all the time and fails to listen to others
Interrupter	One who does not give others a chance to fully express their ideas
Thoughtless Agreer	One who enthusiastically supports any—and every—point of view
Forecaster of Doom	One who sees only the negative aspects of every issue
One-Track Thinker	One who repeatedly returns to the same issue
Supercritic	One who finds fault but fails to make constructive criticisms
Put-Down Artist	One who finds fault with other group members
Silent Observer	One who never expresses his or her ideas and opinions
Wanderer	One who digresses from the main point of the discussion

Working with the Model

Seven group members had researched and prepared prediscussion outlines on the problem, "What special provisions should be made for the education of physically disabled children?" Then they met as a group to discuss the problem. The leader of the group was Lucy. The other members of the group were Edrill, Jeremy, Carmine, Susan, Alvin, and Felipe. Read the following transcript of part of their discussion. As you read, think about the different roles played by each group member.

LUCY: We have agreed on four basic criteria for evaluating possible solutions. I think, then, that we're ready to discuss exactly what the possible solutions are.

EDRILL: I spoke with one taxpayer who suggested that we should make no special provisions at all for educating disabled kids. I think I should mention, by the way, that this person doesn't have any children. I've been noticing that the people who really oppose spending money on education don't have children of their own. You'd think that they would understand that public education affects everyone—not just parents and kids.

JEREMY: I know what you mean. Some of the people in our apartment building think they shouldn't have to pay taxes for the schools—just because their kids have all finished school already. No wonder our school district is short of funds!

LUCY: You're right, that is a problem. But right now we should get back to Edrill's main point. One possible solution that has been suggested is that public schools should not have to make any special provision for educating physically disabled children.

CARMINE: Yes, I read a letter in last month's *Tribune* that expressed the same idea. If disabled kids can't take advantage of whatever the regular classroom provides, then it's up to their parents to educate them.

SUSAN: But that's just not fair! Kids who have physical disabilities need an education just as much as kids without physical disabilities—maybe more. And think about how *different* it would make you feel if you weren't even allowed to go to school.

LUCY: You're making a good point, Susan, but let's wait with the evaluation until we have mentioned all the possible solutions. Alvin, do you have any ideas about other possible solutions we should be considering?

ALVIN: *(shakes his head)*

model

FELIPE: I read several magazine articles about a general program called mainstreaming. This usually involves including physically disabled kids in —

EDRILL: Oh, yeah, mainstreaming really seems to be the answer. It helps disabled kids and nondisabled kids. Of course, some people aren't enthusiastic about mainstreaming, but there are always some people who are afraid of anything different.

LUCY: It's good that you're enthusiastic about one of the solutions, Edrill, but let's give Felipe a chance to finish explaining it. Remember, we want to consider each solution before we begin our evaluations.

FELIPE: Well, with mainstreaming, physically disabled kids are included in regular classrooms as much as possible. But that doesn't mean that they're just left to work things out on their own. They're given any special help they need in addition to the regular classroom instruction.

QUESTIONS

A. Think about how Lucy acted as the leader of the group discussion.
   1. How did she summarize what the group had already accomplished?
   2. How did she guide the group members in continuing the discussion?
   3. How did she try to keep the discussion focused on the problem?
   4. How did she attempt to involve everybody in the discussion?

B. Think about the informal roles played by the other members of the group.
   1. What role did Edrill assume when she first spoke?
   2. How did Jeremy respond to Edrill's irrelevant comments?
   3. Which students assumed these roles at least once in the recorded section of the discussion: Information Giver, Interrupter, Silent Observer?

C. Evaluate each member's contribution in the recorded section of the group discussion.
   1. How did each member help advance the discussion?
   2. What specific suggestions would you make to help each member improve his or her contribution to the discussion?

Guidelines

Whenever you participate in a group discussion, you should consider the variety of roles that each group member might play.

1. The leader of the group discussion has a formal role to fill. He or she is responsible for making arrangements for the group meeting. During the course of the group discussion, the leader is responsible for stimulating participation, resolving conflicts, and keeping the discussion focused on the problem to be considered.

2. The members of a discussion group may assume various informal roles during the course of a problem-solving discussion. These roles may be positive; they may help to advance the discussion. These roles may also be negative; they may detract from the purpose of the discussion. Understanding these different informal roles will help you contribute positively to the group discussion and respond constructively to other group members.

Preparing and Presenting

With the other members of your group, role play different discussion-group roles. Before you begin, each member should select a specific role to play and should announce his or her role to the rest of the group members. One member should choose the role of group leader. Half of the remaining members should choose positive informal roles; the other half should choose negative informal roles.

Work together to act out one section of a problem-solving group discussion. You may base the content of your discussion on the content used in the transcript in the Working with the Model section of this lesson. Or, if one of your group members has completed his or her prediscussion outline, you may base the content of your discussion on one specific section of that student's outline.

Remember that, in this activity, you should concentrate on playing specific roles. Later you will have an opportunity to actually conduct your group discussion and to work with the information you have gathered.

As you and the other group members act out the discussion, think about how it feels to play each kind of role. Also think about how you spontaneously respond to the roles played by other group members, and about how you could respond in a constructive manner.

After the members of your group have acted out their roles for several minutes, change roles. A different member should assume the leader's role. Members who had assumed positive informal roles should adopt negative informal roles; members who had assumed negative informal roles should adopt positive informal roles. Again, announce the specific roles you intend to play, and act out one of the four sections of a problem-solving group discussion.

You may wish to continue changing roles until every member has had an opportunity to act out the role of group leader. If your group does this, be sure that you act out a different role each time.

Evaluating

With the other members of your group, discuss the various roles you acted out. Discuss how the player of each role felt and how the other group members responded to each player. You may wish to respond to the following questions:

1. What did each group leader do to guide the discussion?

2. What problems did each group leader face? How did he or she attempt to solve those problems?

3. What positive informal roles did the members act out? How did the player of each of these roles help advance the discussion?

4. How did the rest of the group members react to those who were playing positive informal roles?

5. What negative informal roles did the members act out? How did the player of each of these roles disrupt the progress of the discussion?

6. How did the rest of the group members react to those who were playing negative informal roles?

Working with Others to Solve a Problem

Whether as a student, as a worker, or as a member of your community, you need to be able to work with other people in order to solve problems. Often, a problem will arouse strong emotions in people, and it is important that you be able to discuss it without quarreling. Here are guidelines to follow when working with others to solve a problem:

- When the group is organized, it should include people who have different interests or attitudes toward the problem. To solve a job-related problem, for example, shop or clerical workers, supervisors, salespeople, and managers might work together.
- Be sure each participant knows enough about the problem to be able to contribute ideas to the group.
- Follow the steps in the problem-solving sequence. (See Speaking Skills, lesson 7.1.) Be sure to answer all the questions in each step before going on to the next step.
- Keep the group's discussion focused on the problem at hand, rather than on other problems or complaints.
- Don't let personality conflicts intrude on the discussion of the problem.

ACTIVITIES

1. Work with several other students. Ask each student to identify the one or two most important problems facing the school. Select the problem that seems most complicated or that causes the greatest difference of opinion. Work with the other students to find a solution to this problem.

2. Ask several people to identify the most important problem that faces your community. Include people of different ages, occupations, and backgrounds in this group. Select one problem, and meet with these people (if your teacher approves) or with other students to find a solution.

career

7.3 Working Effectively in a Small Group

Using Gestures to Communicate

Whenever you speak, you use your hands, face, and body as well as your voice. A good use of gestures can enhance your speech, but awkward or inappropriate gestures can distract and irritate your audience. To make the best possible use of gestures, follow these guidelines:

- Gestures should be *purposeful.* When you practice a speech, practice the gestures that go with it (preferably in front of a mirror). Know when to gesture, and when to keep still. Find a relaxed and comfortable position for your hands when you are not using them.
- Gestures should be *appropriate.* For example, you may use a sweeping movement of your arm to emphasize the scope of a problem, or a raised hand to alert your audience to an important point. At other times, refraining from movement may help concentrate your audience's attention on a serious statement or a complex point.
- Gestures should be *smooth* and *economical.* Practice moving your hands into position for each gesture, and returning them to the rostrum or to your notes when the need for the gesture is over. Don't jerk, point suddenly, fling out your arms, or sway back and forth.

ACTIVITY

1. Prepare a short speech in which you can make use of various gestures. Deliver the speech to two different groups of students. Before the first group, use a range of appropriate gestures to emphasize the content of your speech. Before the second group, remain as motionless as possible while speaking. Ask each group to evaluate your speech and tell you whether or not they found it effective. Compare the results to learn if your gestures helped or harmed your speech.

movement

How to Work Effectively in a Small Group

If a discussion group is to be successful in exploring and solving a problem, all the group members must work together toward that goal. Working together requires that members listen thoughtfully to one another and build on what has already been said. It requires that they wait for one person to finish expressing his or her thoughts before they begin to speak. It also requires that they approach each contribution with interest and with open minds.

In order to work together successfully, discussion group members must be considerate of one another's feelings. They must respect one another's intentions, ideas, and emotions, and they must understand that differences of opinion can be resolved constructively.

Working with the Model

The following transcript records another section of the group discussion on the problem, "What special provisions should be made for the education of physically disabled children?" The members of the group are Lucy (who is the group leader), Edrill, Jeremy, Carmine, Susan, Alvin, and Felipe. Read the transcript, and think about how each group member listens and responds to the contributions of the other members.

LUCY: We seem to have covered the evaluation of our first possible solution. Let's go on to see how our second possible solution, mainstreaming, measures up against our criteria.

JEREMY: In terms of psychological and educational benefits to disabled children, I read some pretty exciting things about mainstreaming. Provided a disabled child is given enough support, being in a so-called regular classroom with other kids the same age can be really positive. The kid's self-image and even the kid's ability to learn are improved.

CARMINE: I read the same kinds of articles. Some very exciting things *can* happen. But that's not the way it always works out. When we consider mainstreaming, we have to think about the disabled kids who end up overwhelmed and frustrated, too.

EDRILL: Oh, don't be so negative, Carmine. Try to look on the bright side of this issue.

185

FELIPE: Carmine's just trying to help us be realistic. Physically disabled kids do have to deal with special problems. If those problems prevent the kids from keeping up with the rest of the class, they're just going to feel defeated. And defeat is never positive—psychologically or educationally!

SUSAN: You're right, Felipe. On the other hand, to make a fair evaluation, we have to assume that mainstreaming will be carried out thoughtfully and carefully. At its best, mainstreaming involves a thorough evaluation of each child's total situation, followed by a placement that will best meet all the child's needs. Disabled kids who cannot benefit from regular classroom work—for *whatever* reason—shouldn't be forced out of a better situation. That's the point that Public Law 94-142 makes about "the least restrictive environment."

LUCY: It looks like, in terms of our first criterion, mainstreaming gets a mixed rating. It can have both positive and negative effects on disabled children. What about in terms of our second criterion—its effects on the nondisabled kids who are involved?

FELIPE: I think mainstreaming gets the same kind of rating here—mixed.

CARMINE: I know what you mean. When it's well done, mainstreaming seems to have a terrific effect on everybody. All the kids—disabled and nondisabled—learn more because they're learning together. And they're learning from each other.

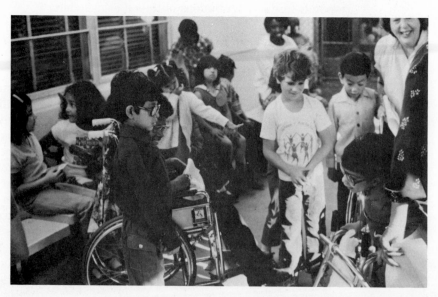

SUSAN: That's right. But when it isn't done carefully—

EDRILL: Oh no! Here comes another put-down.

SUSAN: I'm just trying to be fair. If mainstreaming isn't done right, everybody's education can suffer. And nondisabled kids— instead of developing healthy and accepting attitudes—can build up new kinds of resentments against people who appear to be different.

· · · ·

LUCY: Now that we have evaluated each of the three possible solutions, we need to work on choosing the one solution we consider best.

CARMINE: I think that a program of mainstreaming seems most effective. It benefits both disabled and nondisabled kids, and it clearly complies with the law.

FELIPE: That's true, but there is another criterion to consider. Mainstreaming is clearly the most expensive of the three possible solutions.

SUSAN: According to our phrasing of that criterion, expense is really only a consideration if all the other effects are equal.

LUCY: That's right, Susan. So now we need to be sure that everyone agrees on the superiority of mainstreaming in terms of our other three criteria. Jeremy, what do you think?

QUESTIONS

A. Think about how each member contributed to the group discussion.
   1. Which group members showed that they were listening thoughtfully to the contributions of others? How did they respond to those contributions?
   2. Which group members showed that they were not listening carefully and that they were not concentrating on the group's purpose?
   3. Which group members showed consideration of the feelings of others? How did their consideration help advance the discussion?
   4. Which group member did not show consideration of the feelings of others? How did that lack of consideration disrupt the discussion?

B. Think about how the group members began trying to agree on the best solution to the problem.
   1. What standards did they try to use in judging the possible solutions?
   2. What do you think happened in the rest of the discussion? Which solution do you think the group members chose as best? Why do you think they chose that solution?

C. Think about what changes might enhance the group discussion.
   1. How might each group member's contribution be changed to show involvement in the group's task, consideration for the feelings of others, and respect for the ideas posed by others?
   2. What might the other group members do to decrease the disruptive effect of Edrill's comments?
   3. What might the other group members do to encourage Alvin's involvement in the discussion?

Guidelines

The following guidelines will help you participate constructively in a group discussion:

1. Work with the other group members toward the accomplishment of the group's purpose. Listen thoughtfully to the facts and opinions contributed by others. Be ready to add your own facts and opinions, but also be ready to change your mind in response to new ideas.

2. Be considerate of the feelings of others, and respect the ideas they suggest. Any strain in the relationships between group members may detract from the accomplishment of the group's purpose.

Preparing and Presenting

With the other members of your group, conduct a group discussion about the problem you selected and researched.

Before you begin, choose one member of the group to act as the discussion leader. That person should review the responsibilities of a group leader (see lesson 7.2). The other group members should review the positive informal roles that can be played by discussion group members (see lesson 7.2).

As the group discussion develops, you should consider, in order, the four steps in the problem-solving process. Each group member should refer to his or her outline for specific facts, quotes, and sources. Each of you should remember, however, that your outline is not intended as an outline for the group discussion. Rather, you should use your outline as a reference for the specific information and ideas you gathered in preparing for the discussion.

After the members of the group have evaluated each of the possible solutions raised during the discussion, you should try to agree on the best solution. If there is disagreement about which solution is best, try to combine different solutions to come up with one that everyone accepts, or try to find some additional information about one of the original solutions that will make that solution acceptable to everyone in the group.

Evaluating

With the other members of your group, evaluate your problem-solving discussion. Talk about your responses to the following questions:

1. How did each group member help advance the discussion?

2. What evidence was there that each group member had researched and considered the problem before the discussion?

3. How did the group leader guide the discussion and keep it moving?

4. In what remarks did group members build on something that had just been said?
5. What specific problems did the leader face? How did he or she attempt to solve those problems?
6. What evidence was there that the group members were listening and responding to one another's ideas?
7. What kinds of disagreements arose during the discussion? How did the group members deal with those disagreements?
8. Which step in the problem-solving process did the discussion deal with most thoroughly? Which step (if any) did the discussion fail to deal with thoroughly enough?
9. If the group were to begin its discussion again, what would you advise each member to do to improve his or her contribution?

Developing Agreement
within a Political Organization

Citizens who participate in a local political organization—such as a neighborhood action group, a precinct caucus, or a county committee—must be able to reach agreement on public issues and to take positions on those issues. Only an organization that is united behind a platform or program can be effective. Reaching agreement (or *consensus*) requires careful, serious discussion and the ability to compromise. Here are guidelines for developing agreement:

- All participants should be well informed on the issues.
- Every participant should have a chance to be heard on the issues he or she thinks are important.
- Discussions should focus on the issues rather than on the personalities of the participants. (A skillful chairperson can help keep discussions from degenerating into quarrels.)
- Participants should consider how people outside the organization (including voters) will respond to their position on an issue.
- Participants should try to include the best features of all suggestions in the organization's final position. Individuals should not fight so strongly for their ideas that compromise becomes impossible.
- Participants should follow the steps in the problem-solving sequence (see Speaking Skills, lesson 7.1), whenever possible.

ACTIVITIES

1. Invite a local political organizer or committee member to speak to your class. Ask the person to describe the way "grass-roots" political organizations function, and how they develop their positions on issues. Alternatively, research local and national political organizations at your library, and report to the class on how such organizations reach agreement on issues.
2. Organize two political parties, each with four to six students. Each party should develop a platform, with positions on major local, state, and national issues. Then each party should present its platform to the rest of the class. The class can discuss the platforms and the issues, and vote for the party it prefers.

citizenship

8 Parliamentary Discussion

Meetings of clubs, boards, committees, and legislatures are conducted according to parliamentary procedure. This system assures that the meeting will be orderly, and that every member will have a chance to speak. The rules of parliamentary procedure may seem complicated at first, but knowing and using them is an important skill. If you belong to a public organization, or if you ever deal with one, understanding the parliamentary rules and motions can help you accomplish your aims more effectively.

After working through this chapter, you should be able to

- understand the way a parliamentary body is organized
- know the nine events in a meeting conducted according to parliamentary procedure
- participate in a parliamentary meeting
- introduce parliamentary motions

The Speaking Skills lessons in this chapter will help you master the rules of parliamentary procedure. You will learn to

- prepare and use an agenda
- use the basic parliamentary motions

The Skills for Success lessons in this chapter will help you take part in public meetings. You will learn to

- nominate a candidate for office
- participate effectively in a public meeting

8.1 Planning a Meeting

Using an Agenda

Most meetings of organizations have to deal with several different types of business. For such a meeting to run efficiently, it should follow an *agenda*. An agenda is simply a list of things to be done during the meeting, the order in which they should be done, and (often) the names of the persons responsible for each piece of business.

The chairperson of the meeting draws up the agenda in advance. He or she may be assisted by several other members. This is the usual order of items on an agenda:

1. Call to Order
2. Reading of Minutes of Previous Meeting
3. Treasurer's Report
4. Correspondence
5. Committee Reports
6. Old Business (or Unfinished Business)
7. New Business
8. Announcements
9. Adjournment

For each of these categories, the chairperson should list the number and subject of expected reports, the names of the people reporting or giving background information, and the approximate time each piece of business will take. At any meeting, of course, some items on the agenda may be passed by quickly (for example, there may be no correspondence to read). Generally, new business will take the most time.

ACTIVITY

1. Draw up an agenda for a class organization or student government committee. Include the titles of specific items of business (for example, "School Orchestra Fundraising Drive"), the names of the officers or members who will present each item, and an estimated time for each piece of business. Read the agenda to your class, and ask for their suggestions of other items or details.

problem solving

How to Plan a Meeting

Many clubs and other organizations adopt the rules of parliamentary procedure to conduct their meetings. The meetings of local civic groups and the meetings of your school's student council are probably conducted according to the rules of parliamentary procedure. The meetings of the United States Congress are conducted according to the same rules. Parliamentary procedure is used so widely and in so many diverse situations because it ensures that every group's meetings will proceed fairly and efficiently.

Parliamentary procedure cannot be used effectively in a meeting, however, unless all the participants make specific preparations for that meeting.

The person who will be in charge of conducting the meeting, called the *chairperson,* has the greatest responsibility in preparing for the meeting. The chairperson should write out an *agenda,* a list of things that will be done during the meeting. The nine events usually included in a meeting are shown, in order, in the chart on the following pages. The chairperson's agenda should list each of those nine events with specific notes on who will speak and what will be considered during that portion of the meeting. The written agenda should also include estimates of the time required for each portion of the meeting. These estimates will help the chairperson conduct the meeting efficiently and adjourn the meeting promptly.

Each member who plans to make a specific contribution during the meeting should discuss his or her plans with the chairperson. For example, a member who plans to present a committee report or introduce an item of new business should consult with the chairperson before the meeting. These pre-meeting discussions will help the chairperson plan the meeting accurately and allow time for each person's contribution. After confirming his or her plans with the chairperson, each member should prepare his or her contribution in detail by making notes for a report or by writing out a specific proposal.

All the other organization members should also prepare for the meeting. They should think about the issues that are likely to be considered during the meeting. If necessary, they should also review the rules of parliamentary procedure so that they can participate correctly in the meeting.

THE NINE EVENTS IN A MEETING CONDUCTED ACCORDING TO PARLIAMENTARY PROCEDURE

Call to Order	The chairperson calls the meeting to order. Informal conversation ends and the rules of parliamentary procedure take effect.
Minutes of Previous Meeting	The secretary reads the minutes and the chairperson asks for corrections. If someone has a correction, it is made, and the minutes stand approved as corrected. If there are no corrections, the minutes stand approved as read. If the minutes have been distributed in writing and everyone had copies prior to the meeting, the chair may simply ask for corrections. If there are none, the minutes stand approved as distributed.
Treasurer's Report	The treasurer reports the balance of funds as of the previous meeting, the funds received since that meeting, the amount spent, and the new balance. This is *not* the part of the meeting to deal with issues related to the financial operations of the organization.
Correspondence	The secretary reads letters sent to the organization (or distributes them if they have been duplicated). Issues raised by the letters are not acted on at this time. They are referred to appropriate committees by the chairperson or are scheduled for consideration later in the meeting under "new business."

Committee Reports	Proper advance planning will ensure that only committees with something to report are called on. Committee recommendations may be acted on at this time.
Old Business	Issues considered but not resolved at previous meetings are scheduled for further consideration at this point. Sometimes this part of the agenda is called "unfinished business."
New Business	Issues being considered for the first time are introduced and discussed. When practical, members should be made aware before the meeting of issues scheduled as new business.
Announcements	The chairperson and others may announce upcoming events and other matters of interest to members at this point in the meeting. Time will be saved if these announcements are prepared in writing and distributed to members.
Adjournment	The meeting may be brought to an official close either when all business has been completed or when a majority of those in attendance vote for adjournment. Once the members of an organization have voted to adjourn, they can conduct no further business without convening a new meeting.

Working with the Model

Claire is the president of the Stevenson Service Club. To prepare for one of the club's meetings, Claire wrote the following agenda. Read the agenda carefully, and think about the plan it presents.

model

AGENDA
Stevenson Service Club – April 12, 1982

1. Call to Order (3:15)
2. Minutes of Previous Meeting (5 minutes)
   a. Stan—read minutes
   b. Corrections and approval
3. Treasurer's Report—Tanya (5 minutes)
4. Correspondence—none

model

5. Committee Reports (10 minutes)
   a. Leah—community committee
   b. Miguel—fund-raising committee
   c. Malcolm—school grounds committee
   (No report from new students committee, sports committee, or social committee)
6. Old Business (10 minutes)
   a. New club representative for Student Council
   b. Orientation for foreign exchange students
   c. Banquet for outstanding community members
   d. Open to floor
7. New Business (20 minutes)
   a. Stevenson High fund-raising fair—Maxine
   b. Summer picnic for next year's freshmen—Lyle
   c. Entertainment program for senior citizens
   d. Open to floor
8. Announcements—Gary (5 minutes)
9. Adjournment (4:10)

QUESTIONS

A. Think about the agenda Claire prepared.
   1. How will the written agenda help Claire lead the club members in a productive and efficient meeting?
   2. How will the suggested times help Claire lead the meeting? Imagine that Tanya's report takes only three minutes, instead of five. What do you think Claire will do? Imagine instead that the committee reports take fifteen minutes, instead of only ten. What do you think Claire will do?
   3. Imagine Leah wants the club members to consider another item of old business. When will she have an opportunity to bring that item to the attention of the club?
   4. Imagine that, since the previous meeting, the Stevenson Service Club has received a letter from the Mayfield City Council, requesting assistance in a city clean-up campaign. When would the letter be read? When would a specific proposal regarding participation in the campaign be introduced?
B. Think about how other people should prepare for the meeting.
   1. What should each of these members do before the meeting: Stan, Tanya, Leah, Miguel, Malcolm, Maxine, Lyle, and Gary?
   2. What should the other club members do?

C. Think about your own experiences in attending meetings conducted according to parliamentary procedure.

1. In what specific meetings did the chairperson follow a written agenda? How did the agenda help the chairperson conduct the meeting? What problems, if any, did the chairperson have in following the agenda?

2. In what specific meetings did the chairperson seem not to have a written agenda? How could you tell that he or she did not have one? What problems arose because the chairperson had no written agenda?

Guidelines

Before the meeting of a club or organization, each member should make specific preparations:

1. The chairperson, who will conduct the meeting, should write an agenda, a list of what will happen during the meeting.

2. Members who plan to make specific contributions, such as presenting committee reports or introducing items of new business, should discuss their plans with the chairperson and should prepare their contributions in detail.

3. All the other members of the club or organization should think about issues likely to be raised during the meeting, and should review the rules of parliamentary procedure as necessary.

Preparing and Presenting

Write a complete agenda for a meeting that will be conducted according to parliamentary procedure. You may write the agenda for a meeting of a real club or organization, or you may make up a club or organization. You may wish to use one of the following clubs:

Seaside High School Sailing Club
Central Chess Club
Main High School Debate Club
Ski and Surf Club
Latin Club
Jazz Club

Include in your agenda each of the nine events usually included in the order of business. Plan at least one item of correspondence, two committee reports, two specific items of old business, and two specific items of new business. Also include in your agenda a specific time for beginning the meeting, an estimated number of minutes to be spent on each event, and an estimated time for adjourning the meeting.

Evaluating

Exchange agendas with another student. Read each other's work carefully, and then discuss both agendas. In the course of your discussion, answer the following questions:

1. Which of the two agendas would be easier for a chairperson to use in conducting a meeting? How could the other agenda be made easier to use?

2. Which agenda (if either) is not complete? What should be added to make that agenda complete?

3. Which agenda (if either) includes unnecessary information? What should be taken out of that agenda?

4. Which agenda (if either) does not present a realistic estimate of the time involved in conducting the planned meeting? How should the estimates of time on that agenda be revised?

After you have discussed agendas with your partner, make any changes that are needed to improve your agenda.

Nominating a Candidate for Office

The two purposes of a nominating speech are to explain why your candidate is qualified for a particular office, and to make your audience feel enthusiastic about that person. The speech should create a sense of excitement that (you hope) will carry over into the voting. Follow these guidelines when preparing a nominating speech:

- List the requirements of the office, and point out how well your candidate's experience and personality fulfill each requirement.
- Give examples of your candidate's intelligence, energy, warmth, judgment, patriotism, and loyalty. Relate these details to the office he or she is seeking, rather than giving the candidate's entire biography.
- Emphasize the superiority of your candidate without making personal attacks on the other candidates. Such attacks usually backfire and produce sympathy for the victims.
- Speak with conviction and enthusiasm. Use the candidate's name frequently, so that your listeners will associate it with the qualifications you are describing.
- Don't speak too long, or you will risk losing the audience's attention. Try to create a sense of rising excitement, and end the speech with the name of your candidate.

ACTIVITIES

1. Read or listen to a famous nominating speech for a presidential candidate made during a political convention. Decide what strategies the speaker used to make the candidate appear able, likeable, and electable. Listen for the use of anecdotes, the repetition of key words and phrases, and appeals to the audience's emotions. Report your findings to the class.

2. Write a nominating speech for a candidate for local, state, or national office. (The person can be an actual candidate, or someone you would like to see run for the office.) You and several other students should deliver speeches for different candidates to the class, and let them vote for the candidate who was given the best nomination.

citizenship

8.2 Participating in a Meeting

Learning the Basic Parliamentary Motions

The business of a parliamentary meeting is carried on by means of *motions*—suggestions or proposals made by members who have been recognized by the chairperson. Specific purposes have specific motions. Some motions need seconds; others do not. Some may be debated; others may not. Some require majority approval; others require a two-thirds vote, or only approval by the chairperson. Effective organization members know how to use the following motions.

PURPOSE	MOTION	SECOND	DEBATE	VOTE
If you want to . . .	Then you should move to...	Will you need a second?	May the motion be debated?	Approval requires a vote which is...
1. Introduce business	Introduce a motion	Yes	Yes (A)	Majority
2. Consider motions which were tabled	Take from the table	Yes	No	Majority
3. Delay action.	Lay on the table	Yes	No	Majority
4. Require an immediate vote	Call the previous question	Yes	No	Two thirds
5. Modify a motion	Amend	Yes	Yes (A)	Majority
6. Correct or question a parliamentary error	Rise to a point of order (I)	Yes	No	Decision of chair
7. Clarify outcome of voice vote	Call for division of the house (I)	No	No	Majority, if vote is needed
8. Dismiss meeting for a specific (usually brief) time	Recess	Yes	No (A)	Majority
9. Dismiss a meeting	Adjourn	Yes	No (A)	Majority

(I) May interrupt speaker   (A) May be amended

How to Participate in a Meeting

In a meeting conducted according to parliamentary procedure, most business is accomplished by using motions. A *motion* is a proposal that specific action be taken. During appropriate portions of a meeting, any member may introduce a motion. Usually, the motion must be seconded and may then be discussed by all the members. Changes in the wording or the intent of a motion may be accomplished by *amendments*. Every motion brought before a meeting must be voted on, and the majority vote rules.

It is essential that every member understand the procedure used in introducing and acting upon a motion. Parliamentary motions are explained in detail in *Robert's Rules of Order (Revised)*, the most commonly accepted authority on parliamentary procedure.

During a meeting, the chairperson's main responsibility is to conduct the meeting. The chairperson gives each member who wants it permission to speak, but, with few exceptions, the chairperson may not introduce or second a motion and may not participate in the discussion or the voting, except to break a tie. The chairperson must always strive to be impartial in calling upon speakers. As he or she conducts the meeting, the chairperson must keep in mind one of the primary goals of parliamentary procedure: to ensure that the will of the majority is carried out and that the rights of the minority are protected.

Here is a description of five common parliamentary motions:

Main Motion

Intention:	To obtain action on a proposal.
Member:	"I move _____." The specific proposal should be stated simply and briefly. If the issue is complex, the motion should be written out and given to the chairperson.
Chairperson:	"Is there a second?" Once the chairperson receives a seconding motion, he or she says, "It has been moved and seconded that _____. Is there any discussion? Since there is no further discussion, we will vote. All those in favor of the motion, which is _____, say aye (yes). All those opposed say no." Depending on the outcome of the vote, the chairperson then says, "The motion is carried" or "The motion is defeated."

Motion to Amend a Proposal

Intention: To change a proposal being considered by the group.

Member: "I move to amend the motion by (inserting, adding, substituting _____)." The amendment must be related to the proposal under consideration. It must not be just the opposite of the proposal under consideration.

Chairperson: After the motion to amend the proposal has been seconded, the chairperson says, "It has been moved and seconded to amend the motion by _____. Is there any discussion?" Discussion should be restricted to the amendment until it has been voted on. When the discussion has ended, or if there is no discussion, the chairperson says, "All in favor of amending the motion by _____, say aye. Opposed, say no." Depending on the outcome of the vote, the chairperson then says, "The amendment is carried, the question is now the motion as amended" or "The amendment is lost, the question is now the motion as originally stated, to _____."

Motion to Refer a Proposal to a Committee

Intention: To have a committee study a proposal.

Member: "I move that this matter be referred to the _____ committee." The motion can be worded to specify that a special committee be appointed by the chairperson or the organization to study the proposal. The motion can also include specific directions, such as "and that the committee report by (specified date or time)."

Chairperson: After the motion has been seconded, the chairperson says, "It has been moved and seconded that this matter be referred to the _____ committee. All those in favor of referring this matter, which is _____, to the _____ committee, say aye. Opposed, say no." Depending on the vote, the chairperson says, "The motion is carried, you have voted to _____" or "The motion is lost; the original motion is now before us."

Motion to Delay Action on a Proposal

Intention: To delay action on a proposal. Action may be postponed indefinitely or to a specified time. A proposal may also be "tabled," which stops action on it unless a later vote "takes it from the table."

Member: "I move that this matter be postponed" or "I move that this matter be postponed until (specify time)."

Chairperson: After the motion is seconded, the chairperson says, "It has been moved and seconded to postpone this matter to _____. Is there any discussion?" After discussion has ended, or if there is no discussion, the chairperson says, "All those in favor of postponing this matter to _____, say aye. Opposed, say no." Depending on the vote, the chairperson says, "The motion is carried and we will consider _____ at _____" or "The motion is lost and the original motion is now before us."

Motion to Move the Previous Question

Intention: To stop discussion on a motion and get the members to vote on it.

Member: "I move the previous question."

Chairperson: After the motion is seconded, the chairperson says, "The previous question has been moved." This motion is not debatable. "Shall we stop debate and order an immediate vote? All those in favor raise their hands (or stand). All opposed raise their hands." If two-thirds of those present and eligible to vote, vote in favor, then the motion passes. The chairperson then says, "The motion is carried. We will proceed at once to vote on the motion to _____. All those in favor say aye. Opposed say no." If the previous question is defeated, the chairperson says, "The motion is lost, and we will return to the original motion. Is there any discussion on the motion to _____?"

Working with the Model

Read the following transcript from a portion of the Stevenson Service Club's meeting. Notice how motions are introduced and discussed according to parliamentary procedure.

model

CHAIR: The first item of new business is the Stevenson High fund-raising fair. Maxine.

MAXINE: I move that we sponsor a booth at this year's fund-raising fair.

MALCOLM: I second the motion.

CHAIR: It has been moved and seconded that we sponsor a booth at this year's fund-raising fair. Is there any discussion? Sergio.

SERGIO: Maxine has a good idea, but her motion isn't quite clear. What kind of booth should we sponsor?

CHAIR: Phan.

PHAN: I move to amend the motion to read that we should sponsor a dart-throwing booth at this year's fund-raising fair.

CHAIR: Is there a second to the amendment?

SERGIO: I second the amendment.

CHAIR: It has been moved and seconded that we amend the motion to read that we should sponsor a dart-throwing booth at this year's fund-raising fair. Is there any discussion? Maxine.

MAXINE: The amendment helps make clear exactly what we should do. I think it's a good idea.

CHAIR: Isabel.

ISABLE: I agree that the amendment does clarify the motion, but I'm getting tired of the dart-throwing booth. This will be the fourth year in a row that we've sponsored one. Shouldn't we try something different?

CHAIR: Setsuko.

SETSUKO: The important thing to remember about the fair is that its purpose is to raise money. We have had the same kind of booth for several years, but it's always been very successful. I think the best way to contribute to the fair is to stick with something that works.

CHAIR: Julian

JULIAN: I think Setsuko's right. Besides, we already have most of what we need to set up a dart-throwing booth. If we switch to something new, we will have to commit more time and more money to the project.

CHAIR: Is there any further discussion? Hearing none, I will call for the question. All those in favor of amending the motion to read that we should sponsor a dart-throwing booth at this year's fund-raising fair, say "aye." Those opposed say "no." The amendment is carried. Is there any discussion on the motion as amended?

QUESTIONS

A. Think about what happened in the recorded portion of the meeting.

1. What main motion was introduced?

2. What had to happen before the club members could begin talking about whether or not they should sponsor a booth at the fund-raising fair?

3. What kind of motion did Phan make?

4. Imagine that Phan had said, "I move to amend the motion to read that we should not sponsor a booth at this year's fund-raising fair." What would have been wrong with his motion?

5. Imagine that, when Setsuko contributed to the discussion, she had said, "Don't be crazy, Isabel. Any fool knows that our dart-throwing booth is a big success. You only want to change it so that we can have a baseball pitching contest. Then you'll be able to show off your good throwing arm!" What would have been wrong with Setsuko's contribution?

6. Imagine that, after the chair had asked for any further discussion on the motion as amended, Lyle had said, "I move that we plan a summer picnic for next year's freshman students." What would have been wrong with his motion?

B. Think about what might happen in the next portion of the meeting.

1. Imagine Janey wants to suggest that the proposal for sponsoring the dart-throwing booth be referred to the club's fund-raising committee. What should she say?

2. What would be necessary before Janey's suggestion could be discussed?

3. What might some of the club members say in discussing Janey's motion?

4. Imagine that, after several people have spoken, there seems to be no more discussion on Janey's motion. What should the chairperson say?

5. Imagine that most of the members vote against Janey's motion. What should the chairperson say?

6. Imagine that Nikki wants to end the discussion and to have the club members vote on the main motion as it has been amended. What should she say?

7. After Nikki's motion has been seconded, what should the chairperson say? If the majority of the members vote in favor of Nikki's motion, what should the chairperson say next? Then, if the majority of members vote for the main motion as amended, what should the chairperson say?

Guidelines

Remember these guidelines whenever you participate in a meeting conducted according to parliamentary procedure:

1. A proposal for specific action must be made as a motion. Usually, a motion must be seconded and may then be discussed by all members. Any motion introduced must be voted on.

2. Before he or she may speak during a meeting, a member must be called upon by the chairperson.

3. The chairperson's main responsibility is to conduct the meeting impartially. With few exceptions, the chairperson does not participate in discussion or voting.

4. The chairperson must not be partial in calling upon speakers. Everyone at the meeting should remember that one of the goals of following parliamentary procedure is to carry out the will of the majority while protecting the rights of the minority.

Preparing and Presenting _____

With the other students in your class, participate in a meeting conducted according to parliamentary procedure. The class members should select as the agenda one of those written for lesson 8.1. Then select one student to chair the meeting and other students to fill the specific roles called for in the agenda. (A secretary, a treasurer, at least two committee representatives, and at least two people to introduce specific items of new business will be needed.)

Those students who have specific roles called for in the agenda should plan what they will contribute to the meeting. The treasurer, for example, will need to prepare a report, and the students who are responsible for items of new business will need to plan their motions.

Students who do not have specific roles to play should prepare by reviewing the use of motions in parliamentary procedure, as explained in *Robert's Rules of Order (Revised)*.

When everyone is prepared, the chairperson should conduct the meeting, following the plan in the agenda.

Evaluating _____

After the meeting has been adjourned, form a group with two or three other students. With the other members of your group, discuss the use of parliamentary procedure in the meeting. During the course of your discussion, respond to the following questions:

1. What evidence was there that each participant had prepared for the meeting? How did that preparation help make the meeting run smoothly?
2. What specific problems were prevented by the use of parliamentary procedure?
3. What specific problems (if any) arose as a result of the group's use of parliamentary procedure? How were those problems resolved?
4. In what specific ways did the use of parliamentary procedure help the participants to focus on only one issue at a time?
5. In what specific ways did the use of parliamentary procedure ensure that the will of the majority was carried out? In what specific ways did it protect the rights of the minority?

Participating in a Public Meeting

To participate effectively in a meeting of a local board or governmental agency, you must be prepared, informed, and confident. Public organizations usually have many pieces of business on their agendas, and are impatient with speakers or groups who cannot present their ideas succinctly. Remember these guidelines:

- Know the board or agency's rules and procedures: both the general rules of parliamentary procedure and the specific rules for public participation in meetings.
- Know your issue thoroughly, and be aware of the other issues before the meeting.
- Learn as much as you can about the personalities, interests, and biases of the members of the board or agency.
- Prepare your presentation carefully to make the best use of your allotted time. Practice it before other people to be sure you are speaking smoothly, confidently, and convincingly, and are making effective use of gestures.

ACTIVITIES

1. Attend a meeting of a school board, city commission, or other local organization. Observe the members of the public who address the meeting, and evaluate their presentations. In what ways were they effective? Did they make good use of their allotted time? What effect did they have on the members of the board or committee? Make a brief report on your observations to your class, and discuss with them how the speakers could have been more effective.

2. Select an important local issue on which you want to make your position known. Obtain permission to present your views before an appropriate body, board, or commission. Invite members of your class to attend the meeting. Make the most effective presentation you can, and ask the other students to evaluate your performance and the reaction of the board, using the guidelines above.

citizenship

9 Persuasive Speaking

In a persuasive speech, you will try to make your listeners change their minds on some issue. You may want them to support a candidate, to join a movement, or to look at a problem in the way you do. You must use different methods for different audiences and purposes. Sometimes listeners can be persuaded by logic and evidence. At other times, an appeal to an audience's emotions will be most effective. Often, a speaker will try to make listeners feel that he or she has much in common with them, and is worth listening to. Using one or all of these techniques, you can become a more persuasive speaker in school, at work, and in public meetings.

After working through this chapter, you should be able to

- use appeals to logic
- use appeals to emotion
- use identification
- use identification with appeals to logic and appeals to emotion

The Speaking Skills lessons in this chapter will help you become a more persuasive speaker. You will learn to

- follow the steps in preparing a persuasive speech
- evaluate loaded words
- be aware of different dialects
- understand bias and stereotyping

The Skills for Success lessons in this chapter will help your persuasive speaking as a citizen and on the job. You will learn to

- appeal to a governmental agency
- motivate others to help solve a problem
- evaluate your credibility as a speaker
- make a sales presentation

9.1 Using Appeals to Logic

Preparing a Persuasive Speech

Follow this list of sixteen steps when you prepare a persuasive speech. Not every step may be appropriate to every speech you make, but you should follow them in this order to avoid omitting any important elements.

1. Select a topic narrow enough to be covered in the time allotted you.
2. Find out what positions people hold on this topic.
3. Research the arguments supporting and opposing each position.
4. Decide on your position on the topic.
5. Analyze your audience—its background, interests, and prejudices.
6. With your position and audience in mind, complete your research, using a variety of reliable sources.
7. Decide which arguments will be most effective with your audience.
8. Outline the main arguments of your speech, and the evidence you will use to support each argument.
9. Outline the arguments and evidence you will use to refute the opposing position.
10. Decide what visual aids, if any, will help make your speech more effective.
11. Prepare the introduction and conclusion of your speech.
12. Prepare notes for your speech, and practice it alone, preferably before a mirror.
13. Practice your speech before at least one other person, and ask the person for his or her response.
14. Revise your speech in accordance with the person's response, and practice it again.
15. Deliver your speech before an audience.
16. Analyze your speech and the audience's response, and apply what you learn to future speeches.

planning

How to Use Appeals to Logic

When you make any persuasive speech, your general purpose is to convince your listeners that they should think or act in a certain way. When you plan a persuasive speech, you should begin by clarifying the specific purpose of that speech: Precisely what do you want your listeners to think or do? That specific purpose is called the *position* of your speech.

One effective way to develop a persuasive speech is to support your position with *logical arguments*. Your logical arguments must be objective reasons that directly support your position. These arguments should not involve personal preferences or opinions. In turn, each logical argument in your speech must be supported by *evidence*—factual illustration, statistics, expert testimony, or other specific details about the argument.

In order to plan an effective persuasive speech developed with logical arguments, research your topic thoroughly, consulting a variety of sources. You must also think about your audience. Consider which arguments and which kinds of evidence will be understandable and convincing to your listeners. In addition, you must organize your persuasive speech clearly and carefully. The most effective kind of organization for a persuasive speech developed with logical arguments is shown in the following chart.

Introduction	Draw your listener's attention to the topic of your speech.
	State your position on the topic.
Body	Clearly state each logical argument.
	After the statement of each argument, present evidence to support that argument.
	(In most cases, you should present your most effective argument last, to leave a strong impression with your listeners.)
Conclusion	Restate your position and summarize your arguments in support of that position.

Working with the Model

Until 1858, Jewish citizens were excluded from holding office in the British Parliament. For many years before the law was changed, the members of Parliament debated the issue of whether Jews should be allowed to be elected to the legislature.

In 1830, a member of Parliament from Oxford (referred to in the following speech as "my honorable friend the Member for the University of Oxford") made a speech asserting that it was logical to exclude Jews from office. Three years later, Thomas Babington Macaulay replied to that member's speech. The specific purpose of Macaulay's speech was to persuade his listeners that, contrary to his opponent's main point, it was illogical to exclude Jews from office. In spite of the fact that Macaulay's speech was delivered in the middle of the nineteenth century, it still presents a strong and relevant argument against bigotry in all its many forms.

Read the following excerpt from the introduction and part of the body of Macaulay's speech. Look for Macaulay's position, the three logical arguments he presents, and the evidence he uses to support those arguments.

I recollect, and my honorable friend the Member for the University of Oxford will recollect, that when this subject was discussed three years ago, it was remarked that the strength of the case of the Jews was a serious inconvenience to their advocate, for that it was hardly possible to make a speech for them without wearying the audience by repeating truths which were universally admitted.

My honorable friend the Member for the University of Oxford began his speech by declaring that he had no intention of calling in question the principles of religious liberty. He utterly disclaims persecution, that is to say, persecution as defined by himself. It would, in his opinion, be persecution to hang a Jew, ... or to imprison him, or to fine him; for every man who conducts himself peacefully has a right to his life and his limbs, to his personal liberty, and to his property.

But it is not persecution, says my honorable friend, to exclude any individual or any class from office. ... He who obtains an office obtains it not as a matter of right, but as a matter of favor. He who does not obtain an office is not wronged; he is only in that situation in which the vast majority of every community must necessarily be. There are in the United Kingdom five and twenty million Christians without places [in Parliament]; and, if they do not complain, why should five and twenty thousand Jews complain of being in the same case? In this way my honorable friend has convinced himself that, as it would be most absurd in him and me to say that we are wronged because we are not secretaries of state, so it is most absurd in the Jews to say that they are wronged because they are, as a people, excluded from public employment.

model

Now surely, my honorable friend cannot have considered to what conclusions his reasoning leads.

Does he really mean that it would not be wrong in the legislature to enact that no man should be a judge unless he weighed twelve stone [168 pounds], or that no man should sit in Parliament unless he were six feet high? We are about to bring in a bill for the government of India. Suppose that we were to insert in that bill a clause providing that no graduate of the University of Oxford should be governor general or governor of any presidency, would not my honorable friend cry out against such a clause as most unjust to the learned body which he represents? And would he think himself sufficiently answered by being told, in his own words, that the appointment to office is a mere matter of favor, and that to exclude an individual or a class from office is no injury? Surely, on consideration, he must admit that official appointments ought not to be subject to regulations purely arbitrary, to regulations for which no reason can be given but mere caprice, and that those who would exclude any class from public employment are bound to show some special reason for the exclusion.

My honorable friend has appealed to us as Christians. Let me then ask him how he understands that great commandment which comprises the law and the prophets. Can we be said to do unto others as we

model

would that they should do unto us, if we wantonly inflict on them even the smallest pain? That by excluding others from public trust we inflict pain on them my honorable friend will not dispute. As a Christian, therefore, he is bound to relieve them from that pain, unless he can show, what I am sure he has not yet shown, that it is necessary to the general good that they should continue to suffer.

But where, he says, are you to stop if once you admit into the House of Commons people who deny the authority of the Gospels? ... I will answer my honorable friend's question by another. Where does he mean to stop? Is he ready to roast unbelievers at slow fires? If not, let him tell us why; and I will engage to prove that his reason is just as decisive against the intolerance which he thinks a duty as against the intolerance which he thinks a crime. Once admit that we are bound to inflict pain on a man because he is not of our religion, and where do you stop? Why stop at the point fixed by my honorable friend rather than at the point fixed by the Member for Oldham, who would make the Jews incapable of holding land? And why stop at the point fixed by the honorable Member for Oldham rather than at the point which would have been fixed by a Spanish inquisitor of the sixteenth century? When once you enter on a course of persecution, I defy you to find any reason for making a halt till you have reached the extreme point.

QUESTIONS

A. Think about the introduction of Macaulay's speech, contained in the first three paragraphs.

   1. How does Macaulay direct his listener's attention to the topic of his speech?

   2. What is Macaulay's position on that topic? In which sentence does Macaulay state his position?

B. Think about the three arguments Macaulay presents in the final three paragraphs of the excerpt. Notice that each paragraph presents one logical argument (objective reason) in support of Macaulay's position. Each argument, however, is stated at or near the end of the paragraph.

   1. What is the first argument in support of Macaulay's position?

   2. What evidence supports that first argument?

   3. What is the second argument in support of Macaulay's position?

   4. In supporting that second argument, Macaulay uses the phrase "that great commandment which comprises the law and the prophets" to refer to what we call "the golden rule." What is that rule?

   5. What evidence supports Macaulay's second argument?

   6. What is the third argument in support of Macaulay's position?

   7. What evidence supports that third argument?

C. Think about an appropriate conclusion for this portion of Macaulay's speech.

1. If you were preparing the conclusion, how would you restate Macaulay's position?

2. How would you summarize Macaulay's arguments in support of that position?

Guidelines

When you plan a persuasive speech developed with logical arguments, you should keep in mind the following guidelines:

1. Decide on and clearly state the specific purpose of your speech. The sentence that states your specific purpose is called the statement of your position.

2. Research the topic of your speech. Knowing as much as possible about the topic will allow you to select the best arguments and evidence in support of your position.

3. Think about your audience. Select arguments and evidence that your listeners will understand and accept.

4. Organize your speech carefully. Follow the plan shown in the chart on page 215.

Preparing and Presenting

Select a topic for a persuasive speech. If you wish, you may choose one of the following topics:

- equal rights for women
- the rights of minors
- the use of nuclear power

- government surveillance of private citizens
- citizens' rights to own handguns

Think about your chosen topic, and decide what you would like to convince listeners to think or do in respect to that topic. Then write a one-sentence statement of your position.

Plan a persuasive speech that uses appeals to logic in support of your position. Begin by researching your topic; consult at least four different sources.

After you have gathered information, think about the audience (your fellow students) for whom your speech is intended. Evaluate your possible arguments and evidence in terms of the interests and experiences of your listeners. Select at least three major arguments in support of your position. Select at least two items of evidence in support of each argument.

Write an outline for your persuasive speech. Organize your speech according to the plan shown on page 215. (Your outline should have three main parts: I. Introduction; II. Body; III. Conclusion.)

Evaluating

Exchange outlines with another student. Read your partner's speech outline carefully, considering the planned speech in terms of the following questions:

1. How is the topic of the speech introduced? How might this introduction be made more effective or more interesting?

2. What is the statement of position? What changes (if any) are needed to clarify the position?

3. What logical arguments support the position? Which arguments (if any) are personal preferences or opinions rather than objective reasons? Which arguments (if any) might not be understandable or convincing to an audience of your fellow students?

4. What kinds of evidence support each argument? Which arguments (if any) are not directly supported by factual illustrations, statistics, expert testimony, or other specific details? Which items of evidence (if any) might not be understandable or convincing to an audience of your fellow students?

5. What is included in the conclusion of the speech? How might the conclusion be made more clear or more effective?

With your partner, discuss the two speech outlines. Listen carefully as your partner evaluates your work. Then make any changes that will improve your plan for a persuasive speech.

Appealing to a Governmental Agency

At some time you will probably need to appeal to a governmental official or agency to take action on a problem. Whether you and your community receive the help you want will depend on your understanding of the agency's powers and the persuasiveness of your presentation. Keep the following guidelines in mind.

- Be sure you understand your problem, and that all your facts and figures are accurate.
- Learn which agency or official can help you. Don't waste time appealing to people who are powerless.
- Learn about the personality, powers, and biases of the official you will be speaking to.
- Have a specific action that you want the official to take.
- Make an appointment to see the official, and arrive on time.
- Present your case in a well-organized manner, using your strongest facts and arguments. Be concise, and end your presentation with a summary of your case and request for action.
- Speak effectively and sincerely, but avoid emotional displays. Be respectful, but not awestruck.
- When you have finished your presentation, ask for a specific date or time when you can learn whether action has been taken.
- Follow up your appeal by speaking to or phoning the official to see what action has been taken.

ACTIVITIES

1. Arrange to meet with a city or county supervisor, a school board member, or another public official who has the power to take action on local problems. Ask about the ways citizens persuade this official to help solve problems, and which methods are most effective.

2. Working with several other students, identify a local problem that you believe needs action by a public agency. You might ask for action on poor streets, defective traffic signals, or other problems. Prepare a concise, well-organized presentation on the problem. If your teacher decides that you should make the presentation, make an appointment to speak to the appropriate official. You may present your case with a single spokesperson. However, if the problem is complex, you may divide the presentation among several people. Report on your presentation to the class.

citizenship

9.2 Using Appeals to Emotion

Evaluating Loaded Words

Many words and phrases have two different meanings. The first meaning, or *denotation,* is the dictionary definition of the word. The second meaning, or *connotation,* is what the word suggests to people because of its favorable or unfavorable associations.

The word *bureaucracy* is a good example. The denotation of *bureaucracy* is a group of appointed government officials who help make policy and administer programs. To many people, however, *bureaucracy* has the connotation of unhelpful officials who waste taxpayers' money and complicate people's lives with governmental red tape. A politician needs only to identify someone as a *bureaucrat* to make an audience dislike that person. In political speeches of the 1970s and 1980s, *bureaucracy* and *bureaucrat* are *loaded words.*

Other loaded words have positive connotations. American audiences will have favorable associations for such expressions as *patriotism* and *free enterprise.* Many speakers use loaded words, not to inform or persuade their listeners, but to produce an instant reaction that may not be justified by their facts or arguments.

ACTIVITIES

1. Keep a list of the loaded words and phrases you read or hear during the course of a week. Divide your list into two parts, "Positive" and "Negative." Write down loaded words you hear in speeches and conversations, on radio or television, and that you read in newspapers, magazines, books, and advertising. Compare your list with the lists of other students. Decide which words are most frequently used, and with what connotations.

2. Listen to or read a speech delivered at a Democratic or Republican national convention. Make a list of all the loaded words and phrases you hear, and note their connotations and the context in which they are used. Then discuss your findings with a student who listened to a speech given at the other party's convention. Compare your lists of words, and try to draw up a basic vocabulary of loaded words and phrases for each party.

How to Use Appeals to Emotion

Rather than appealing to the listeners' minds, as logical arguments do, some persuasive speeches appeal to the listeners' emotions. Emotional appeals are based upon the three kinds of basic needs all people have: physical needs, psychological needs, and social needs. *Physical needs* involve the life and health of an individual's body; examples of physical needs include the need for food and the need to avoid physical pain. *Psychological needs* involve an individual's inner life; examples of psychological needs include the need for love and the need for self-respect. *Social needs* involve an individual's relationship to a group; examples of social needs include the need for freedom and the need for acceptance by others. Appeals to emotion are intended to convince listeners that accepting the speaker's position will satisfy one or more of these basic needs.

When you plan to use appeals to emotion in a persuasive speech, you must constantly consider your position, the specific purpose of your speech. You should be sure that each appeal you choose will lead your listeners to accept that position.

Being able to make such judgments, of course, involves knowing your audience thoroughly. You must be familiar with your listeners' most important needs, with their interests, and with their fears. If you misjudge your audience, your appeals to their emotions will not be successfully persuasive.

In organizing a persuasive speech with appeals to emotions, you may want to develop your position before you state it. For example, you might begin by interesting listeners in the topic of your speech. Then you might present statements, examples, or short anecdotes (brief stories) that appeal to specific emotions and that will sway your listeners in favor of your position. By the time you reach the conclusion of your speech, you should have already succeeded in persuading your listeners to accept your position. This may be the most effective time to state that position directly to the audience.

When you present a persuasive speech developed through appeals to emotion, you should use particularly vivid language. You may also want to employ voice tones and gestures that depict greater intensity than you might show in other kinds of speeches. Be careful, however, that you do not confuse forceful speaking with shouting.

Also be careful, as you plan and present a persuasive speech with emotional appeals, that you avoid unfair and dishonest persuasive techniques. Such techniques as telling lies or half-truths, calling names, using obscenities, and making irrelevant personal attacks are unethical and, in many cases, harmful.

Working with the Model

In 1976, Representative Barbara Jordan of Texas was the keynote speaker at the Democratic National Convention. Read the following excerpt from the speech she made on that occasion. As you read, think about the specific purpose of Jordan's speech and about the appeals she uses to achieve that purpose.

There is something special about tonight. What is different? What is special? I, Barbara Jordan, am a keynote speaker.

A lot of years passed since 1832, and during that time it would have been most unusual for any national political party to ask that a Barbara Jordan deliver a keynote address ... but tonight here I am. And I feel that, notwithstanding the past, my presence here is one additional bit of evidence that the American Dream need not forever be deferred.

Now that I have this grand distinction, what in the world am I supposed to say? ...

I could list the many problems which Americans have. I could list the problems which cause people to feel cynical, angry, frustrated; problems which include lack of integrity in government; the feeling that the individual no longer counts; the reality of material and spiritual poverty; the feeling that the grand American experiment is failing or has failed. I could recite these problems, and then I could sit down and offer no solutions. But I don't choose to do that. ...

The citizens of America expect more. They deserve and they want more than a recital of the problems.

We are a people in a quandary about the present. We are a people in search of our future. We are a people in search of a national community.

We are a people trying not only to solve the problems of the present: unemployment, inflation ... but we are attempting on a larger scale to fulfill the promise of America. We are attempting to fulfill our national purpose; to create and sustain a society in which all of us are equal....

Let's all understand that these guiding principles cannot be discarded for short-term political gains. They represent what this country is all about. They are indigenous to the American idea. And these are the principles which are not negotiable. ...

model

And now we must look to the future. Let us heed the voice of the people and recognize their common sense. If we do not, we not only blaspheme our political heritage, we ignore the common ties that bind all Americans.

Many fear the future. Many are distrustful of their leaders, and believe that their voices are never heard. Many seek only to satisfy their private work wants, to satisfy private interests.

But this is the great danger America faces: that we will cease to be one nation and become instead a collection of interest groups; city against suburb, region against region, individual against individual, each seeking to satisfy private wants.

If that happens, who then will speak for America?

Who then will speak for the common good? . . .

Are we to be one people bound together by common spirit sharing in a common endeavor, or will we become a divided nation?

For all of its uncertainty, we cannot flee the future. We must not become the new puritans and reject our society. We must address and master the future together. It can be done if we restore the belief that we share a sense of national community, that we share a common national endeavor. It can be done.

There is no executive order, there is no law that can require the American people to form a national community. This we must do as individuals, and if we do it as individuals, there is no president of the United States who can veto that decision.

As a first step, we must restore our belief in ourselves. We are a generous people, so why can't we be generous with each other? We need to take to heart the words spoken by Thomas Jefferson:

"Let us restore to social intercourse that harmony and that affection without which liberty and even life are but dreary things."

A nation is formed by the willingness of each of us to share in the responsibility for upholding the common good.

A government is invigorated when each of us is willing to participate in shaping the future of this nation.

In this election year we must define the common good and begin again to shape a common future. Let each person do his or her part. If one citizen is unwilling to participate, all of us are going to suffer. For the American idea, though it is shared by all of us, is realized in each one of us.

And now, what are those of us who are elected officials supposed to do? We call ourselves public servants, but I'll tell you this: we as public servants must set an example for the rest of the nation. It is hypocritical for a public official to admonish and exhort the people to uphold the common good if we are derelict in upholding the common good. More is required of public officials than slogans and handshakes and press releases. More is required. We must hold ourselves strictly accountable. We must provide the people with a vision of the future.

If we promise as public officials, we must deliver. If we as public officials propose, we must produce. If we say to the American people, "It is time for you to be sacrificial; sacrifice"—if the public official says that, we (public officials) must be the first to give. We must be. And again, if we make mistakes, we must be willing to admit them. We have to do that. What we have to do is strike a balance between the idea that government should do everything and the idea, the belief, that government ought to do nothing. Strike a balance.

Let there be no illusions about the difficulty of forming this kind of a national community. It's tough, difficult, not easy. But a spirit of harmony will survive in America only if each of us remembers that we share a common destiny; if each of us remembers, when self-interest and bitterness seem to prevail, that we share a common destiny.

model

I have confidence that we can form this kind of national community. . . .

We cannot improve on the system of government handed down to us by the founders of the Republic; there is no way to improve upon that. But what we can do is to find new ways to implement that system and realize our destiny.

Now, I began this speech by commenting to you on the uniqueness of a Barbara Jordan making the keynote address. Well, I am going to close my speech by quoting a Republican president, and I ask you that as you listen to these words of Abraham Lincoln, relate them to the concept of a national community in which every last one of us participates: "As I would not be a slave, so I would not be a master. This expresses my idea of Democracy. Whatever differs from this, to the extent of the difference is no Democracy."

QUESTIONS

A. The specific purpose of Jordan's speech is to persuade her listeners that they must work together in forming a national community based on the principles of democracy. Think about how the speech is organized around that purpose.

   1. Which single sentence in Jordan's speech do you consider the direct statement of her position?

   2. How does the introduction of Jordan's speech capture the listeners' interest in her position?

   3. How does the main portion of her speech develop that purpose?

   4. How does the conclusion emphasize that position?

B. Think about the appeals to emotion which Jordan uses to develop her persuasive speech.

   1. Read the following appeals to emotion from Jordan's speech. On which kind of basic need—physical, psychological, or social—is each appeal based?

     "to create and sustain a society in which all of us are equal"

     "the reality of material . . . poverty"

     "problems which cause people to feel cynical, angry, frustrated"

     "only if each of us remembers that we share a common destiny"

   2. Find four other examples of appeals to emotion in Jordan's speech. On what kind of basic need is each appeal based?

C. Think about the audience to whom Jordan's speech is addressed.

   1. Who are the people in the audience?

   2. How do the appeals Jordan uses show her understanding of those people?

Guidelines

These guidelines will help you plan and present an effective persuasive speech developed with appeals to emotion:

1. Appeals to emotion are based on the three kinds of basic needs common to all people: physical needs, psychological needs, and social needs. When you select the specific appeals to use in your speech, you must think carefully about the needs, interests, and fears of the people in your audience.

2. Use vivid language, a forceful voice, and clear gestures when you present your speech.

3. Carefully avoid unfair persuasive techniques, such as lying, calling names, using obscenities, and making irrelevant personal attacks.

Preparing and Presenting

Choose a product, real or imaginary, to use as the topic of a persuasive speech. Select a specific audience, such as preschool children or wealthy middle-aged adults, for your speech. Think about the emotional appeals that will most effectively convince the members of that audience of their need for your product. Plan a brief persuasive speech, developed with at least two specific appeals to emotion, that will persuade the people in your audience to use the product.

After you have planned and rehearsed your speech, select a partner. Have your partner listen as you give your persuasive speech; then listen as your partner gives his or her persuasive speech.

Evaluating

After you and your partner have both given your persuasive speeches, discuss the effectiveness of each speech. In the course of your discussion, answer the following questions:

1. What position was presented in the speech? In which part of the speech was the position directly stated? In what other part of the speech might the position have been more effectively presented?

2. What specific emotional appeals were used to develop the speech? On what kind of basic need was each appeal based?

3. For what specific audience was the speech intended? How well were the appeals to emotion suited to the members of that audience? What other appeals to emotion might have been better suited to that audience?

4. What changes in choice of words, in tone of voice, or in gestures might have made the presentation of the speech more effective?

5. What unfair persuasive techniques (if any) were used in the speech? How might those unfair techniques have been avoided?

Motivating Others to Help Solve a Problem

Some problems that you have at school, in your community, or on the job require more than one person to solve them. You may need the talents and influence of several specific people to reach a solution. Or you may simply need a number of people to support you (for example, if you are circulating petitions). You need to motivate others to join you in solving a problem. Every problem is different, but some principles for motivating people are always important:

- Reach the people who can actually help you. They must have the knowledge, ability, time, and interest that you need.
- Use personal appeals to interest these people in your cause. Persuade them that it is their cause, too. Convince them that what you want them to do is both right and practical.
- Have a specific course of action you want people to follow. Don't leave them wondering what to do.
- Be open to other people's suggestions, and always treat them with respect and interest.
- Be honest about possible difficulties or dangers, but don't frighten people so that they are afraid to act.
- Remind people of the success that they and others have had in the past when solving similar problems. Show them that if you follow the right steps, you can reach your goal.

ACTIVITIES

1. Identify a problem that affects your school or community, and outline a possible solution or solutions. Try to motivate five other students to join you in solving this problem. Make notes on the methods of persuasion you used and the way each student reacted. Report to your class on your success or lack of success (it may be best to refer to "Student A," "Student B," and so forth in your report). Ask the class for their reactions and suggestions for motivating others.
2. Invite a community leader to speak to your class. This person can be a member of a neighborhood committee, a political organizer, or an activist on an issue of public interest. Ask the speaker how he or she motivates people to join in solving problems, and which methods work best with different types of people.

career

9.3 Using Identification

Being Aware of Different Dialects

Every person in the world speaks a *dialect*—that is, a special version of his or her language. American English is one of the dialects of the English language. Within the United States, there are a number of regional dialects, including New England, Boston, New York, Southern, Midwestern, and Hawaiian. Any dialect has several characteristics that distinguish it from other dialects:

1. *A population of speakers.* A dialect is spoken and understood by people in a city or region, or from a particular ethnic background.

2. *A special vocabulary.* It contains words from older forms of English (as in Southern and Appalachian English) or from foreign languages (for example, French in Louisiana or Spanish in the Southwest).

3. *Special pronunciations.* Certain vowels and consonants are always pronounced the same way in a given dialect (for example, *car* sounds rather like *caah* in Boston and *caw* in the South).

4. *Special grammatical forms.* A dialect may have forms borrowed from a foreign language, surviving from older English, or developed in a particular region (for example, the Southern form "you all," for the plural of "you"). Nationally used textbooks and broadcasting are making such forms more rare.

There are many areas of life in which speaking a distinctive dialect can be a disadvantage. Successful speakers often tone down their regional dialects. As a result, although their origins are still recognizable, they have eliminated expressions and pronunciations that might confuse or distract their listeners.

ACTIVITY

1. During one or two weeks, see how many different dialects you can find on television programs. Try to identify the region or group associated with each dialect. Note how dialects are used on dramatic or comedy shows. For example, do they dramatize a lack of communication, or are they used to make fun of certain characters? Compare your observations with those of other students.

language

How to Use Identification

The effectiveness of a persuasive speech can be greatly enhanced if the listeners think of the speaker as a person very much like themselves (or very much like their best images of themselves). As such, the speaker becomes a person whom the listeners can trust and believe.

Whenever you present a persuasive speech, you should encourage the members of your audience to identify with you. To do so, you must establish your own credibility, or believability, in the minds of the audience. You must also evoke the goodwill of the audience. Specific techniques for achieving these goals are listed in the chart below.

You can also use your method of delivery to encourage identification. If you project self-confidence and a genuine enthusiasm when you speak, your listeners will want to believe you.

HOW TO ENCOURAGE IDENTIFICATION	
To Establish Credibility	To Gain Goodwill
• Speaker has an established reputation. • Speaker has demonstrated knowledge of the topic. • Speaker is sincere. • Speaker appears trustworthy to audience members.	• Speaker stresses interests in common with audience. • Speaker identifies self with person or cause audience admires. • Speaker compliments audience on its positive qualities.

Working with the Model

In 1933, in the middle of the Great Depression, Franklin Delano Roosevelt was inaugurated into his first term as President. Read the following excerpt from the beginning of his inaugural address. As you read, notice how directly Roosevelt encourages the members of his audience to identify with him.

I am certain that my fellow Americans expect that on my induction into the Presidency I will address them with a candor and a decision which the present situation of our Nation impels. This is preeminently the time to speak the truth, the whole truth, frankly and boldly. Nor need we shrink from honestly facing conditions in our country today. This great Nation will endure, will revive and will prosper. So, first of all, let me assert my firm belief that the only thing we have to fear is fear itself—nameless, unreasoning, unjustified terror which paralyzes needed efforts to convert retreat into advance. In every dark hour of our national life a leadership of frankness and vigor has met with that understanding and support of the people themselves which is essential to victory. I am convinced that you will again give that support to leadership in these critical days.

In such a spirit on my part and on yours, we face our common difficulties. They concern, thank God, only material things. Values have shrunken to fantastic levels; taxes have risen; our ability to pay has fallen; government of all kinds is faced by serious curtailment of income; the means of exchange are frozen in the current of trade; the withered leaves of industrial enterprise lie on every side; farmers find no market for their produce; the savings of many years in thousands of families are gone.

More important, a host of unemployed citizens face the grim problems of existence, and an equally great number toil with little return. Only a foolish optimist can deny the dark realities of the moment.

Yet our distress comes from no failure of substance. We are stricken by no plague of locusts. Compared with the perils which our forefathers conquered because they believed and were not afraid, we still have much to be thankful for.

QUESTIONS

A. Think about the audience to whom this speech is directed.

1. Who are the listeners in Roosevelt's audience?
2. How does Roosevelt show that he knows his audience well?

B. Think about the techniques Roosevelt uses to establish his own credibility.

1. What is Roosevelt's established reputation at the time of this speech? How does he refer to that reputation in the first sentence of his speech?
2. What is Roosevelt's demonstrated knowledge of his topic? How does he refer to that knowledge?
3. How does the following sentence indicate Roosevelt's sincerity? "Only a foolish optimist can deny the dark realities of the moment." In what other ways does Roosevelt show his sincerity?

C. Think about the techniques Roosevelt uses to evoke the goodwill of his audience.

1. How do the following sentences stress the interests and efforts Roosevelt has in common with his listeners?

   "Nor need we shrink from honestly facing conditions in our country today."

   "In such a spirit on my part and on yours we face our common difficulties."

   Find at least two other sentences in which Roosevelt emphasizes his unity with his listeners.
2. Reread the last two sentences in the first paragraph of the speech. With whom is Roosevelt identifying himself? Why could he expect the members of his audience to admire those leaders?
3. What positive quality in his listeners does Roosevelt compliment in the final sentence of the first paragraph?

Guidelines

When you give a persuasive speech, you should encourage your listeners to identify with you, to regard you as a person like themselves who can be trusted and believed. These guidelines will help you:

1. Establish your own credibility.
2. Evoke the goodwill of your listeners.
3. Speak with self-confidence and genuine enthusiasm.

Preparing and Presenting

With a partner, select a persuasive speech to analyze. For example, you may select a campaign speech, a sales presentation, or a persuasive speech made before a legislative body. You may choose a speech that you attended or one that you heard broadcast on television or radio. If you wish, the speech may be one presented by a fictional character in a television drama or a film.

Listen carefully to the speech that you and your partner select. As you listen, think about how the speaker encourages identification on the part of his or her listeners.

After the speech, write a four-paragraph analysis of the speaker's success in encouraging audience identification. In the first paragraph, examine the speaker's efforts to establish his or her own credibility. Consider each of the techniques listed in the chart on page 231, and cite specific examples from the speech.

In the second paragraph, examine the speaker's efforts to evoke the goodwill of the audience. Consider each of the techniques listed in the chart on page 231, and cite specific examples from the speech.

In the third paragraph, examine the speaker's method of delivery. Consider the self-confidence and the enthusiasm he or she displayed while speaking, and, once again, cite specific examples.

In the final paragraph of your analysis, summarize the effectiveness of the speaker's attempts to encourage audience identification. Also suggest specific changes in the content or delivery of the speech that might have improved the audience's identification with the speaker.

Evaluating

Read your partner's analysis, and compare it with your own. Discuss with your partner the points of agreement and of disagreement in the two analyses. During the discussion, respond to the following questions:

1. How did you and your partner evaluate the speaker's effectiveness in establishing his or her credibility? Which examples most clearly typify the techniques he or she used, or failed to use?

2. How did you and your partner evaluate the speaker's effectiveness in evoking the goodwill of the audience? Which examples most clearly typify the techniques he or she used, or failed to use?

3. How did you and your partner evaluate the effectiveness of the speaker's delivery? How did the members of the audience seem to react to the speaker's self-confidence and enthusiasm, or to the speaker's lack of self-confidence and enthusiasm?

4. What specific suggestions for improving audience identification did you and your partner make? Which of your partner's suggestions seem most appropriate? Which of your suggestions seem most appropriate?

5. How did the speaker's success (or failure) in encouraging audience identification enhance (or detract from) the effectiveness of his or her persuasive speech?

Evaluating Your Credibility as a Speaker

To be an effective speaker, you must be *credible* to others. The following chart contains ten questions to evaluate a speaker's credibility. Each question may be answered by a score of 0 (poorest) to 10 (best).

Quality	Rating
1. How well does the speaker know his or her subject?	
2. How accurately does the speaker report information?	
3. Does the speaker give due credit to sources of information and ideas?	
4. Does the speaker use sound logic?	
5. Does the speaker avoid deceptive techniques and loaded language?	
6. Are the speaker's facts and ideas consistent on different occasions?	
7. Does the speaker avoid gossip, rumor, and innuendo?	
8. Does the speaker show respect for others?	
9. Does the speaker avoid bragging?	
10. How would you rate the speaker's overall credibility, in speaking and in life?	

ACTIVITY

1. Use the preceding chart to evaluate five well-known speakers (for example, a politician, a city or state official, a newscaster, a business person, and a celebrity). Add up their scores in each category, and see how they rank on a scale of 0 to 100. Compare your evaluation with those of other students in your class, and discuss why you evaluated each speaker as you did.

career

9.4 Using Identification with Appeals to Logic and Appeals to Emotion

Understanding Bias and Stereotyping

A *bias* is a prejudice either for or against certain people, institutions, or ideas. A biased person has already made up his or her mind, often with very little information, and may be difficult to persuade. A bias towards a particular group of people—all members of a race, age group, nationality, religion, or profession—can lead to *stereotyping*. Stereotypes are all too common in speech and writing. Consider these:

''All cheerleaders are silly airheads.''
''Football players are subhuman.''
''Women only go to college to get married.''

People tend to cling to destructive prejudices even in the face of overwhelming evidence against them. As a speaker, you need to ask yourself several questions about bias and stereotypes:

- What biases do I show in my speech and arguments, and how can I eliminate them?
- What are the biases of my audience, and how can I make them more open-minded toward my ideas?
- What stereotypes am I guilty of using, and how can I be more responsible in my speech?
- What stereotype might my audience have about me, my background, or the subject of my speech, and how can I persuade them to change their minds?

ACTIVITIES

1. During the course of a week, take notes on the examples of bias and stereotyping you hear in people's speech, in movies, and on television. Draw up a list of examples, and compare it with the lists of other students.
2. Make a list of your own biases and use of stereotypes. Think about why you developed these biases and stereotypes, and the ways in which they may affect your behavior. Decide what steps you could take to eliminate them from your speech and thinking.

attitude

How to Use Identification
with Appeals to Logic and Appeals to Emotion

As you listen to and evaluate persuasive speeches, you will probably find that the most convincing speeches do not rely only on logical arguments or only on appeals to emotion. In many cases, a combination of these two methods of development results in the most effective persuasive speech.

When you plan a persuasive speech, consider including both logical arguments and appeals to emotion. Select a logical argument for each main point that is based on common sense or fact. Select an appeal to emotion for each main point that involves a basic physical, psychological, or social need. As you choose your main points, remember to consider both your position and your audience. Be certain that each main point will be clearly understandable and convincing to your listeners.

When you plan your speech, also think about the techniques you can use to encourage your listeners to identify with you. Consider how you can best appear credible and self-confident to the members of your audience, and consider how you can evoke their goodwill. If your listeners regard you as familiar and trustworthy, they will be more readily persuaded by your speech.

Working with the Model

In 1894 Captain Alfred Dreyfus, a French army officer, was accused of selling military secrets to Germany. Although much of the evidence against him had been forged, Dreyfus was convicted by a secret court martial, and condemned to life imprisonment on Devil's Island. Proof of Dreyfus' innocence was found in 1897, but the army refused to reopen the case. This controversy divided France into two factions: those who believed Dreyfus had been convicted largely because he was a Jew, and those who believed the army should be supported at any cost.

In 1898 the novelist Emile Zola published an article entitled *I Accuse!* He accused politicians and officers, by name, of framing Dreyfus, concealing evidence, and deliberately encouraging public anti-Semitism. Zola knew he would be charged with libel, and he wanted to use his trial to reopen the Dreyfus case. Zola was convicted, and fled to England to avoid imprisonment. Shortly afterwards, Dreyfus was pardoned, and eventually he was entirely cleared.

As you read the following excerpts from Zola's speech to the jury, observe the way he uses appeals to logic, appeals to emotion, and identification to argue his case.

model

If I am standing here before you, it is by my own wish. I alone decided that this dark, monstrous scandal should be brought under your jurisdiction. I alone, of my own free will, chose you—the highest source of French justice—in order that France might at last know everything, and reach a verdict. My acts have had no other purpose, and my person is nothing. I have sacrificed my person so that I could place in your hands, not only the honor of the army, but the imperiled honor of the nation. . . .

You know the legend that has grown up: Dreyfus was condemned justly and legally by seven infallible officers, whom we cannot even suspect of error without insulting the entire army. He pays with deserved tortures for his abominable crime. And since he is a Jew, a Jewish syndicate has been established, an international syndicate of people without national allegiances, in order to save the traitor at the price of shameless bribery. Next, this syndicate piles crime on crime, buying consciences, throwing France into disastrous confusion, determined to sell her to the enemy, to plunge France into a general war, rather than to renounce its terrible plan.

There it is. It's very simple—even childish and imbecile, as you see. But with this poisoned bread the dirty press has been nourishing our people for months. And we must not be astonished if we are witnessing a dangerous crisis, for when you sow folly and lies, you reap madness.

Certainly, gentlemen, I do not insult you by thinking that you have been taken in by such nursery tales. I know you, I know who you are. You are the heart and mind of Paris, of my great Paris, where I was born, which I love with an infinite tenderness, which I have studied and written about for forty years. And I know what is now going on inside your brains; for before coming to sit here as the defendant, I was seated there, in the jury box where you are. There you represent the average point of view, you illustrate wisdom and justice in the mass. Soon I will be with you, in thought, in the room where you deliberate. I am convinced that your effort will be to safeguard your interests as citizens, which are, naturally, the interests of the entire nation. You may make mistakes, but you will make mistakes with the idea that in serving your own welfare, you serve the welfare of all.

I see you with your families in the evening, under the lamplight. I listen to you chatting with your friends. I accompany you into your factories and shops. You are all working people, some in trade, some in industry, some in the professions. And your anxiety over the deplorable state into which business has fallen is legitimate. Everywhere the

model

present crisis threatens to become a disaster. Receipts fall off, business deals become more difficult. So the thought which you have brought here, the thought I read on your faces, is that there has been enough of this scandal, and you must put an end to it.

You have not reached the point of saying, like many: "What does it matter to us whether an innocent man is on Devil's Island?" But you tell yourselves, just the same, that the agitation by us, who hunger and thirst for truth, is not worth all the evil we are accused of causing. And if you condemn me, gentlemen, only one thought will underlie your verdict: the desire to calm your own seas, to revive business, the belief that in striking at me you will be putting an end to a campaign that is harmful to the interests of France.

I do not defend myself. But what a blunder you would make, if you believed that in striking at me you would reestablish order in our unhappy country! Don't you understand now that the country is dying of the darkness in which they so obstinately keep her? The mistakes of government officials pile up on top of mistakes; one lie necessitates another, and the mass becomes overwhelming. A judicial blunder has been committed; and in order to hide it, it has been necessary to commit a new offense every day against common sense and justice . . .

model

Today they ask you to condemn me, in my turn, because, seeing my country on such a terrifying course, I have cried out in my anguish. Condemn me, then! But it will be another mistake, a mistake whose burden you will bear throughout history. And my condemnation, instead of restoring the peace which you desire, which we all desire, will only sow new passion and disorder. The cup, I tell you, is full to the rim. Do not make it overflow! . . .

The Dreyfus case—ah, gentlemen, the Dreyfus case has become very small at this moment. It is very far away, compared to the terrifying question which it has raised. It is no longer a question of the Dreyfus case. It is a question of whether France is still the France of the Declaration of the Rights of Man, the France which gave liberty to the world, and which ought to give the world justice. Are we still the most noble, the most fraternal, the most generous nation? Are we going to protect our reputation in Europe for justice and humanity? Are not all our victories now called into question? Open your eyes, and realize that the French soul, to be in such confusion, must have been shaken to its depths by these terrible dangers. A nation is not turned upside down in this way unless its moral existence is in peril. This is an hour of extraordinary gravity; the safety of the nation is at stake.

And when you have grasped this, gentlemen, you will feel that only one remedy is possible: to speak the truth, to render justice. Everything that holds back the light, everything that piles darkness on darkness, will only prolong and aggravate the crisis. The role of good citizens, of those who feel the overriding necessity to put an end to this business, is to demand broad daylight. There are many of us who believe this. Men of letters, philosophers, scientists are rising on every side in the name of intelligence and reason. And I am not speaking of foreigners, of the shudder that has shaken all Europe. Yet the foreigner is not necessarily the enemy. Let us not consider the nations who might be our enemies tomorrow. But great Russia, our ally, or generous little Holland, or all the sympathetic northern peoples, or the French-speaking lands of Switzerland and Belgium—why are their hearts so full, so overflowing with brotherly suffering? Do you imagine that France is isolated from the world? When you cross the frontier, do you want them to forget your traditional reputation for justice and humanity?

Perhaps, gentlemen, like so many others, you are waiting for a clap of thunder—the proof of Dreyfus' innocence, falling from the sky like a bolt of lightning. Truth does not behave in that way. She requires some searching, some intelligence. The proof! You know very well where it is, where we could find it! . . . And if it is impossible for the present to seek it out where it is, the government—which is ignorant of nothing, which is as convinced as we are of the innocence of Dreyfus—when it

model

sees fit, and when there are no risks, will find the witnesses who will at last give us light.

Dreyfus is innocent, I swear it! I stake my life on it, I stake my honor! In this solemn hour, before this tribunal which represents human justice, before you, gentlemen of the jury, who are the very incarnation of my country, before all France, before the whole world, I swear that Dreyfus is innocent! By my forty years of labor, by any authority that labor may have conferred upon me, I swear that Dreyfus is innocent! By all that I have achieved, by the name that I have made for myself, by the works I have added to French literature, I swear that Dreyfus is innocent! Let all that melt away, let my works perish, if Dreyfus is not innocent! He is innocent!

Everything seems to be against me: the two legislative Chambers, the civil power, the military power, the newspapers with the widest circulation, the public opinion which they have poisoned. And I have on my side only the ideal—an ideal of truth and justice. But I am content, for I will win!

I did not want my country to be the victim of lies and injustice. You may condemn me here. One day France will thank me for having helped to save her honor.

QUESTIONS

A. Think about the appeals to logic that Zola makes in his speech.
1. In what part of the speech does he appeal to the jurors' ability to tell truth from falsehood?
2. In what passages does he explain how the present crisis came about?
3. In what passage does he try to account for the lack of proof on his side of the case?
4. Why do you think Zola makes as few appeals to logic as he does?

B. Think about the appeals to emotion in this speech.
1. In what passages does Zola appeal to the jurors' sense of fairness?
2. In what passages does he appeal to their patriotism and national pride?
3. What other emotions does Zola appeal to?

C. Think about Zola's use of identification in this speech.
1. How does he present himself to the jurors?
2. How does he explain his ability to understand the jurors' thoughts and feelings?
3. In what passages does Zola ask to be judged on the basis of his talent and reputation?

D. At the time he made this speech, Zola was fairly certain he would be convicted. If he believed this, why do you think he made this speech? Why do you think he made the specific appeals that he did? In what ways do you think the speech might have been different if Zola had thought he would be acquitted?

Guidelines

Very often, logical arguments and appeals to emotion can be combined to develop a particularly effective persuasive speech. When you combine these methods of development, remember to keep the following guidelines in mind:

1. Use logical arguments in presenting main points that are based on common sense or fact. Be sure each logical argument directly supports your position and will be understandable and convincing to your audience.

2. Use appeals to emotion in presenting main points that are based on basic physical, psychological, or social needs. Be sure each appeal to emotion directly supports your position and will be understandable and convincing to your audience.

3. Plan to use specific techniques that will encourage your audience to identify with you. If you establish their identification with you early, your listeners will be particularly willing to be persuaded by your speech.

Preparing and Presenting

With three or four other students, select a topic on which you can all prepare persuasive speeches. You and the other members of your group may wish to choose one of the following topics:

- violence on television
- the budget for national defense
- cigarette smoking in public buildings
- career-directed education for high school students
- a national draft for two years of public service

Working independently, plan a persuasive speech on the topic that you and the other group members have chosen. Decide on your position on that topic. Also select an audience for the persuasive speech in which you will present that position. You may choose your fellow students as an audience, or you may choose another kind of group.

If necessary, do research on the topic of your speech. Then select three or more main points that will persuade your listeners to accept your position. Your main points should include both logical arguments and appeals to emotion.

Write a complete outline for your speech. In your outline, include notes on the methods you will use to encourage the members of your audience to identify with you.

With the rest of your group, discuss the speech outline prepared by each group member. Talk about the statement of position, the logical arguments, the appeals to emotion, and the methods for encouraging audience identification presented in each student's outline. Help each group member improve his or her outline as necessary.

After you have revised and improved your own speech outline, practice presenting your speech. Ask the other members of your group to listen as you speak and to suggest specific ways in which you might improve your tone of voice, rate of speaking, use of gestures, and projection of self-confidence and enthusiasm.

Finally, present your speech to the other students in your class. If you have selected an audience other than your fellow students, identify your intended audience before you begin your speech.

Evaluating

With the other members of your group, discuss the effectiveness of the speech you gave to the rest of the class. The following questions will help you evaluate your speech:

1. How might the statement of position have been more convincingly phrased? How might it have been more effectively placed in the speech?

2. What logical arguments were presented to support the position? Which logical arguments, if any, were not appropriate to the topic or to the audience? What other logical arguments, if any, should have been presented?

3. What appeals to emotion were presented to support the position? Which appeals to emotion, if any, were not appropriate to the topic or to the audience? What other appeals to emotion, if any, should have been presented?

4. What techniques were used to encourage the audience to identify with the speaker? How successful were those techniques? What other techniques, if any, should have been used?

5. How persuasive was the delivery of the speech? What changes in voice or gestures would have made the speech more convincing?

6. Consider the over-all impression made by the speech: How persuasive was the speech? What one change would have been most important in improving the effectiveness of the speech?

Making a Sales Presentation

Very few products or services can sell themselves. First-rate sales-people can inspire customers with a desire to buy and the feeling that they are making the right decision. Effective sales presentations are based on extensive practice, experience, and knowledge of human psychology. Several principles, however, are always true:

- A good sales presentation has the qualities of a good persuasive speech. It uses facts, figures, and other evidence to promote a product. It meets and answers the listeners' objections to the product, and it is delivered with conviction and enthusiasm.

- An effective salesperson uses questions and observations to learn about his or her customers. How much money do they have to spend? Are they seriously interested in buying, or only comparison shopping? What are they looking for in a product—for example, do they value glamour or efficiency more highly?

- If there is more than one customer, a good salesperson finds out what features each person is most interested in, then emphasizes those features when speaking to that customer.

- A good salesperson never argues with customers—even if they are wrong. The salesperson should continually observe the customers' reactions, and change the presentation accordingly.

- A good salesperson knows when to stop talking and let the customers make up their minds. Whether or not the presentation results in a sale, the salesperson should give the customers a business card and urge them to stay in touch.

ACTIVITIES

1. Working with three or more other students, select several products to shop for. (You should consider stereo equipment, bicycles, televisions, used cars, and other products students might reasonably be expected to buy.) Visit the stores individually, and listen to the sales presentations. Then evaluate the presentations according to the guidelines above, and report your findings to the class.

2. Work with another student. Each of you should prepare a different sales presentation for a product. Try to make the presentations equally appealing to customers. Then deliver your presentations before the class. Have the other students vote for the presentation more likely to make them buy the product.

career

10 Debates

A debate is more than an argument between persuasive speakers. It is a competition that requires skill, preparation, and alert listening. A good debater must be able to research and organize evidence in order to use it at very short notice. He or she has to listen carefully to opposing arguments in order to detect their weaknesses. A debater must persuade an audience with facts, and rebut the opponent's evidence with stronger evidence. Developing debating skills is good preparation for a career in law, government, or business. Learning the basic principles of debate can give you confidence and flexibility as a speaker.

After working through this chapter, you should be able to

- understand the terms used in debate
- prepare a debate brief
- understand how debate speeches are organized
- make a constructive speech or a rebuttal speech

The Speaking Skills lessons in this chapter will help you become more effective in debate and other persuasive speaking. You will learn to

- recognize errors in reasoning
- recognize errors in debate arguments

The Skills for Success lessons in this chapter will help you apply debate skills to public life. You will learn to

- avoid common research mistakes
- participate in a candidate debate

10.1 Preparing for Debates

Recognizing Errors in Reasoning

Avoid the following common errors in your own speech, and be able to recognize them in the speech of others.

1. *Begging the question* means stating a position that needs to be proved as though it had already been proved; for example:

   > The issue of this campaign is whether Mayor Grey, who has had a disgraceful four years in office, deserves another chance.

   The real "issue," however, is whether Grey's record can be shown to be disgraceful. The speaker who avoids having to prove this is begging the question.

2. *Reasoning backward* assumes that because members of a particular group have a characteristic in common, anyone with that characteristic must belong to the group; for example:

   > Communists are always talking about peace. Senator Flower talks about peace. Therefore Senator Flower must be a communist.

   Obviously, it is possible to talk about peace without being a communist. Unsound though it is, backward reasoning leads to many dangerous accusations.

3. *Confusing "after" with "because"* is a common error; for example:

   > During the governor's term of office, the cost of living has doubled. Are you going to reelect a man who made your poorer?

   The fact that something happened *after* a person became governor does not mean that it happened *because* he became governor. The speaker has to demonstrate the cause-and-effect relationship.

ACTIVITY

1. Listen to or read a persuasive speech by a candidate or public official. See how many of the preceding errors in reasoning you are able to identify in the speech. If you find no errors, locate at least one passage where the speaker could easily have made an error, and decide what the speaker might have said if he or she had been less careful. Report on your findings to the class.

listening

How to Prepare for a Debate

A debate is a competition between persuasive speakers. A formal debate usually involves two teams, each with two members, presenting in a specific sequence their arguments for and against a given resolution.

The following chart presents the most important terms used in a formal debate. Study the terms and their explanations.

Debate Terms

Proposition	The formal statement of the issue to be debated. During the debate, the speakers take opposing sides on the proposition. The proposition for a debate should be a concisely worded statement that contains only one idea. It is a statement of policy, not of fact. It should propose a specific change in existing conditions or policies.
Affirmative	The side of the debate that argues for the change advocated in the proposition. During the debate, the affirmative side presents arguments and evidence to support the proposition.
Negative	The side of the debate that argues against the change advocated in the proposition. During the debate, the negative side presents arguments and evidence to oppose the proposition.
Argument	The statement of an objective reason that directly supports the position of either the affirmative side or the negative side.
Evidence	Facts, statistics, expert testimony, or other specific details that directly support an argument.
Brief	A complete outline of all the necessary definitions, arguments, and evidence on both sides of a proposition.
Refutation	An effort by speakers to answer or disprove arguments presented by the other side in a debate.

Constructive Speech	The first speech given by each debater. Both affirmative and negative speakers use their constructive speeches to present the arguments in support of their positions. Except for the first speaker in the debate, they may also include some refutation in their constructive speeches.
Rebuttal Speech	A speech in which refutation is the primary activity. Usually, each debater gives one constructive speech and, later, one rebuttal speech, half as long as the constructive speech. In his or her rebuttal speech, the debater may also try to bolster arguments refuted by the other side, clarify positions, and summarize arguments.

Successful participation in a debate requires thorough and careful preparation. Each debater must consider the proposition closely and must research both sides of the issue. In order to argue persuasively either for or against the proposition, and in order to convincingly refute opposing arguments, all the debaters must be completely familiar with both the affirmative and the negative positions.

Each debater should consult a wide variety of sources in researching the issue of the debate. When he or she has completed the research, the debater should organize all the information, arguments, and evidence into a complete outline, the debate *brief.*

The following outline shows the specific parts of a complete brief. A formal brief should be written as a sentence outline. Its purpose is to help the debater understand both sides of the debate issue; it also serves as a source of the specific information the debater will include in the outline for his or her debate speech.

Parts of a Brief

I. Statement of the proposition.

II. Introduction.

  A. Tell why the issue is important.

  B. Give a short history of the issue.

  C. Define controversial or vague terms. Include various possible definitions where necessary.

  D. State the main arguments.

   1. List the arguments for the affirmative side. Common arguments are that the proposed change is needed, that the change is practical, that the change is desirable, and that the advantages of making the change are greater than the disadvantages of making it.

   2. List the arguments for the negative side. Common arguments are that the proposed change is not needed, that the change is impractical, that the change is undesirable, that the disadvantages of making the change are greater than the advantages of making it, and that there are solutions better than those proposed by the affirmative side.

III. Body. (This is the longest, most detailed portion of the brief.)

  A. State again each argument for the affirmative. After each argument, list the specific evidence that supports it. Cite the source for each item of evidence.

  B. State again each argument for the negative. After each argument, list the specific evidence that supports it. Cite the source for each item of evidence.

IV. Conclusion.

  A. Summarize the position and arguments of the affirmative side.

  B. Summarize the position and arguments of the negative side.

Working with the Model

Read the following outline. It shows the beginning of the brief Camilla prepared for a formal debate.

model

Debate Brief

I. Statement of the proposition: The teachers in Elementary School District 212 should be allowed to use corporal punishment to discipline their students.

II. Introduction.

    A. Consideration of the use of corporal punishment to discipline students is important for two major reasons.

        1. Discipline problems in the elementary schools have increased steadily during the past five years.

        2. A group of teachers and parents has organized a campaign to change the current regulation against corporal punishment.

    B. Since Elementary School District 212 was established forty-three years ago, corporal punishment has never been permitted. On two occasions (approximately twenty years ago and eight years ago), unsuccessful efforts have been made to allow corporal punishment.

model

C. The following definitions may be applied.

 1. "Teachers" should be considered the main classroom instructors for students in kindergarten through eighth grade. Some may want to include aides, classroom assistants, student teachers, or school administrators in this definition.

 2. Using "corporal punishment" may be defined as hitting students, in a controlled and supervised situation, either with the open hand or with a wooden paddle.

D. The following are the major arguments for each side.

 1. The affirmative side can be expected to present these arguments.

  a. The use of corporal punishment will improve students' behavior.

  b. A majority of the students' parents approve of the use of corporal punishment.

  c. Corporal punishment does not violate the rights of students.

  d. Abuses in the use of corporal punishment are easily prevented.

 2. The negative side can be expected to present these arguments.

  a. The use of corporal punishment will not significantly improve students' behavior.

  b. Corporal punishment violates the rights of students.

  c. The right to use corporal punishment is often abused.

  d. Forms of discipline other than corporal punishment can more effectively improve students' behavior.

III. Body.

A. The affirmative arguments are supported by these items of evidence.

 1. The use of corporal punishment will improve students' behavior.

  a. After corporal punishment was ended in Los Angeles schools (1975), students' fighting and "general disregard for good behavior" increased markedly, according to Board of Education member Bobbi Fiedler (*U.S. News & World Report*, June 2, 1980).

  b. The superintendent of a school district in which corporal punishment is allowed notes that such punishment rarely has to be used more than once with the same child (Brenton, *Today's Education,* November/December 1978).

253

QUESTIONS

A. Think about what you have read in Camilla's debate brief.
   1. What is the issue of the debate?
   2. What is the proposition?
   3. What does the wording of the proposition indicate about the current use of corporal punishment in Elementary School District 212?
   4. What information on the importance and the history of the issue is included in the brief?
   5. Which terms are defined in the brief? What changes, if any, would you suggest for the definitions in the brief? What other terms, if any, do you think should be defined?
   6. What arguments for the affirmative are listed in the introduction? What arguments for the negative are listed in the introduction? What other arguments, if any, would you add?
   7. What indication, if any, about which side Camilla will support is included in the brief?

B. Think about what might be included in the rest of the brief.
   1. What arguments will be included in the body of the brief?
   2. What kinds of evidence might be included to support each argument?
   3. What information should be included after each item of evidence?
   4. What will be included in the conclusion of the brief?

C. Think about a debate you have heard, either in person or on television or radio.
   1. How well prepared did the debaters seem to be?
   2. What indication was there that the debaters were familiar with both sides of the issue?

Guidelines

When you prepare to participate in a formal debate, you should remember the following guidelines:

1. A well-stated proposition has the following characteristics:
   • It is a statement, not a question.
   • It contains only one idea.
   • It is worded so that the persons who argue for it (the affirmative) advocate a change from existing conditions.
   • It is precisely stated; ambiguous terms are avoided, as are overly broad statements.
   • It must present a debatable issue, one that is not a question of fact and one that does not give either side a clear advantage.

2. Debaters on both the affirmative team and the negative team should research the issue of the debate thoroughly, consulting a variety of sources.

3. Each debater should organize the information he or she has gathered into a debate brief, a complete outline presenting the background of the issue and the arguments and evidence that support both sides of the issue.

Preparing and Presenting

Form a group with three other students. Together, select one of the following topics, or choose another topic that your teacher approves.

- government-supported day-care programs
- the closing times for polling places during national elections
- government control of oil companies
- national health insurance
- restrictions on the use of automobiles
- statewide requirements for graduation from high school

With the other members of your group, write a debate proposition on the issue you have chosen.

Then work independently to research that issue. Consult at least six different sources, and take notes on the information, arguments, and evidence you find.

Use your notes to write a debate brief. Your brief should be a sentence outline and should include all the parts shown in the outline on page 251.

Evaluating

With the other members of your group, decide who will be the two members of the affirmative team and who will be the two members of the negative team. Then compare your brief with the brief prepared by your teammate. Together, discuss the two briefs. During your discussion, you should answer the following questions:

1. Which brief presents the more complete explanation of the importance of the issue?

2. Which brief includes the more accurate history of the issue?

3. Which terms are defined in each brief? How do the definitions of those terms differ?

4. Which main arguments for the affirmative side are missing from each brief? What irrelevant arguments for the affirmative side are included?

5. Which main arguments for the negative side are missing from each brief? What irrelevant arguments for the negative side are included?

6. Which arguments for the affirmative side are not fully supported by relevant evidence? In which sources might evidence to support those arguments be found?

7. Which arguments for the negative side are not fully supported by relevant evidence? In which sources might evidence to support those arguments be found?

With your teammate, combine the information in the two briefs. Also take out any irrelevant information, and do research to add any other needed information.

Avoiding Common Research Mistakes

To take part effectively in group discussions, meetings, and other business situations, you need to have accurate facts and figures available. Inaccurate, out-of-date, or incomplete information can cause you embarrassment and damage your credibility. Study the following list of *don'ts* to avoid common research errors:

- Don't begin your research without a specific goal in mind.
- Don't ignore what you already know about a topic. Use your knowledge to locate areas where more research is needed.
- Don't hesitate to ask for help from teachers, librarians, and experts.
- Don't consult obsolete or unreliable sources, even if they are more readily available.
- Don't consult sources that are too much alike—for example, only encyclopedias, or only news magazines.
- Don't record everything indiscriminately. Select only information that can help you.
- Don't record any fact without understanding it in its context.
- Don't record any important piece of information without verifying it with an independent source.
- Don't record information without also recording the author, title, date and page number of the source.

ACTIVITY

1. Using at least three different *types* of sources, research one of the following topics. Obtain enough facts, statistics, and expert opinions for a ten-minute oral presentation on the subject.
   - deregulation of the airline and trucking industries
   - feasibility of solar power as an energy source for cities and factories
   - the all-volunteer army *versus* the draft

career

10.2 Participating in Debates

Recognizing Errors in Debate Arguments

Be alert to the following errors, and be prepared to point them out in your refutation. (Also see Speaking Skills, lesson 10.1.)

1. *Oversimplifying the issue* results in statements that may sound persuasive, but that distort the truth; for example:

   > On this issue, we have a clear choice between a policy that will lead to national disgrace and disaster, and a policy that will lead to strength, peace, and prosperity.

   Unless the debater can offer facts to support this simplistic statement, the judges and listeners will not be persuaded.

2. *Misleading statistics* sound factual, but they may not prove what the debater wants them to. For example, magazines often conduct surveys to learn whether Americans are content with their jobs, incomes, and personal lives. Not surprisingly, most of the responses come from people with enough leisure and money to read magazines and answer questionnaires. Such people are often contented with their lives, but their answers do not provide useful information about the population as a whole. If an opponent uses such a survey as evidence, you should point out how unreliable it is.

3. *False analogy* means using a figure of speech to make a comparison, then reasoning from the comparison as though it were a fact:

   > Politics is like a football game. In football, if a player doesn't follow the signals, the coach pulls him off the field. Obviously any politician who doesn't obey the head of the party should be kicked out of the party.

   Although there may be a superficial resemblance, the real world of politics is infinitely more complicated than a game of football.

ACTIVITY

1. Read or listen to a transcript of a debate, and try to detect these three errors. Then see whether the debater's opponent pointed out the error in argument. Report on your findings to the class.

How to Participate in a Debate

Once the debaters have researched the issue and written their briefs, they must prepare the speeches they will make during the debate. The members of each team should divide the important arguments between themselves, so that all the arguments will be presented but none will be repeated. Each debater presents and supports his or her major arguments during the constructive speech and refutes the opposing team's arguments during the rebuttal.

The traditional pattern for speeches in a debate is as follows:

Constructive Speeches (6 minutes each)

First Affirmative

First Negative

Second Affirmative

Second Negative

Rebuttal Speeches (3 minutes each)

First Negative

First Affirmative

Second Negative

Second Affirmative

The debaters should carefully outline their constructive speeches, remembering all the methods and techniques of persuasive speaking. Except for the first affirmative speaker, each debater should allow some time in his or her plan for refutation of the previous speaker's arguments.

In the rebuttal, each debater attempts to refute the arguments presented by the other side and to rebuild the case of his or her own team. These rebuttal speeches, obviously, cannot be outlined in advance; they must show direct responses to the arguments and evidence presented by the other team. Debaters can, however, prepare for their rebuttal speeches by studying their briefs. Each debater's brief should clearly indicate what arguments and evidence the opposing team is likely to present. It should also include specific items of evidence that will be useful in refuting the opposing team's arguments.

Debaters should also prepare for their rebuttal speeches by listening carefully and critically during the debate. It is essential that each debater hear and understand the arguments of the other side in order to refute those arguments successfully.

The last two speakers in a debate (Second Negative and Second Affirmative) should also be prepared to summarize the cases developed by their teams. Both before and during the debate, these two debaters should make notes that will help them present clear and convincing summaries.

Working with the Model

Camilla, Vince, Fran, and Elena participated in a debate on the following proposition: The teachers in Elementary School District 212 should be allowed to use corporal punishment to discipline their students.

The following excerpt is from the beginning of Vince's speech of rebuttal during that debate. As you read the excerpt, think about the argument Vince is attempting to refute. Also think about the evidence he uses in that attempt.

Vince's Rebuttal

model

Camilla would have us believe that the use of corporal punishment in schools will develop positive behavior among the students. This is simply not the case. Recently, the National Education Association appointed a task force to study the effects of corporal punishment in the schools. That task force found that, instead of decreasing aggression on the part of students, corporal punishment actually increased the students' aggression. Members of the National Center for the Study of Corporal Punishment reached similar conclusions.

Hitting is, after all, an aggressive act. Elementary school students look on their teachers as role-models. When they see their teachers acting aggressively, they learn to act aggressively themselves. A university professor of psychology stated this problem most directly. "Violence breeds violence," he said. "There's a greater chance that children who are hit will hit other children, will retaliate directly against teachers, will take their hostility out on the school buildings."

QUESTIONS

A. Think about what the excerpt from Vince's speech tells about the debate.
1. Is Camilla a debater on the affirmative team or the negative team?
2. Is Vince a debater on the affirmative team or the negative team?
3. What was one of the main arguments presented by the affirmative team members during their constructive speeches?

B. Think about how Vince tries to refute Camilla's argument.
1. When and how does he restate Camilla's argument?
2. When and how does he state his objection to the argument?
3. What specific evidence does Vince use to refute Camilla's argument?
4. Since Vince could not have outlined his rebuttal speech before the debate, where do you think he found the evidence that he used?
5. What other kinds of evidence might Vince have used?
6. How are the organization and presentation in this part of Vince's rebuttal speech like those for a persuasive speech developed with appeals to logic? (See lesson 9.1.)

C. Camilla will give her rebuttal speech after Vince has finished his.
1. How do you think she will try to rebuild the affirmative case?
2. What kinds of evidence might she use?

D. Think about a debate that you have heard, either in person or on television or radio.
1. How did the debaters organize and present the arguments and evidence in their speeches?
2. How did they attempt to refute the arguments of their opponents?
3. How did they try to rebuild their own cases?

Guidelines

The following guidelines will help you when you participate in a formal debate.

1. Before the debate, discuss your brief with your teammate, and decide which major arguments each of you will present. Also decide which of you will be the first speaker and which the second speaker for your side. The responsibilities of the first speaker include introducing your side's case during his or her constructive speech. The responsibilities of the second speaker include summarizing your side's case during his or her rebuttal speech.
2. Outline your constructive speech, using the methods of planning and organization appropriate to a persuasive speech developed with logical arguments (see lesson 9.1).

3. To prepare for your rebuttal speech, study your brief carefully before the debate. During the debate, listen carefully and critically to the debaters for the other side.

4. When you make your constructive and rebuttal speeches, present your arguments and evidence clearly, and speak with confidence.

Preparing and Presenting

With your teammate, decide who will present and develop each major argument in your case. Also decide who will speak first and who will speak second.

Outline your own constructive speech, and practice presenting it while your teammate listens. Together, discuss improvements that might be made in both your constructive speeches. Also discuss the arguments you expect the other side to present and the evidence you plan to use to refute those arguments.

Finally, with the other members of your group, conduct your debate before the rest of your class. Have one of the students serve as time keeper during the debate, signaling each speaker as the end of his or her allotted time approaches.

Evaluating

Have each student in your debate audience complete the form below. After the debate, study the other students' responses, and discuss with the other members of your group how each debater might have improved his or her participation.

Debate Proposition: _____

_____

Before the Debate

I am

_____ strongly in favor of

_____ in favor of

_____ uncertain about

_____ against

_____ strongly against

the change advocated in the proposition.

After the Debate

I am

_____ strongly in favor of

_____ in favor of

_____ uncertain about

_____ against

_____ strongly against

the change advocated in the proposition.

I

_____ changed

_____ did not change

my opinion for the following reasons:

1. _____

2. _____

3. _____

4. _____

Participating in a Candidate Debate

A well-planned candidate debate can give the public valuable information on the issues and the candidates' positions. A debate should be planned according to these guidelines:

1. Determine the setting, questioners, question format, and number of participants well in advance. All the candidates should agree to the conditions.

2. Candidate debates have from three to five questioners, who may be journalists, officials, or local citizens. The questioners should discuss the questions they will ask, to be sure they are covering all the major issues. The chairperson introduces the candidates and questioners, times the candidates' reponses, and selects audience questions.

3. In most candidate debates, the same question is asked of each candidate, who has a set time for his or her response. Questioners may ask follow-up questions. In two-candidate debates, each candidate is usually allowed a shorter time (one or two minutes) to respond to what the other candidate has said.

4. Hold the candidates to their allotted times, politely but firmly.

5. Encourage the candidates to answer the questions, rather than deliver prepared speeches. When asking a follow-up question, you can politely remind the candidate that he or she has not answered the original question.

6. If members of the audience are to question the candidates, they should write their questions out and have them approved by the questioners. Most candidates will be unwilling to take unscreened questions.

ACTIVITY

1. Role-play a debate between candidates running for state or federal office. Students should take the parts of two candidates, three questioners, and a chairperson. Each of you should research the major issues and be prepared to ask or answer questions. Conduct the debate in front of the class, and allow time for at least two questions. Ask the other students to evaluate the conduct of the debate and the quality of the questions and responses.

citizenship

11 Critical Listening

Freedom of speech also includes the freedom to listen. In a society where every person is allowed to speak his or her mind, it is vital that citizens listen critically to what they hear. Critical listening means constantly evaluating a speaker's words. The critical listener is alert for distorted facts, faulty use of evidence, and the techniques of propaganda. If you listen critically to politicians and other public figures, you will be able to distinguish trustworthy speakers from irresponsible ones. You will be able to cast your vote wisely, and support positions you truly understand.

After working through this chapter, you should be able to

- evaluate persuasive appeals
- give a speech analyzing a persuasive appeal
- identify techniques of propaganda
- analyze techniques of propaganda

The Speaking Skills lesson in this chapter will help you use critical listening skills. You will learn to

- use four basic approaches to decision making
- choose the most appropriate technique for decision making

The Skills for Success lesson will show you how you can use your critical listening skills as a citizen. You will learn to

- evaluate political appeals
- distinguish between sound and unsound arguments

11.1 Evaluating Persuasive Appeals

Learning Four Approaches to Decision-Making

Here are four approaches to decision-making and the circumstances under which you might follow them:

1. *Trial-and-Error:* trying a likely solution to your problem, and, if it doesn't work, trying alternative solutions until you find one that does work. This approach can waste both time and money, but if people are working under pressure or difficulties (for example, getting a car out of a muddy ditch), it may be the only way.

2. *Incremental:* taking a small step toward a decision, seeing if that is successful, taking the next small step, and so on until you reach a decision. This method, too, is time-consuming, but when strong feelings are involved (as in labor-management negotiations or international diplomacy), the step-by-step approach is usually best.

3. *Rational:* analyzing all facts and problems logically, based on certain *premises* (or assumptions) and the *inferences* (or conclusions) that can be made from them. This is the method scientists use. If the premises are correct, the scientific method should always lead to the correct decision.

4. *Scanning:* identifying all possible solutions and the standards for evaluating them, rejecting the solutions which do not meet the standards, then testing the other possible solutions in the same way. By rejecting unworkable solutions, you should arrive at the most satisfactory decision. If you cannot choose between two or more possible decisions of equal value, you will have to test your solutions by some other means.

ACTIVITY

1. Invite a person who makes decisions as part of his or her job to speak to your class. You might invite a judge, a parole officer, a supervisor, or a doctor. Ask the person how he or she makes decisions. Take notes on the answer, and see which approach or approaches the person's method belongs to.

How to Evaluate Persuasive Appeals

A speaker who wants your money, your vote, or your support may use every technique to sway you emotionally and intellectually. The speaker may use facts, statistics, emotional appeals, loaded language, generalizations, the names of famous people, and sometimes even outright lies in order to win you over. To evaluate persuasive appeals, you must be *alert* and *informed*. Be aware of the speaker's intentions, and continually compare what the speaker is saying with what you know to be true. Be especially alert to the techniques of propaganda.

Propaganda is a one-sided argument that tries to win people over to a cause, such as a political movement. Its primary appeal is to the emotions, and when propagandists use facts they prefer to distort them. These are the principal techniques of propaganda:

1. *Loaded words and phrases.* Sometimes called "buzz words," these are expressions that produce an instant, unthinking reaction in an audience. Listeners will probably react positively to such words and phrases as *all-American, free enterprise, family man, justice, equality,* and *peace.* Most people will probably react negatively to *communism, oppression, bureaucracy, politician,* and *inflation.* Such words can be used in a meaningful way. But some audiences will react only to the good or bad associations of the words, not to the ideas behind them.

2. *Name calling.* Like the use of loaded language, name calling means attaching a label to a person. Labels such as *bureaucrat, subversive, big spender, warmonger,* and *extremist* can badly damage a politician's reputation. Yet the propagandist who uses such labels might not be able to find facts to justify them.

3. *Faulty generalizations.* There are two kinds of faulty generalizations.

   Hasty generalizations are based on too little evidence:

   > "After his first week in office, everyone agrees that Mayor Watson's policies are leading this city towards bankruptcy."

   Glittering generalizations are based almost entirely on prejudice. Some common generalizations are completely contradictory:

   > "This country is run by an establishment of millionaires and liberal professors."
   > "This country is run by an establishment of millionaires and conservative industrialists."

Because faulty generalizations may contain a small grain of truth, people are often willing to accept them unquestioningly. This saves propagandists the trouble of using evidence to support their positions.

4. *The bandwagon.* Propagandists often urge people to jump on the bandwagon—to join in a movement or crusade simply because everyone else is doing it. People who want to feel part of a winning team are very vulnerable to this appeal. Often, those who do not join are made to feel insulted or threatened.

5. *Transference.* Many speakers, including propagandists, try to transfer the positive qualities associated with a place or party to their own cause:

"Here in Philadelphia, in the shadow of Independence Hall ..."
"We Republicans, the party of Abraham Lincoln ..."
"We Democrats, the party of Franklin Delano Roosevelt ..."

Of course, such historic associations probably have little or nothing to do with what the speaker is advocating in the present. Propaganda uses such transference as a substitute for sound argument. Listeners are asked to use their emotions, not their minds.

6. *Testimonials.* A testimonial, or endorsement, by a movie star, sports hero, or other celebrity may draw everyone's attention to a candidate or campaign. Many voters feel that people who are glamorous, competent, and intelligent on the screen must be that way in real life. In fact, celebrities are no more or less competent to judge public issues outside their own fields than the rest of us are. Propagandists try to use the magic of celebrities' names to lure people to support dubious causes.

7. *The big lie.* The big lie is an outright, often outrageous falsehood, repeated loudly and often. Many people feel that if a politician or ruler sounds positive about a statement, it must be true. Propagandists who use the big lie exploit this feeling. A candidate may use the big lie technique to slander an opponent. A dictator may use it to blame his country's troubles on members of a single race, religion, or party. No matter how absurd it seems to those who know better, the big lie is extremely dangerous, especially when it can be spread by newspapers, radio, and television.

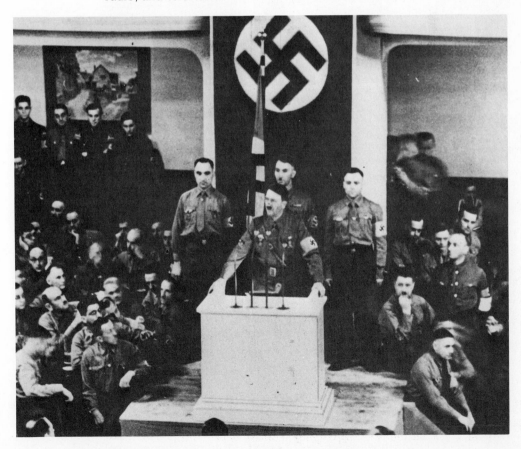

Working with the Model

Benito Mussolini, the head of the Fascist party, became dictator of Italy in 1922 after leading his Black Shirts in a march on Rome. Under Fascism, all other political parties were suppressed, and newspapers and radio became tools of government propaganda. King Victor Emmanuel III became a figurehead without real authority. Government, education, and industry were all dedicated to increasing Mussolini's power, enlarging the Italian army, and conquering weaker nations. In 1935 Mussolini invaded Ethiopia, whose ill-equipped people were soon defeated. In August, 1936, spectacular war games were conduced at Avellino, Italy. On August 30, Mussolini delivered the following speech to an audience of 20,000, and it was broadcast throughout the country. In the speech, Mussolini refers to the region as "Hirpinia"—the ancient Roman name for southern Italy. As you read the speech, observe Mussolini's persuasive appeals, and his use of propaganda techniques.

model

The grand maneuvers of the fourteenth year of Fascism have ended. They have taken place, from the first to the last day, in an atmosphere vibrant with enthusiasm. The generous hospitality of the Hirpinian people has surrounded the participating soldiers. Comrades of Hirpinia, your fervent patriotism and your dedication to the regime make you worthy of having the grand maneuvers of the first year of the Fascist Empire held in your magnificent territory!

Tomorrow, on the plains of Volturara, before His Majesty, Victor Emmanuel, King of Italy and Emperor of Ethiopia, will pass more than 60,000 men, 200 tanks, 400 pieces of heavy artillery, 400 mortars, 3000 machine guns, and 2800 armored cars. This concentration of men and arms is imposing, but it represents, at most, a modest and almost insignificant number compared with the total of men and arms on which Italy can surely count.

I invite Italians to take this declaration of mine absolutely to heart. Not despite the African war, but as a consequence of the African war, all the armed forces of Italy today are more efficient than ever. At any time, in the course of a few hours and after a simple order, we can mobilize eight million men. It is a formidable bloc that fourteen years of Fascist rule have prepared at white heat with great sacrifice. The Italian people should know that their internal peace will be protected, and with it the peace of the world.

With the most crushing of victories, in one of the most just wars, Italy, with war in Africa, has acquired an immense, rich, imperial territory, where for many decades she will be able to carry out the achievements of her labors and of her creative ability. For this reason, but only for this reason, we will reject the absurdity of eternal peace, which is foreign to our creed and to our temperament.

model

We desire to live a long time at peace with all. We are determined to offer our lasting, concrete contribution to the project of collaboration among peoples. But after the catastrophic failure of the disarmament conference, in the face of an armaments race already under way and irresistible from this time on, and in the face of political situations whose outcome is uncertain, the order of the day for Italians, for Fascist Italians, can be only this: We must be strong! We must be always stronger! We must be so strong that we can face any eventualities, and look directly in the eye whatever may happen. To this supreme principle must be subordinated, and will be subordinated, all the life of the nation.

The conquest of the empire was not obtained by compromises on that table of diplomacy. It was obtained by fine, glorious, and victorious battle, fought with the spirit that has overcome enormous material difficulties and an almost world-wide coalition of nations. It is the spirit of the Black Shirt revolution, the spirit of this Italy, the spirit of this populous Italy, warlike and vigilant on sea, on land, and in the heavens! It is the spirit I have seen shining in the eyes of the soldiers who have maneuvered in these past days, the spirit we shall see shine when King and country call them.

Before concluding this meeting, I ask you: Were our old accounts settled? [*The crowd shouted:* "Yes!"]

And have we marched straight ahead until now? [*The crowd:* "Yes!"]

I tell you—I promise you—we shall do the same tomorrow and always!

QUESTIONS

A. Think about the purpose of Mussolini's speech.

1. Of what fact or feeling is Mussolini trying to persuade his audience?

2. Find at least two passages in the speech that show Mussolini is trying to appeal to a nationwide audience.

3. This speech was widely reprinted in Europe and America. What passages suggest that Mussolini was thinking of an international audience as well?

B. Think about the appeals to emotion in this speech.

1. Why do you think Mussolini would refer to the province by its ancient Roman name?

2. In the second paragraph, why does Mussolini list the numbers of men and weapons? What effect is he trying to create?

3. Find at least three passages in which Mussolini speaks of the Italian people in a way that is meant to encourage a feeling of unity.

4. Mussolini speaks of Italians overcoming "enormous difficulties" with "great sacrifice." What do you think such difficulties and sacrifices might have been? Do you think the sacrifices were voluntary? Why or why not?

5. If the King of Italy had no real power, why does Mussolini refer to him twice in this speech? Of what propaganda technique is this an example?

6. What is the purpose of Mussolini's questions to the audience at the end of the speech? Suppose you had been in the audience; would you have wanted to answer "No"? What would you have done?

C. Think about the propaganda techniques in this speech.

1. Find at least five examples of loaded words or phrases. What emotions are these words meant to produce?

2. Find at least three places where Mussolini uses faulty generalizations or exaggerations. What would have been the effect if he had paid more attention to the facts?

3. Find three uses of the bandwagon technique in the speech.

4. Find at least one use of the big lie in this speech.

Guidelines

When evaluating a persuasive appeal, you should ask yourself the following questions:

• *Is the speaker making promises that he or she cannot fulfill?* A candidate may say, "If you vote for me, I'll turn this country around within a year." But listeners who understand complex national problems realize that no one person, no matter how competent, could solve them in such a short time. The better informed you are, the more easily you can tell serious promises from empty ones.

- *Is the speaker suppressing or distorting facts in order to be more persuasive?* Speakers naturally want to emphasize their own achievements and belittle those of their opponents. They may misuse facts and figures in order to do this. For example, suppose a candidate announces, "When I was mayor of Metropolis, we virtually wiped out violent crime!" A check of newspapers might show a drop in the crime rate, but this is not the same as "wiping out" crime—nor does it prove that the mayor had anything to do with it. Such a use of facts is a *distortion* of the truth. Suppose another candidate announces, "Since Smith's party took over this city in 1964, the murder rate has doubled." That sounds like a frightening statistic, until you learn that during the same period the city's population tripled. By *suppressing,* or withholding, the additional fact about the population, the candidate has turned a fact into a falsehood.

- *Does the speaker use innuendo to attack others?* Responsible speakers will attack their opponents directly, using facts in order to persuade their listeners. Irresponsible speakers may use *innuendo*—attacking a person by implication or association. For example, a candidate may say, "The mayor was seen having lunch with a man whose lawyer once represented organized-crime figures." The innuendo in this statement suggests a connection between the mayor and organized crime, but the connection is in fact very flimsy.

- *Does the speaker offer positive alternatives?* It is easy to attack people and parties that are currently in office. It is difficult to suggest new programs that would work better. Be wary of speakers who are eager to criticize, but who can offer only vague promises and suggestions for improvement.

- *Is the speaker being consistent with previous speeches and writings?* A speaker who changes his or her positions in front of different audiences may only be interested in telling people what they want to hear. Compare the speaker's earlier speeches and writings with what he or she is saying today. Television reporters often do this, using videotape from their files. Remember, though, that consistency does not guarantee integrity. It is possible for a speaker to be consistently wrong or dishonest.

- *Is the speaker using the techniques of propaganda?* These techniques, explained at the beginning of this lesson, include:

loaded words and phrases	transference	the big lie
name calling	testimonials	the bandwagon
faulty generalizations		

The use of one or more propaganda techniques does not automatically prove that a speaker is irresponsible. Loaded language, faulty generalizations, and the transference of good qualities to people or programs that do not deserve them are all traditional in political speechmaking. You should, however, be suspicious of speakers who rely heavily on such techniques. Name calling and the big lie are techniques that have no place in responsible speech.

Preparing and Presenting

Find a persuasive speech on an issue that arouses strong emotions. You may look in books or in periodicals such as *Vital Speeches*. You may also listen to or watch recorded speeches. The speech should not run much over ten minutes. It should be on an issue that you either understand or can do research to learn about. Read or listen to the speech several times, and ask yourself the questions in the Guidelines section of this lesson. Make notes on the different persuasive appeals used by the speaker. Make an outline for a presentation in which you explain the persuasive appeals and give specific examples.

When you make your presentation to the class, begin by reading aloud or playing the speech you have studied. Ask the other students whether they found the speech persuasive, and why. Then present your own observations.

Evaluating

Compare your observations with those of the other students in the class. If they disagree with you, be prepared to support your findings by using specific examples from the speech as evidence.

Using Critical Listening

Candidates, politicians, and activists will frequently appeal to you for your support and vote. They may ask you to contribute to a campaign, write letters in support of a bill, sign a petition, or help elect someone to public office. Political speakers will use every skill and argument they have in order to persuade you. To tell the worthwhile appeals from the worthless ones, you must ask yourself these questions:

- Is the speaker using the techniques of propaganda? (see lesson 11.1 for a list of these techniques).
- Is the speaker making promises that he or she cannot fulfill?
- Does the speaker use innuendo or distortions of fact to attack others?
- Does the speaker offer positive alternatives to the people or positions he or she attacks?
- Is the speaker being consistent with his or her previous speeches and writings, or is the speaker simply telling the audience what it wants to hear?

ACTIVITIES

1. Listen to a recorded speech or editorial from radio or television. Decide what position the speaker is actually taking, and what he or she wants the members of the audience to do. Analyze the speech by asking yourself the questions listed above. Then decide whether you agree with the speaker because of or in spite of what he or she said. Describe your findings to the class, and compare your reactions to theirs.

2. Working with another student, prepare two brief speeches advocating the same position. One speech should use the techniques of good persuasive speaking, and the other should use deceptive and unsound arguments. Deliver your speeches before the class. Have them vote for the more persuasive speech, and ask them to explain their reasons.

citizenship

PART 4

Speaking to Entertain

12. Narrative Speaking

13. Oral Interpretation

14. Listening for Enjoyment

A Case Study

THINK AND DISCUSS

Study these six panels from the comic strip *Family Circus*. What do you think is happening on the television screen in each of the panels?

What is the little boy's reaction to each of the programs? Is he reacting in the way the broadcasters would like him to? Is he reacting to each situation in the way an adult would?

In the last panel, why do you think the boy has left the room? Do you know teenagers or adults who also prefer not to watch the news?

In Part Four, "Speaking to Entertain," you will learn to entertain others by using your voice for story-telling, oral interpretation, and radio drama. You will also think about an issue raised by this Case Study: how well or badly your television time is spent.

12 Narrative Speaking

You are probably used to telling stories and anecdotes, sometimes to entertain and sometimes to make a point. Narrative speaking is the art of telling a story well. A good narrative speaker plans his or her story carefully. He or she thinks about the incidents of the story, the order in which they occur, and the details that will make them vivid to the audience. The speaker practices delivering the story, until his or her voice and gestures are as effective as possible. The ability to tell a story well can enhance any kind of speech you give, whether informative, persuasive, or entertaining.

After working through this chapter, you should be able to

- identify the important elements of a story
- organize a story, using specific details to make it clear
- deliver a story in the most effective manner

The Speaking Skills lesson in this chapter will help make your narrative speaking more effective. You will learn to

- recognize the important types of images
- use sensory images

The Skills for Success lesson in this chapter will help you use narrative and other speaking skills with co-workers. You will learn to

- understand the way businesses deal with work problems
- use constructive communication at work

12.1 Telling a Story

Using Sensory Images

We perceive the world through our five senses—sight, hearing, touch, taste, and smell. The most effective speakers and writers also appeal to our senses by using words and phrases that recall familiar sights, sounds, textures, tastes, and odors. Such words and phrases are *sensory images*. Sensory images can make an otherwise dull story vivid and real to your audience. For example, the following description has no appeal to the senses:

On the table were a centerpiece, a kettle, bread, meat, and two kinds of vegetables.

Now see how sensory images can make this description come to life:

Sight: The centerpiece of yellow, orange, and rust-colored flowers was set in a border of dark brown pine cones.

Sound: The teakettle, coming to the boil, bubbled and whistled on the hotplate.

Touch: A dozen crusty rolls sat in a basket under a coarse cotton towel.

Taste: Near the head of the table was a platter of roast duck, with the dark, rich flavor of wild game.

Smell: At the other end, clouds of sweet, buttery steam rose off bowls of mashed potatoes and boiled ears of corn.

ACTIVITY

1. Select five magazine advertisements that use sensory images to make a product seem attractive to readers. Try to find at least one image for each of the five senses. Report to the class on the way sensory images are used in these advertisements. Ask students to suggest other images that might have been used, and discuss whether these would have been more or less effective.

language

How to Tell a Story

Whether you tell a story to illustrate a point or simply to entertain, you should plan and practice your story carefully. To plan a story, begin by identifying for yourself the essential elements: *who* is involved; *when* and *where* does the story take place; *what* happens. Next, decide what the most important or most exciting part of your story is. Then organize the events of your story in chronological order so that they lead up to that most important part. Finally, choose specific details that will make the story clear to your listeners. Avoid details—however interesting—that are not essential to the development of your story.

Once you have planned your story, you should practice telling it. As you practice, keep in mind the most important part of your story. Remember that everything in the story and everything in your telling of the story should lead up to that part. For example, you might try speaking slowly at first; then quicken your rate of speech as you move toward the most important part. Also try pausing just before you tell the most important part. Experiment with facial expressions and gestures that will emphasize the development of your story. As you practice, have a friend listen and comment on the effectiveness of your speaking techniques and actions.

Working with the Model

Moss Hart was a well-known American playwright. In his autobiography, *Act One,* Hart included the following story about an incident from his childhood. As you read the story, think about how Hart presented it.

model

It was the Christmas after my aunt had left the house, and since it was she who always supplied the tree and the presents for my brother and myself, this first Christmas without her was a bleak and empty one. I remember that I was more or less reconciled to it, because my father had worked only spasmodically throughout the year. Two of our rooms were vacant of boarders and my mother was doing her marketing farther and farther away from our neighborhood. This was always a sign that we were dangerously close to rock bottom, and each time it occurred I came to dread it more. It was one of the vicious landmarks of poverty that I had come to know well and the one I hated the most. As the bills at our regular grocer and butcher went unpaid, and my mother dared not even be seen at the stores lest they come to the doorways and yell after her publicly; she would trudge ten or twelve blocks to a whole new neighborhood, tell the new grocer or butcher that we had just moved in to some fictitious address around the corner, and establish credit for as long as she could. Thus we were able to exist until my father found work again, or all the rooms were rented, and she could pay our own grocer and butcher, and gradually the others. This time, however, they had all of them gone unpaid and my mother was walking twenty blocks or more for a bottle of milk.

Obviously Christmas was out of the question—we were barely staying alive. On Christmas Eve my father was very silent during the evening meal. Then he surprised and startled me by turning to me and saying, "Let's take a walk." He had never suggested such a thing before, and moreover, it was a very cold winter's night. I was even more surprised when he said as we left the house, "Let's go down to a Hundred and Forty-ninth Street and Westchester Avenue." My heart leapt within me. That was the section where all the big stores were, where at Christmastime open pushcarts full of toys stood packed end-to-end for blocks at a stretch. On other Christmas Eves I had often gone there with my aunt, and from our tour of the carts she had gathered what I wanted the most. My father had known of this, of course, and I joyously concluded that this walk could mean only one thing—he was going to buy me a Christmas present.

On the walk down I was beside myself with delight and inner relief. It had been a bad year for me, that year of my aunt's going, and I wanted a Christmas present terribly—not a present merely, but a symbol, a token of some sort. I needed some sign from my father or mother that they knew what I was going through and cared for me as much as my aunt and my grandfather did. I am sure they were giving me what mute signs they could, but I did not see them. The idea that my father had managed a Christmas present for me in spite of everything filled me with a sudden peace and lightness of heart I had not known in months.

We hurried on, our heads bent against the wind, to the cluster of lights ahead that was 149th Street and Westchester Avenue, and those lights seemed to me the brightest lights I had ever seen. Tugging at my father's coat, I started down the line of pushcarts. There were all kinds of things that I wanted, but since nothing had been said by my father about buying a present, I would merely pause before a pushcart to say, with as much control as I could muster, "Look at that chemistry set!" or, "There's a stamp album!" or, "Look at the printing press!" Each time my father would pause and ask the pushcart man the price. Then without a word we would move on to the next pushcart. Once or twice he would pick up a toy of some kind and look at it and then at me, as if to suggest this might be something I might like, but I was ten years old and a good deal beyond just a toy: my heart was set on a chemistry set or a printing press. There they were on every pushcart we stopped at, but the price was always the same and soon I looked up and saw we were nearing the end of the line. Only two or three more pushcarts remained. My father looked up, too, and I heard him jingle some coins in his pocket. In a flash I knew it all. He'd gotten together about seventy-five cents to buy me a Christmas present, and he hadn't dared say so in case there was nothing to be had for so small a sum.

As I looked up at him I saw a look of despair and disappointment in his eyes that brought me closer to him than I had ever been in my life. I wanted to throw my arms around him and say, "It doesn't matter . . . I understand . . . this is better than a chemistry set or a printing press . . . I love you." But instead we stood shivering beside each other for a moment—then turned away from the last two pushcarts and started silently back home. I don't know why the words remained choked up within me. I didn't even take his hand on the way home, nor did he take mine. We were not on that basis. Nor did I ever tell him how close to him I felt that night—that for a little while the concrete wall between father and son had crumbled away and I knew that we were two lonely people struggling to reach each other.

QUESTIONS

A. Think about the organization of the story.
  1. Identify the *who, when, where,* and *what* of the story. When is each of these story elements presented?
  2. In what order are the story events organized?
  3. What is presented as the most important part of the story?
  4. How does the organization emphasize the most important part of the story? Imagine that Hart had continued his story by presenting several more events that took place on Christmas. How might those additions have altered the effect of the story?

B. Think about the development of the story.
  1. What specific details show how poor Hart's family was? How do those details help make the story clear to you?
  2. What specific details show that the gifts Hart wanted were too expensive? What effect do those details have on the development of the story?
  3. Imagine that the story included several specific details about Hart's tour of the pushcarts on previous Christmas Eves. What effect would those details have had on the story?

Guidelines

As you prepare to tell a story, remember the following guidelines:

1. Plan to include the essential story elements (*who* is involved; *when* and *where* the story takes place; *what* happens) and to avoid any unnecessary information.
2. Plan your story to lead up to the most important or most exciting part. Arrange the events of the story leading up to that part in chronological order.
3. Include specific details that will help make the story clear to your listeners. Avoid details that do not directly develop the story.
4. Practice telling your story, being sure to emphasize the most important part.

Preparing and Presenting _____

Think of a story you would like to tell. If possible, choose a story from your own experiences—something that happened to you or something that you observed. You may choose a story because it is amusing or interesting, or because it illustrates a point you want to make.

Carefully plan the organization and development of your story. Then practice telling your story to another student. Ask that listener to evaluate the organization and development of your story, as well as your effectiveness in telling it. Encourage your listener to make specific suggestions that will help you improve your story and your delivery.

After you have practiced and improved your story, tell it to a group of other class members.

Evaluating _____

Ask your classmates to answer these questions about your story:

1. How were the essential story elements introduced? Which necessary elements (if any) were left out? What unnecessary information (if any) was presented?

2. How were the story events organized? What changes in organization might make the story more effective?

3. What specific details were included in the story? What effect did the details have? In which parts of the story should more details have been used? In which parts were there too many details?

4. What was the purpose of the story? Was it intended to illustrate a specific point? If so, what was the main idea of the story?

5. What techniques of speaking and moving were used to emphasize the most important part of the story?

Using Constructive Communication at Work

Even the best-run businesses have some problems of inefficiency and poor communication. As a worker, you will have to decide when such problems are worth speaking up about, and to whom you should speak. No two companies are alike, but three rules should always be followed:

1. *Make suggestions rather than complaints.* If you make only negative remarks, your employers may think you are simply in a bad mood. Making constructive suggestions, on the other hand, shows that you care about your job and think of ways to perform it more efficiently. For example, instead of saying, "The people in Keypunch are clumsy idiots," say, "I think we could increase efficiency in Inventory if a quality-control checker looked over the cards as they came out of Keypunch."

2. *Understand the company's system for dealing with problems.* Whatever your position, you will have a foreman, supervisor, or manager to whom you should report. Don't try to go over or around this person. Supervisors have their jobs because the company's management trusts them. Only when top management openly invites worker response should you make direct complaints or suggestions to highly placed people. In all cases, you should talk about efficiency and productivity rather than personalities.

3. *Avoid gossip.* Like schools, some businesses are filled with gossip, both petty and malicious. Taking part in such gossip can only hurt you professionally. Successful employees have no time for idle talk, and they know the dangers of discussing business secrets. If you become the object of gossip, it is best to ignore it, no matter how painful. Your friends will not listen to malicious rumors, and those who listen are not your friends.

ACTIVITY

1. Working with two other students, identify a problem that affects your school. Working independently, develop three reports on this problem. Each student's report should be directed to the person or organization responsible, and should contain constructive suggestions. Present your reports for class evaluation. Have the students tell which report would be most effective, and why.

career

13 Oral Interpretation

Oral interpretation is the art of reading aloud a story, poem, or speech. To be an effective interpreter of an author's work, you must be sensitive to the emotions and ideas in the selection, and to the language in which they are conveyed. You should practice your reading until you can use your voice and gestures in the most effective manner.

Radio drama is one kind of oral interpretation. Because listeners must use their imaginations to visualize scenes and characters, putting on an effective radio play is an exciting challenge. Scenery, mood, action, and emotions all have to be presented through sound. You can use voices, music, and sound effects to create a gripping drama. The skills that you develop with radio drama can give you more control of your voice and can help you prepare for stage or other dramatic presentations.

After working through this chapter, you should be able to

- understand an author's ideas and emotions
- prepare and give an oral reading
- use voice and sound effects in radio dramas
- rehearse and present a radio drama

The Speaking Skills lessons in this chapter will help you make more effective use of your voice. You will learn to

- understand figurative language
- recognize when and how to speak louder
- improve your articulation and pronunciation
- improve the rate, pitch, and variety of your voice

The Skills for Success lessons in this chapter will help you communicate effectively on the job and at public meetings. You will learn to

- read minutes and committee reports
- accept constructive criticism
- read a speech or report written by someone else
- use a microphone or public address system

13.1 Understanding an Author's Ideas and Emotions

Understanding Figurative Language

Figurative language makes ideas more vivid by comparing them to things most people have seen, touched, or felt. Such techniques of comparison are called *figures of speech*. Most figures of speech compare something familiar with something unfamiliar. These are the most important figures of speech:

A *simile* compares two unlike things, using the word *like* or *as*.

> Mike prowled around the room like a cat looking for its rubber mouse.

> Her voice was as cold and sharp as an icicle.

A *metaphor* compares two unlike things, without using *like* or *as*.

> This debate is a swamp of confusion and contradiction.

> Roger tiptoed downstairs through a jungle of shadows.

Personification is a kind of metaphor in which something inanimate is given the qualities of a human being.

> Mother Nature showed her contempt for my shack by flattening it with a storm.

An *analogy* is an extended comparison, often explaining a process.

> A living cell is like a city under siege, letting food and other vital supplies enter its walls, but repelling hostile invaders—in this case, microbes.

ACTIVITY

1. Invent figures of speech to make each of the following ideas or objects more vivid or understandable:

a jet plane	a dark night
a crowded street	a political convention
a field of grain	a nuclear explosion

   Compare your figures of speech with other students'. Decide which ones would be most effective in a speech.

How to Understand an Author's Ideas and Emotions

When you give an oral reading, your goal should be to convey the ideas and emotions in your selection as completely as possible. Your audience should gain as much from your reading as they would by reading the selection themselves. The first step in your preparation for giving a successful oral reading is to understand both the ideas and the emotions the selection contains.

Begin by looking for the major idea in your selection. Most selections contain one major idea supported by several minor ideas. If your selection is from a story or essay, each paragraph will usually contain a single idea that supports the major idea of the selection.

To understand the ideas in your selection, you must understand the words in which they are written. Use an unabridged dictionary to check the meaning of any words you don't understand fully. The meaning of a word is called its *denotation.* You must understand the denotation of each word the author has used if you are to fully grasp the ideas of the selection. In order to understand the feelings the author wishes to convey about these ideas, you must also be aware of what the words suggest. Such suggestions are called the *connotations* of a word. For example, *slender* and *thin* have almost identical denotations. *Slender,* however, suggests a pleasingly slim form. *Thin* can suggest a slimness that is not pleasing. A word's connotation is the emotional message it carries.

Reread your selection to find any *figures of speech* your author may have used. Figures of speech make ideas more vivid by presenting them through an unusual comparison. A figure of speech also contains an emotional message. This message helps to present the author's feelings about the ideas he or she is expressing.

Then look for other devices the author may use to create emotional emphasis, and see what emotions are expressed through them. For example, has the author repeated sounds, words, or phrases to emphasize or build emotion? Has the author used a light, tripping rhythm to suggest humor, or a slow, heavy one to convey solemnity? Answering these questions will help you discover the emotions in your selection.

When you feel you understand the ideas and emotions in your selection, spend some time reading about its author. If possible, find out how your selection came to be written. This knowledge will deepen your understanding of the selection and improve your oral reading.

Working with the Model

Here are two selections for you to study at home and discuss in class. The first selection is from the inaugural address of President John F. Kennedy. In the second selection, a poet remembers his grandmother and the times he spent with her when he was a child. Read each selection at home, first silently and then aloud. Come to class prepared to answer and discuss the questions following the selections.

model

From the Inaugural Address

Mr. Chief Justice, President Eisenhower, Vice President Nixon, President Truman, reverend clergy, fellow citizens, we observe today not a victory of party, but a celebration of freedom—symbolizing an end, as well as a beginning—signifying renewal, as well as change. For I have sworn before you and Almighty God the same solemn oath our forebears prescribed nearly a century and three quarters ago.

The world is very different now. For man holds in his mortal hands the power to abolish all forms of human poverty and all forms of human life. And yet the same revolutionary beliefs for which our forebears fought are still at issue around the globe—the belief that the rights of man come not from the generosity of the state, but from the hand of God.

We dare not forget today that we are the heirs of that first revolution. Let the word go forth from this time and place, to friend and foe alike, that the torch has been passed to a new generation of Americans—born in this century, tempered by war, disciplined by a hard and bitter peace, proud of our ancient heritage—and unwilling to witness or permit the slow undoing of those human rights to which this Nation has always been committed, and to which we are committed today at home and around the world.

Let every nation know, whether it wishes us well or ill, that we shall pay any price, bear any burden, meet any hardship, support any friend, oppose any foe, in order to assure the survival and the success of liberty.

This much we pledge—and more.

To those old allies whose cultural and spiritual origins we share, we pledge the loyalty of faithful friends. United, there is little we cannot do in a host of cooperative ventures. Divided, there is little we can do—for we dare not meet a powerful challenge at odds and split asunder.

To those new States whom we welcome to the ranks of the free, we pledge our words that one form of colonial control shall not have passed away merely to be replaced by a far greater iron tyranny. We shall not always expect to find them supporting our view. But we shall always hope to find them strongly supporting their own freedom—and

from where do human rights come? What does the statement that such rights do not come from the "generosity of the state" mean? Compare what President Kennedy says about human rights with this paragraph from the Declaration of Independence.

> "We hold these truths to be self-evident, that all men are created equal, that they are endowed by their Creator with certain unalienable Rights, that among these are Life, Liberty and the pursuit of Happiness."

4. Explain the meaning of each figure of speech from President Kennedy's speech: "iron tyranny"; "those who foolishly sought power by riding the back of the tiger ended up inside"; "peaceful revolution."

5. Often in a poem, the major idea is not stated in any one group of words. Rather, the major idea may be the total impression created by all the ideas and descriptions in the poem. What is the major idea in the poem by Leonard Adamé? What supporting ideas contribute to the major idea?

6. *Papas* means potatoes. What do *tortillas* and *café* mean?

7. What does Adamé mean when he says his grandmother would rock and hum until her hands "calmed"? What does he mean by saying her father's hopes "sank/with cement dust/to his insides"? What do these lines tell you about how the grandmother's father earned his living in his new country?

B. Think about the emotions expressed in each of these selections.

1. The connotations of words convey emotional meanings. These phrases come from President Kennedy's speech: "the torch has been passed," "the ranks of the free," "master of its own house," "strengthen its shield of the new and the weak." What idea does each phrase convey? What emotion is suggested by the connotation of each phrase? How does the new president want Americans to view their country on his inaugural day?

2. President Kennedy begins his speech by saying he has just taken the presidential oath written by the founders of our country. After speaking of the past, he turns to the future. In speaking of the future, he uses the word *pledge* (another kind of oath) many times. What connotations does the word *pledge* suggest? Why do you think the president spoke of the oath he has just taken in the way he did? How might that statement make his audience feel about his pledges for the future?

3. President Kennedy uses repetition to create drama and emotional emphasis in his speech. Notice how he repeats the word *know* here: "Let all our neighbors *know* that we shall join with them to oppose aggression or subversion anywhere in the Americas.

And let every other power *know* that this hemisphere intends to remain the master of its own house." Find three other examples of repetition used for emotional emphasis in President Kennedy's speech. Discuss how repetition heightens emotional emphasis in each case.

4. Adamé says "always her eyes / were clear / and she could see / as I cannot yet see." What are the connotations of *see* in these lines?

5. In this poem, Adamé presents his memories of his grandmother. Each memory has a slightly different emotional message. How can you tell by looking at the poem where one memory ends and another begins? What clue does this give you about how to find the emotional messages in a poem?

6. Adamé's poem tells about his memories of his grandmother, and about her memories of Mexico. From one point of view, this poem is about how a people's cultural heritage is preserved through their memories. Explain how this idea is presented in the last stanza of the poem. What emotion or emotions do you find accompanying this idea in the last stanza?

C. Think about the background of each selection.

1. How does knowing that President Kennedy was inaugurated during one of the most prosperous periods in American history affect your evaluation of his speech? How might his speech have been different if his inauguration had occurred during the Depression, as did President Roosevelt's? (See the Model in lesson 9.3 for Roosevelt's first inaugural address.)

2. How does knowing that Adamé escaped from the poverty and disappointment suffered by his grandmother affect your evaluation of his poem?

Guidelines

When preparing for an oral reading, make sure you have a complete understanding of your selection.

1. Be sure to correctly identify the major idea of your selection.

2. Identify figurative language the author has used, and evaluate what ideas and emotions this figurative language is meant to convey.

3. Make sure you understand what overall mood or emotion the author means to convey. Note specific words and phrases that suggest this mood to you.

4. Evaluate how the author uses phrasing, repetition, contrast, rhythm, or rhyme to convey ideas and emotions.

5. Add to your understanding of your selection by doing research on its author and the circumstances under which it was written.

Preparing and Presenting

Work with a partner. The two of you should choose one of the following selections to prepare for oral interpretation. (You may choose another selection instead, with your teacher's approval.)

Working separately, you and your partner should each study the selection to discover its ideas and emotions. Each of you should read the selection at home, first silently and then aloud. Discover the major idea of your selection, and as an example of this idea, write the lines or words in which it is presented. Then find each supporting idea, and at least one group of words as an example of each supporting idea.

Then think about the emotions in your selection. Decide what the major mood or emotion is, and find an example of a figure of speech, phrase, line, sentence, or group of words in which this emotion is expressed. Then find any supporting emotions, and one example (one group of words) that expresses each.

Next, do some reading on your author and the circumstances under which your selection was written. Your reading may lead you to look at your selection in a new way, so that your interpretation of its ideas and emotions changes slightly.

Finally, arrange all your information in an outline. Your finished outline should look something like this:

I. Your Statement of Major Idea (example from selection)
   A. Supporting Idea (example)
   B. Supporting Idea (example)
   C. Supporting Idea (example)

II. Major Emotion
   A. Supporting Emotion (example)
   B. Supporting Emotion (example)
   C. Supporting Emotion (example)

III. Author Background That Relates to Selection
   A.
   B.
   C.

IV. Circumstances Under Which Selection Was Written
   A.
   B.
   C.

Here is the group of selections. Each selection is preceded by suggestions on its interpretation; however, remember that there are often several valid ways to interpret a selection, just as there are usually several valid ways to play a character in a stage drama.

HUMOR

The following selections are all humorous. Notice how the poets use a light, tripping rhythm to suggest humor. Notice too how Mark Twain keeps his audience wondering how his story will end, so that the humor of its final outcome is heightened by a release from suspense.

Father William

"You are old, Father William," the young man said,
   "And your hair has become very white,
And yet you incessantly stand on your head—
   Do you think, at your age, it is right?"

"In my youth," Father William replied to his son,
   "I feared it might injure the brain;
But now that I'm perfectly sure I have none,
   Why, I do it again and again."

"You are old," said the youth, "as I mentioned before,
   And have grown most uncommonly fat;
Yet you turned a back-somersault in at the door—
   Pray, what is the reason of that?"

"In my youth," said the sage, as he shook his gray locks,
   "I kept all my limbs very supple
By the use of this ointment—one shilling the box—
   Allow me to sell you a couple."

"You are old," said the youth, "and your jaws are too weak
   For anything tougher than suet;
Yet you finished the goose, with the bones and the beak;
   Pray, how did you manage to do it?"

"In my youth," said his father, "I took to the law,
   And argued each case with my wife;
And the muscular strength which it gave to my jaw
   Has lasted the rest of my life."

"You are old," said the youth, "one would hardly suppose
   That your eye was as steady as ever;
Yet you balanced an eel on the end of your nose—
   What made you so awfully clever?"

"I have answered three questions, and that is enough,"
   Said his father; "don't give yourself airs!
Do you think I can listen all day to such stuff?
   Be off, or I'll kick you downstairs!"

—Lewis Carroll

Don't Cry, Darling,
It's Blood All Right

Whenever poets want to give you the idea that something is particularly
      meek and mild,
They compare it to a child.
Thereby proving that though poets with poetry may be rife
They don't know the facts of life.
If of compassion you desire either a tittle or a jot,
Don't try to get it from a tot.
Hard-boiled, sophisticated adults like me and you
May enjoy ourselves thoroughly with *Little Women* and *Winnie-the-Pooh*.
But innocent infants these titles from the reading course eliminate
As soon as they discover that it was honey and nuts and mashed potatoes
      instead of human flesh that Winnie-the-Pooh and Little Women ate.
Innocent infants have no use for fables about rabbits or donkeys or
      tortoises or porpoises.
What they want is something with plenty of well-mutilated corpoises.

301

Not on legends of how the rose came to be a rose instead of a petunia is their fancy fed.

But on the inside story of how somebody's bones got ground up to make somebody else's bread.

They'll go to sleep listening to the story of the little beggarmaid who got to be queen by being kind to the bees and the birds,

But they're all eyes and ears the minute they suspect a wolf or a giant is going to tear some poor woodcutter into quarters or thirds.

It really doesn't take much to fill their cup;

All they want is for somebody to be eaten up.

Therefore I say unto you, all you poets who are so crazy about meek and mild little children and their angelic air,

If you are sincere and really want to please them, why just go out and get yourselves devoured by a bear.

—Ogden Nash

**From a Speech He Gave
on His Seventieth Birthday**

I have had a great many birthdays in my time. I remember the first one very well, and I always think of it with indignation; everything was so crude, unaesthetic, primeval. Nothing like this at all. No proper appreciative preparation made; nothing really ready. Now, for a person born with high and delicate instincts—why, even the cradle wasn't whitewashed—nothing ready at all. I hadn't any hair, I hadn't any teeth, I hadn't any clothes, I had to go to my first banquet just like that.

Well, everybody came swarming in. It was the merest little bit of a village—hardly that, just a little hamlet, in the backwoods of Missouri, where nothing ever happened, and the people were all interested, and they all came; they looked me over to see if there was anything fresh in my line. Why, nothing ever happened in that village—I—why, I was the only thing that had really happened there for months and months and months; and although I say it myself that shouldn't, I came the nearest to being a real event that had happened in that village in more than two years.

Well, those people came, they came with that curiosity which is so provincial, with that frankness which also is so provincial, and they examined me all around and gave their opinion. Nobody asked them, and I shouldn't have minded if anybody had paid me a compliment, but nobody did. Their opinions were all just green with prejudice, and I feel those opinions to this day.

Well, I stood that as long as—you know I was courteous, and I stood it to the limit. I stood it an hour, and then the worm turned. I was the worm; it was my turn to turn, and I turned. I knew very well the strength of my position: I knew that I was the only spotlessly pure and innocent person in that whole town, and I came out and said so. And they could not say a word. It was so true. They blushed; they were embarrassed. Well, that was the first after-dinner speech I ever made.

—Mark Twain

SERIOUS LITERATURE

Like most well-written poems, the Yeats poem can be understood in several ways. It is a story about a magical event, but it is also a statement of how a man cannot settle for anything less than an ideal he has glimpsed for only a moment.

The Song of Wandering Aengus

I went out to the hazel wood,
Because a fire was in my head,
And cut and peeled a hazel wand,
And hooked a berry to a thread;
And when white moths were on the wing,
And moth-like stars were flickering out,
I dropped the berry in a stream
And caught a little silver trout.

When I had laid it on the floor
I went to blow the fire aflame,
But something rustled on the floor,
And some one called me by my name:
It had become a glimmering girl
With apple blossom in her hair
Who called me by my name and ran
And faded through the brightening air.

Though I am old with wandering
Through hollow lands and hilly lands,
I will find out where she has gone,
And kiss her lips and take her hands;
And walk among long dappled grass,
And pluck till time and times are done
The silver apples of the moon,
The golden apples of the sun.

—William Butler Yeats

MOOD AND ATMOSPHERE

Each of the following selections carefully creates an atmosphere or major emotion, using such emotions as fear, suspense, and mystery. In the first poem, notice that the speaker in the first two stanzas is the witch, and that the speaker in the last stanza is her victim. The mood results partly from the witch's attempt to track her victim, and partly from the results of her attempt. The short lines of the second poem make the mushrooms seem almost timid—until you read the last stanza. The second poem makes heavy use of repetition, assonance, and rhyme to convey ideas and emotions. If you choose this poem, decide what emotional effect is created by these devices.

The Witch

I have walked a great while over the snow,
And I am not tall nor strong.
My clothes are wet, and my teeth are set,
And the way was hard and long.

I have wandered over the fruitful earth,
But I never came here before.
Oh, lift me over the threshold, and let me in at the door!

The cutting wind is a cruel foe;
I dare not stand in the blast.
My hands are stone, and my voice a groan,
And the worst of death is past.
I am but a little maiden still;
My little white feet are sore.
Oh, lift me over the threshold, and let me in at the door!

Her voice was the voice that women have,
Who plead for their heart's desire.
She came—she came—and the quivering flame
Sank and died in the fire.
It never was lit again on my hearth
Since I hurried across the floor,
To lift her over the threshold, and let her in at the door!

—Mary Elizabeth Coleridge

Mushrooms

Overnight, very
Whitely, discreetly,
Very quietly

Our toes, our noses
Take hold on the loam,
Acquire the air.

Nobody sees us,
Stops us, betrays us;
The small grains make room.

Soft fists insist on
Heaving the needles,
The leafy bedding,

Even the paving,
Our hammers, our rams,
Earless and eyeless,

Perfectly voiceless
Widen the crannies,
Shoulder through holes. We

Diet on water,
On crumbs of shadow,
Bland-mannered, asking

Little or nothing.
So many of us!
So many of us!

We are shelves, we are
Tables, we are meek,
We are edible,

Nudgers and shovers
In spite of ourselves.
Our kind multiplies:

We shall by morning
Inherit the earth.
Our foot's in the door.

—Sylvia Plath

RHYTHM AND RHYME

These selections will give you a chance to study how poets use rhythm and rhyme to convey ideas and emotions. The poem by Leigh Hunt presents a modern idea (or viewpoint) in a traditional poetic form for story-telling: the ballad. In the second poem, notice how Poe creates distinctly different moods in describing each group of bells.

The Glove and the Lions

King Francis was a hearty king, and loved a royal sport,
And one day, as his lions fought, sat looking on the court.
The nobles fill'd the benches, with the ladies in their pride,
And 'mongst them sat the Count de Lorge, with one for whom he sigh'd:
And truly 'twas a gallant thing to see that crowning show,
Valor and love, and a king above, and the royal beasts below.

Ramp'd and roar'd the lions, with horrid laughing jaws;
They bit, they glared, gave blows like beams, a wind went with their paws;
With wallowing might and stifled roar they roll'd on one another,
Till all the pit with sand and mane was in a thunderous smother;
The bloody foam above the bars came whisking through the air;
Said Francis then, "Faith, gentlemen, we're better here than there."

De Lorge's love o'erheard the King, a beauteous, lively dame,
With smiling lips and sharp bright eyes, which always seem'd the same;
She thought, "The Count, my lover, is brave as brave can be;
He surely would do wondrous things to show his love of me;
King, ladies, lovers, all look on; the occasion is divine;
I'll drop my glove, to prove his love; great glory will be mine."

She dropp'd her glove, to prove his love, then look'd at him and smiled;
He bow'd, and in a moment leap'd among the lions wild;
The leap was quick, return was quick, he has regain'd his place,
Then threw the glove, but not with love, right in the lady's face.
"By heaven," said Francis, "rightly done!" and he rose from where he sat;
"No love," quoth he, "but vanity, sets love a task like that."

—Leigh Hunt

The Bells

I.

Hear the sledges with the bells—
        Silver bells!
What a world of merriment their melody foretells!
        How they tinkle, tinkle, tinkle,
            In the icy air of night!
        While the stars that oversprinkle
        All the heavens, seem to twinkle
            With a crystalline delight;
            Keeping time, time, time,
            In a sort of Runic rhyme,
To the tintinnabulation that so musically wells
        From the bells, bells, bells, bells,
            Bells, bells, bells—
From the jingling and the tinkling of the bells.

II.

        Hear the mellow wedding bells
            Golden bells!
What a world of happiness their harmony foretells!
        Through the balmy air of night
        How they ring out their delight!—
            From the molten-golden notes,
                And all in tune,
            What a liquid ditty floats
        To the turtle-dove that listens, while she gloats
                On the moon!
        Oh, from out the sounding cells,
What a gush of euphony voluminously wells!
            How it swells!
            How it dwells
            On the Future!—how it tells
            Of the rapture that impels
        To the swinging and the ringing
            Of the bells, bells, bells—
        Of the bells, bells, bells, bells,
            Bells, bells, bells—
To the rhyming and the chiming of the bells!

III.

Hear the loud alarum bells—
    Brazen bells!
What a tale of terror, now their turbulency tells!
    In the startled ear of night
    How they scream out their affright!
        Too much horrified to speak,
        They can only shriek, shriek,
            Out of tune,
In a clamorous appealing to the mercy of the fire,
In a mad expostulation with the deaf and frantic fire,
        Leaping higher, higher, higher,
        With a desperate desire,
    And a resolute endeavor
    Now—now to sit, or never,
By the side of the pale-faced moon.
        Oh, the bells, bells, bells!
        What a tale their terror tells
            Of Despair!
    How they clang, and clash, and roar!
    What a horror they outpour
On the bosom of the palpitating air!

Yet the ear, it fully knows,
   By the twanging,
   And the clanging,
How the danger ebbs and flows;
Yet the ear distinctly tells,
   In the jangling,
   And the wrangling,
How the danger sinks and swells,
By the sinking or the swelling in the anger of the bells—
   Of the bells—
Of the bells, bells, bells, bells
   Bells, bells, bells—
In the clamor and the clanging of the bells!

IV.

Hear the tolling of the bells—
   Iron bells!
What a world of solemn thought their monody compels!
  In the silence of the night,
  How we shiver with affright
At the melancholy menace of their tone!
  For every sound that floats
  From the rust within their throats
    Is a groan.
And the people—ah, the people—
They that dwell up in the steeple,
    All alone,
And who, tolling, tolling, tolling,
  In that muffled monotone,
Feel a glory in so rolling
  On the human heart a stone—
They are neither man nor woman—
They are neither brute nor human—
    They are Ghouls:—
  And their king it is who tolls:—
  And he rolls, rolls, rolls,
    Rolls
  A paean from the bells;
And his merry bosom swells
  With the paean of the bells!
And he dances, and he yells;
Keeping time, time, time,
In a sort of Runic rhyme,
  To the paean of the bells:—
    Of the bells:

Keeping time, time, time
In a sort of Runic rhyme,
   To the throbbing of the bells—
Of the bells, bells, bells—
   To the sobbing of the bells:—
Keeping time, time, time
  As he knells, knells, knells,
In a happy Runic rhyme,
   To the rolling of the bells—
   Of the bells, bells, bells:—
   To the tolling of the bells—
Of the bells, bells, bells, bells,
   Bells, bells, bells—
To the moaning and the groaning of the bells.

—Edgar Allan Poe

Evaluating

Exchange outlines with your partner. Read your partner's outline carefully, then answer the following questions. As you answer each question, remember that there is no single "correct" interpretation of a selection. If both you and your partner can support your evaluations of the major idea and emotion with examples from the selection, you may both have arrived at valid interpretations, even if your evaluations are different.

1. What did you identify as the main idea and supporting ideas of the selection? If your partner stated these ideas differently, modify your outline to reflect your partner's evaluation, if you feel that doing so will enrich your own interpretation.

2. What did your partner identify as the main emotion and supporting emotions of the selection? If your partner stated these emotions differently, modify your outline to reflect your partner's evaluation, if you feel that doing so will enrich your own interpretation.

3. What information (if any) did your partner discover about the author that you did not? If your partner's information adds to your understanding of the selection, modify your evaluation of its ideas and emotions accordingly.

4. What information (if any) did your partner discover about the circumstances under which your selection was written? If your partner found some information you did not and if this information adds to your understanding of the selection, modify your evaluation of its ideas and emotions accordingly.

Reading Minutes and Committee Reports

The reading of minutes and the reading of committee reports are two of the items on the standard meeting agenda. Unfortunately, such reports are usually time-consuming and of limited interest. For these reasons, many organizations vote to waive the reading of the minutes, and large organizations often distribute minutes and reports in printed form rather than having them read aloud.

If you are called upon to read minutes or committee reports, follow these guidelines:

- Propose to the meeting that you be allowed to read a summary or selected highlights of the documents, rather than the entire text. If you receive permission, read a summary that you have written in advance, or selected passages that you have already marked.
- If the members of the organization have printed copies of the minutes or reports in front of them, do not read the documents aloud. Instead, draw the members' attention to the most important passages.
- When you read committee reports, speak loudly enough that everyone can hear you, pronounce your words distinctly, and give your voice sufficient variety to hold your listeners' attention.

ACTIVITIES

1. Obtain a copy of the minutes or a committee report of a school government organization. Read it to the class, with as much clarity and variety as you can. Ask the class for their reactions and any ways in which you could have improved your reading.
2. Obtain two or more committee reports from a school or health board, state agency, or congressional committee. Working with several other students, study and summarize the reports. Think of ways in which the information in these reports could be presented in order to win support for specific programs or ideas. Discuss these suggestions with the other students, then follow the best suggestions while presenting the reports to the rest of your class.

career

13.2 Preparing and Giving an Oral Reading

Knowing When and How to Speak Louder

To be an effective speaker, you must learn to control the volume, or loudness, of your voice. This does not simply mean being able to speak loudly. Too loud a voice will soon irritate your audience, just as too soft a voice will keep them from understanding you. The secret is to vary the loudness of your voice to suit each part of your speech. For example, the parts of your speech that express excitement, high spirits, surprise, indignation, or determination should probably be somewhat louder than average. Moments that are sad or solemn should probably be somewhat softer. Do not vary your volume over too wide a range. Your listeners should always be able to hear you comfortably— without either straining to understand you or wincing at the noise.

How you vary the loudness of your voice is also important. If you take shallow breaths and force air through your throat, your throat muscles will tighten and your voice will become high-pitched and harsh. Instead, take deep breaths, relax your throat muscles, and use your abdominal muscles to push the air up out of your lungs. (This is how opera singers are able to fill huge auditoriums with their voices.) This technique will enable you to speak more loudly without tiring. The relaxed muscles will also give you more control over the pitch and expression of your voice.

As you speak, look at your listeners' faces to see how they are reacting to your voice. If the nearest members of the audience are cowering in their seats, you may be too loud. If those in the rear are cupping their hands behind their ears, your voice is probably too soft.

ACTIVITY

1. Take a speech you have written, or make a copy of a fairly emotional speech from a textbook or other collection. Mark one or more pages to show the volume at which the speech should be read. (You might underline loud passages, and put a line of dots under soft ones.) Practice this portion of the speech, then deliver it before the class. After observing the students' reactions, change your markings to make your delivery more effective.

voice

How to Prepare and Give an Oral Reading

Now that you have analyzed the ideas and emotions in your selection, there is one more step to complete before you are ready to give your oral reading. You must prepare a reading copy of your selection, a copy marked to show exactly how you will read the selection to your audience. To do this, you must decide how you will use your voice to convey the ideas and emotions you've identified in the selection.

The first thing to remember is that your audience won't be able to see the punctuation in your selection. Therefore, you must read it so that they can hear every period, comma, or other punctuation mark. Begin by making a copy of your selection. Read through your selection and draw a vertical line after every punctuation mark.

Next, look at the examples of important ideas and emotions you listed in the outline for lesson 13.1. Draw a vertical line after any idea or emotion that is important enough to require a pause. (Any major idea or emotion will probably require a pause.) Finally, read your selection aloud, and draw a vertical line after any word at which it seems natural to pause.

Next, identify the emotional climax or most important statement in your selection. This passage may be a single sentence or several sentences long. It contains the single most important idea or emotion in your selection. When you practice giving your reading, you should build up to this passage.

Last, you should decide what reading rate and emotional tone are appropriate for your selection. For example, in Poe's "The Bells" you would read the description of the silver bells at a fast rate and in a lighthearted tone; you would read the description of the iron bells at a slow rate and in a solemn tone. Remember that the emotional tone your voice suggests is created by the rate, pitch, and energy with which you read each part of your selection.

Now you are ready to prepare your reading copy. First, type or print your selection, ending a line every time you reach a vertical mark. (You do not need to transfer the vertical marks to your reading copy.) Be sure to leave ample margins, and plenty of space between lines.

Next, mark any place where you want to pause for emphasis with a double line (II). Then, underline any words or phrases you want to emphasize (many of these words or phrases will come from the examples in your outline). Draw brackets on each side of the climax of your selection, so you can see what passage you want your reading to build up to.

313

Finally, make notes in the margin at each point where you want your voice to be softer or louder, where you want to vary the rate of your reading, or where you want to suggest a particular emotional tone.

Working with the Model

Douglas decided to prepare President Kennedy's inaugural speech as his oral reading. Study the following section of his reading copy.

So let us begin <u>anew</u>—|| *moderate rate, with great energy exhort audience*

remembering on both sides that civility is not a sign of

   weakness,

and sincerity is always subject to proof.

Let us never <u>negotiate</u> out of <u>fear</u>. *louder, with emphasis*

But let us never <u>fear</u> to <u>negotiate</u>.||

model

Let both sides explore what problems unite us,

instead of laboring those problems which divide us. ||

Let both sides,

for the first time,

formulate serious and precise proposals

for the inspection and control of arms—

and bring the absolute power to destroy other nations

under the absolute control of all nations. ||

Let both sides seek

to invoke the wonders of science

instead of its terrors.

Together let us explore the stars,

conquer the deserts,

eradicate disease,

tap the ocean depths,

and encourage the arts and commerce. ||

Let both sides unite

to heed in all corners of the earth

the command of Isaiah—

to "undo the heavy burdens

and to let the oppressed go free." ||

And if a beachhead of cooperation   *confident tone*

may push back the jungle of suspicion,

let both sides join in creating a new endeavor,

not a new balance of power,

but a new world of law,

where the strong are just || *emphasize*

and the weak secure || *ending of*

and the peace preserved. || *each line*

QUESTIONS

A. Think about how Douglas plans to use his voice to convey the ideas and emotions in his selection.

1. Douglas has divided his selection to help his listeners grasp which words belong together. He has typed one word group per line. Discuss how Douglas decided which words belong together. For example, how many of the lines in his reading copy end with a period, comma, or other punctuation mark? What lines end with an important word or phrase? What lines represent grammatical units, such as phrases or clauses? What line divisions represent places where it would be natural to pause?

2. What part of his selection did Douglas mark as the climax? Why do you think he chose this part? Do you think Douglas should have marked another passage as the climax? If so, identify the passage you think he should have marked, and explain why you think it is the climax.

3. On a separate piece of paper, list the words and phrases Douglas has underlined. Looking only at your list, write the idea or emotion each item suggests. Then reread the selection, and compare it with the list of emotions you have just made. How well do you think Douglas has identified the most important words presenting the ideas and emotions of his selection? What other words, if any, would you have underlined in the selection? Explain your choices.

4. At what points in his reading does Douglas plan to pause for emphasis? Explain how you think each of these pauses will help convey an important idea or emotion.

5. Read the notes Douglas has made on rate, loudness, and emotional tone. Explain how each of these notes will help him convey an important idea or emotion. What other notes on delivery (if any) should he have made? Why?

B. Think about what nonverbal communication would be appropriate for Douglas's selection.

1. Some speakers like to indicate on their reading copy places where they want to look up at their audience. At what places in his selection might Douglas have made such a notation?

2. Some speakers like to note places where they will make certain movements or gestures during their reading, while others prefer to let their interpretation be more spontaneous. What gestures would have been appropriate for Douglas's reading, and where in his selection would he have made them?

3. Discuss why Douglas decided not to include notes on nonverbal communication on his reading copy. For example, what problems

can you think of that might arise if a speaker had too many marks on the reading copy?

Guidelines

Work from your reading copy when you practice your oral reading. Follow these guidelines when you practice:

1. When you begin a practice session, put your reading copy on a stand at arm's length. If you will not have a stand or podium to use when you give your reading, put your reading copy in a stiff, clear plastic cover so you can hold it easily.

2. Ask a classmate to listen to you as you practice. This classmate should note whether you are using enough eye contact with your audience. He or she should also point out any mannerisms that may distract the audience from your efforts to convey your author's ideas and emotions.

3. If possible, tape-record your practice session to find out whether you are emphasizing the sections you intended to and whether you are building effectively to the climax of your selection.

4. Be aware of the meaning of words and phrases as you speak them.

5. Vary the pitch, rate, and loudness of your voice to convey the author's ideas and emotions and to hold your listeners' interest.

6. Become familiar enough with your material so you can look up frequently to see your listeners' responses.

Preparing and Presenting

Prepare a reading copy of the selection you chose for oral interpretation in lesson 13.1. Remember to mark off the groups of words that go together, and then write or type one word group per line in your reading copy. Underline the words and phrases you want to emphasize, and mark any places where you want to pause for emphasis. Decide what passage represents the climax of your selection, and draw brackets on each side of this passage. Make notes in the margin to indicate where you want to vary rate, pitch, and emotional tone.

Practice your oral reading in front of a classmate, following the procedures set down in the Guidelines section of this lesson. Write your classmate's suggestions on your reading copy, then conduct a final practice session alone. Before you come to class, make enough copies of your reading copy for everyone in the class. When you give your oral reading, ask your classmates to take notes on your presentation.

Evaluating

Ask the class to use the notes they made during your oral reading to answer the first three questions. Then distribute the copies of your reading copy. Give the class time to read your reading copy, and then ask them to answer the remaining questions.

1. What was the most important idea in the selection? Give one example of how the speaker emphasized words or phrases, paused for emphasis, or varied vocal rate or pitch to convey this idea.

2. What was the most important emotion in the selection? Give one example of how the speaker used his or her voice to convey this emotion.

3. How did the speaker use such nonverbal communication techniques as gesture and eye contact to convey the ideas and emotions in the selection?

4. Do you agree with the speaker's interpretation of the major idea and emotion of the selection? Explain why or why not.

5. Do you agree with the way the speaker prepared the reading copy? What, if anything, would you have done differently in preparing it?

Accepting Constructive Criticism

Both at school and at work, friends, teachers, co-workers, and supervisors will criticize your performance. *Constructive criticism* points out the weaknesses in a person's work, and suggests ways in which he or she could improve. In order to benefit from constructive criticism, you should understand that it is meant to be helpful. Remember these guidelines:

1. Listen carefully. Find out what specific criticisms of your performance the other person is making.

2. Ask the other person for specific suggestions for improvement. Ask him or her to clarify any point you do not fully understand.

3. Do not immediately defend your actions or performance. Think about whether the criticism is true. If you have been acting according to certain rules or standards, you should explain those. However, you should not make excuses for everything you have done.

4. Try to correct your performance according to the other person's suggestions. Then ask in a friendly way whether you are doing what he or she suggested. For example, ask, "Is this closer to what you had in mind?" rather than "Is this good enough for you?"

5. If you have real doubts as to whether the person's criticism is justified, check it with someone else. This second person should understand the problem and be objective. Don't ask a friend who will tell you only what you want to hear.

ACTIVITY

1. Think of an instance in which you benefited from constructive criticism. Possible subjects might include clothing, table manners, study habits, mechanical skills, punctuality, or performance on a team. Prepare a brief speech in which you describe the criticism, your reaction to it, and the ways in which you changed your behavior in response to it. Deliver the speech to the class, and ask the other students to discuss similar instances from their own experience.

career

13.3 Using Voice and Sound Effects in Radio Dramas

Improving Your Articulation and Pronunciation

Good *articulation* is the art of speaking so that every sound is clear and distinct. Because speakers with good articulation are easy to understand, their listeners usually pay close attention to them. You can improve your articulation by following these steps:

1. Rehearse your speech aloud, both alone and before another person. Note any parts of the speech in which you had trouble saying certain words, or where you were difficult to understand. If possible, tape-record your speech.

2. Most poor articulation results from not moving your lips and tongue. Practice these movements until each sound is clear and distinct. Rewrite any sentences that you find difficult to say.

3. When you deliver your speech, observe your listeners' expressions to see whether they have trouble understanding particular passages. Work to improve those passages in future speeches.

Good *pronunciation* means pronouncing each word correctly and in a manner the audience will easily understand. Remember these rules for pronunciation:

1. If you have any doubts about the pronunciation of a word in your speech, look it up in a dictionary.

2. Write difficult pronunciations on your note cards, and practice them until they become easy.

3. If the dictionary gives you a choice of pronunciations, choose the one your listeners are most familiar with.

ACTIVITY

1. Working with a partner, prepare and deliver a brief speech. Ask your partner to note any passages where your articulation or pronunciation made the speech hard to understand. Study your partner's notes, and decide which words and sentences cause you the most trouble. Look up any words you are unsure of, and practice to improve your articulation and pronunciation in those areas.

voice

How to Use Voice and Sound Effects in Radio Dramas

Actors and actresses know how much depends on the effective use of the voice. In radio drama, the voice is especially important, since it must be used to convey the action of the story as well as the emotions of the characters.

There are three characteristics of your voice that you can use to convey a character's emotions. First, you can vary your *rate of speaking.* Reading your lines quickly can show that your character is excited or in a hurry. A slow rate can indicate thoughtfulness or depression. You can pause in your delivery to create suspense, to show surprise, or to get your listeners' attention right before an important moment in the drama.

You can also vary the *pitch* of your voice to indicate what kind of character you're portraying. A low voice can help you portray an older character, while a high voice is best for portraying a child. A low voice can also show

that your character is a serious person, while a high voice can suggest a nervous or excited person. Use a medium pitch for everyday conversation and for dialogue spoken by a narrator.

You can also portray a character's emotional state by varying the *volume* of your voice. Although you must always speak loud enough to be heard, you can heighten the effect of moderate changes in volume by varying the intensity of your voice. (If you are using a microphone, remember not to make great variations in the volume of your voice.) For example, the most precious secret of a dying industrial spy might be delivered at a low volume, but with great intensity.

Remember that radio actors must sometimes use their voices to let the audience know what's happened. An actor in a ghost story might actually have to say, "The walls of the room are closing in on me," because the audience could not see this happening. That same actor would have to faint with a groan and fall with a loud thump, because without these sounds the audience would have no way of knowing that the character had fainted.

Besides helping the audience understand the play, sound effects also make the action of the play seem more real. Effects like the ringing of a telephone or the slamming of a door make the radio audience feel they're actually present at the scene of the unfolding action. Using sound effects will greatly enhance the impact of your play.

Music can be used as a sound effect. For example, you would have music in the background if your characters were at a dance. However, background music unassociated with the action can be used to create a mood, and a short passage of rising and falling music often indicates the beginning or end of a scene.

Working with the Model

In the 1930s, the English author Lawrence du Garde Peach wrote many radio plays. Read this scene from his play *The "Mary Celeste,"* paying close attention to how he instructs the actors to use their voices. Also notice what sound effects he indicates for the scene.

SCENE XVI

(The voices in this scene should be hushed and suggest fear and anxiety.)

STEWARD: I tell you I know an unlucky ship when I see one. Wouldn't ha' sailed on her, on'y I bin out of a ship since—

GOTTLIEB: It iss the sea, not the ship.

STEWARD: You make me tired. As if the sea ain't always unlucky.

VOLKERK: You're right. There was a barque sailed out of Boston—the *Aran Hill* her name was—she killed five men one voyage. I'll say she was unlucky. Fell off the main t'gallant yard, the last of 'em did, right on top o' the durned Mate. Killed him too. That was the only bit of luck the rest of the crew had the whole trip.

STEWARD: That's right. I've knowed o' ships like that. Say, have you ever heard of a haunted galley? Aboard the old *Falcon*—it was in San Francisco I first saw her, blast her—there was the ghost of a drowned cook used to hang round the galley half the time. Jumped her at Monterey, I did.

VOLKERK: I believe you. Everyone knows as drowned sailors comes back to the ships that killed 'em. It don't matter where the ship goes. I reckon they gets along under the sea.

STEWARD: I've knowed men as have seed 'em. All drowned and wet, with seaweed on 'em, and no eyes.

GOTTLIEB: You don't have to talk like that.

STEWARD: What's wrong with it? It's true, I tell you. Didn't you ever hear of the old *Spindrift?* Lost, she was, with all hands off the Bank, only they raised her a'terwards. And blame me if the whole durned crew didn't come back and take her over, all drowned, her first night out. When she put back, the new crew was all raving. You mark my words, we hain't seen the last of Bos Lorenzen this trip, nor Harbens. They'll come back—drowned. They didn't go natural, neither, and that makes it worse. And if you sees one of 'em a-lookin' at you over the side, you take my tip and don't you look back.

GOTTLIEB: What for will they come back?

STEWARD: I guess they can't help it. They *gotta* come back. It ain't like being buried on land, there ain't nothing to keep 'em down. It's the sea drawin' of 'em. I've knowed ships come home a'ter a long voyage with the crew so skeart they dursn't break open the hatches for fear o' what they'd find. Every night drowned sailors used to come and jibber at 'em through the port holes or over the stern when they was at the wheel. Half eaten, some of 'em was, by fishes.

VOLKERK: *(suddenly—sharply)* What's that?

STEWARD: Where?

VOLKERK: In the fore peak!

STEWARD: Aw, it ain't nothin'. Quit it, can't ye?

GOTTLIEB: My father, he was drowned at sea, and he come and tap at our window every night for six days afterwards till they find him and bury him at Groningen.

VOLKERK: *(hoarsely)* Look!

GOTTLIEB: Coming over the side!

STEWARD: It's an arm! All white! And wet! *(Suddenly shouting.)* Give me that axe! I'll—! *(There is a loud thud as the axe comes down on the rail.)*

VOLKERK: It's gone!

324

model

GOTTLIEB: There's blood!

STEWARD: *(very frightened)* Boys, it was Harbens—climbing aboard!

MATE: *(coming up)* What's the matter? *(The three sailors begin to tell him excitedly that they have seen the drowned body of Harbens trying to climb aboard.)*

(Fade.)

QUESTIONS

A. Think about how the actors should use their voices to convey action and emotion in this scene.

1. At the beginning of the scene the sailors are swapping stories of the supernatural. What speaking rate would be appropriate for this part of the scene? What rate would be appropriate towards the end of the scene, after Volkerk says "Look!"? What change in the characters' emotions makes a change in rate appropriate?

2. Towards the end of the scene, the playwright gives several directions on how the actors should use their voices. For example, he indicates that Volkerk should say "Look!" *"hoarsely."* What kind of pitch would you use for a hoarse voice? When the steward delivers his last line in the scene, he should sound *"very frightened."* What pitch would you use to make the steward sound "very frightened?"

3. The playwright puts Volkerk's line "What's that?" in italics. At what volume do you think the playwright wants these lines delivered? Where in the scene does the playwright give directions on vocal volume for the actor playing the steward? What directions on volume does the playwright give at the beginning of the scene? What difference in volume should occur between the beginning and end of the scene, and why?

4. How do the actors' lines help the audience know what's happening after Volkerk says "Look!"? What information is presented in words that would probably be presented visually if the play were on television?

B. Think about the sound effects in this scene.

1. What sound effect does the playwright indicate?

2. Discuss what other sound effects you might use in this scene. (For example, you might want to play a tape of waves slapping against the side of a boat throughout the scene.)

3. The author ends the scene by having the excited conversation of the three sailors fade out. How might you have used music to end the scene? What kind of music do you think would be appropriate to begin this scene? What music would be appropriate to end it?

Guidelines

Follow these guidelines as you decide how to use voice and sound effects in a radio drama:

1. Prepare your broadcast copy as a reading copy, using the marks for interpretation explained in lesson 13.2.

2. Remember that in a radio play you cannot rely on great changes in volume to convey excitement, since high volume will cause distortion in the sound. One way to monitor the volume levels you use is to tape your lines. After listening to your tape, you can adjust your interpretation if any of your changes in volume are too great.

3. You may wish to use commercial recordings for some of your sound effects. You will probably find, however, that you can develop interesting and realistic effects yourself by experimenting with a variety of materials. Some of the most frequently used sound effects include doors opening and closing; a telephone ringing; a doorbell ringing; paper rattling; the clinking of dishes or glasses; the pouring of liquid; and the sound of a fire burning. (A book from the library on sound effects can give you many practical suggestions.)

Preparing and Presenting

Work with three or four other students. Select a scene from a novel, play, or short story to present in radio drama form. Your scene should have several characters with intense feelings and should be at least one-half dialogue. The scene should also contain some action, and should take from three to five minutes to read aloud.

Make enough copies of your selection for everyone in your group. Your group should discuss the selection, identifying the action (what happens) and the emotions of each of the characters. Each group member should then choose one of the characters to portray. (Some selections may also require a narrator to give the audience necessary background information.) One group member should be responsible for music and sound effects.

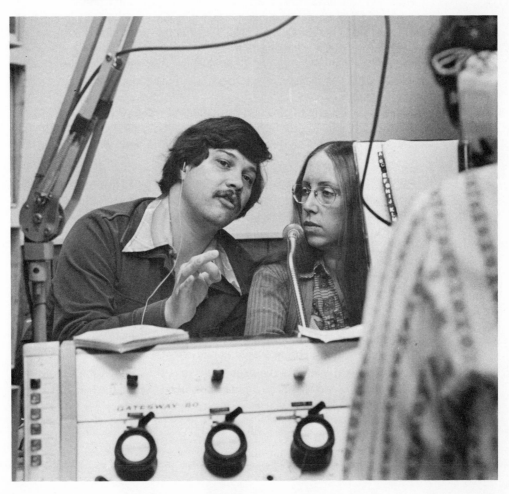

Each person should then prepare a reading copy, marked to show the interpretation to be used for the character he or she will play. The group member working on sound effects and music should mark his or her reading copy to show where effects will be used, and what they will be. The group should then meet to read through the play. They should make any changes needed in the actors' interpretations to make the action seem smoother or more logical. At this meeting the group should also decide whether the sound effects and music work for the scene, and make any necessary changes.

During the next few days, group members should practice their parts. Someone should read through the entire scene several times with the sound effects person, so that that person can practice inserting music and sound effects at precisely the right moments.

After several days, the group should meet for a final rehearsal of the scene, including all music and sound effects. Rehearse the scene once; then perform it a second time, and if possible, tape this second performance. If a tape recorder is not available, rehearse your scene twice.

Before the day you present your scene, make enough copies of your selection (in its original form, not the dramatic version) for everyone in the class.

Present your scene to the class by playing the tape you have made. If you did not make a tape, present your scene by performing it, complete with sound effects and music, behind a screen or from another room.

Evaluating _____

Distribute the copies of your selection to your classmates, and give them enough time to read it. Then ask them to answer these questions:

1. How did the group members use vocal rate, pitch, and volume to convey the emotions of the characters? Which of these three characteristics was used most effectively? Explain why.

2. How did group members use their voices to help the audience grasp the action of the play? Where else in the scene should the actors have used their voices to help the audience understand the action?

3. How appropriate and complete were the sound effects? Where else in the scene would you have used sound effects?

4. For what purposes did the group use music in presenting the scene? How else do you think music could have been used in the scene? Explain your answer.

Reading a Speech or Report
Written by Someone Else

As a worker or organization member, you may be called upon to read aloud a speech or report written by someone else. You may have time to prepare this presentation, or you may have little or no time. Follow these guidelines in each of the three cases:

1. If you have a day or more to prepare the presentation, read the speech through several times. If necessary, type or neatly print the text to make it easier to read. Ask the author to explain any passages that you do not understand or that your listeners might not understand. If possible, have the author rewrite these parts, or get permission to rewrite them yourself. Practice delivering the speech, concentrating on the meaning of the words and sentences. You should practice until you are able to look at the audience more than 50 percent of the time you are reading.

2. If you have only an hour or so in which to prepare the presentation, read the speech over as many times as you can. Mark the important passages that you will emphasize. Look up any words whose pronunciation you are unsure of. Deliver the speech in a clear, relaxed manner. Do not rush, and do not speak in a monotone.

3. If you are given no time at all in which to prepare the speech, do your best to read it in a natural, relaxed manner that your audience can understand. Avoid hurrying and mumbling. Do not complain about the lack of preparation, the subject matter, or the author's style.

ACTIVITY

1. Practice reading a selection from a magazine article or speech written by someone else. Remember that you are not allowed to cut, condense, or adapt this selection. After practicing your presentation several times, deliver it before the class. Ask the other students to evaluate your presentation in terms of clarity, variety, and interest.

career

13.4 Rehearsing and Presenting a Radio Drama

Improving Your Voice: Rate, Pitch, and Variety

Knowing when to speak louder, and how to improve your articulation and pronunciation, are important speaking skills (see Speaking Skills, lessons 13.2 and 13.3). It is also important to speak in a varied and interesting manner. Controlling the rate and pitch of your speech can help you emphasize important points. It can also add variety that will hold your audience's attention (see pages 15–22).

The *rate* of speech is the number of syllables you speak per minute. Nervous people, or those reading a prepared speech, tend to speak too rapidly to be easily understood. When you practice a speech, vary the rate at which you speak. Decide which passages will be most effective at a faster rate, and which will be best at a slower. In general, you should change your rate slightly every few sentences. You should also practice when to *pause*. A slight pause before or after a word or sentence helps to emphasize it.

The *pitch* of your voice is the highness or lowness of the sound. In general, speakers of English raise their voices when asking a question, and lower them at the end of a sentence or when making a statement. You should vary the pitch of your voice slightly within each sentence. This will keep your voice from becoming monotonous to your listeners. A rise or drop in pitch can also help emphasize individual words or phrases.

Rate, pauses, and pitch are all ways of creating *variety* in your speech. Variety in speaking shows your listeners that you have practiced your presentation and understand it thoroughly. It also shows that you are self-controlled and confident. For all these reasons, your listeners are likelier to find you interesting and persuasive.

ACTIVITY

1. Practice reading a brief passage from a novel or short story, using all the appropriate kinds of vocal variety to make it effective. Present your reading before the class. Ask them to evaluate its effectiveness, and to suggest ways in which it could have been more effective.

voice

How to Rehearse and Present a Radio Drama

When your group presents a complete radio drama, you will need to use the techniques you learned in lesson 13.3. They will help you decide how the actors should use their voices, and what sound effects and music will work best in the play.

A complete drama, whether on the stage, on radio, or on television, will require several rehearsals. Rehearsals give the director a chance to be sure that all the elements of the play—the actors' interpretation of their characters, the narrator's delivery, the sound effects, and the music—will work effectively for a listening audience.

At the first rehearsal, the group should *decide on roles* and *distribute scripts.* The group should choose a director to keep the action coordinated and help the actors' interpretations mesh. Two or more group members should be chosen to handle sound effects and music. Then actors should be chosen for the different roles in the play. (Sometimes an actor may have to portray more than one character. When this happens, that person should develop a distinctive voice for each of the characters he or she portrays.)

The first rehearsal is also the time to provide group members with scripts. Your group may decide to present a published radio drama, or may prefer to adapt a stage play or short story into a radio drama. In either case, each person should receive an identical copy of the final script. (Some groups prefer to number each line in the script, for easy reference during rehearsal.) Before the second rehearsal, each group member should *mark the script* to indicate his or her interpretation of the assigned role.

At the second rehearsal, the actors and narrator should *read the script aloud.* (If the sound effects person has any effects ready, he or she should supply these during the reading.) Words or phrases that are difficult to read should be changed at this rehearsal. If an actor's interpretation doesn't seem to fit the character, or if several actors' interpretations don't work well together, the director may want to guide the actors in changing their interpretations. At the end of the second rehearsal, the director should inform the entire group of the work to be done before the final rehearsal. The director may suggest that several actors work together to improve a particular scene. He or she may also suggest changes in sound effects or places where effects are needed.

At the final rehearsal, *final sound effects should be tested* and the *play timed.* If the play is running too long or too short, the director can adjust

331

the actors' rate of delivery, the amount of narration, the length of music opening and closing scenes, or the sound effects to make the play fit the allotted time. At the final rehearsal, the sound effects person should also check to see that the microphones are functioning properly, so that the actors can work with them easily and the sound effects will come across as intended.

You should rehearse until your performance falls within fifteen to twenty seconds of the time allowed you. During the actual performance, the director can lengthen or shorten the performance time by signaling to the actors to speed up or slow down their delivery, or by adjusting the length of musical interludes.

Working with the Model

Eight students have met to rehearse a radio play, their adaptation of the short story "The Open Window," by the English author Saki (H. H. Munro). Jessica is the director, and Luis is the narrator. Carl, Roger, Mona, Yvonne, Todd, and Cynthia play characters. Todd and Cynthia also double on sound effects.

At the first rehearsal, the group assigned roles and read through the script, marking their copies and discussing interpretations. By the second rehearsal, the students know their parts well, and most of the sound effects are ready. Jessica has already had the actors and narrator perform the first two pages of the script. Read this transcript of part of the rehearsal.

JESSICA: Before we go on, I'd like to briefly review what we've done so far. "The Open Window" is set in England at about the turn of the century. You've all done your accents well. They're not 100 percent British, but I think they'll *suggest* the English upper classes to our listeners.

The play opens with the narrator telling us about a young man with a silly name, Framton Nuttell. Framton has "bad nerves," as they used to say, and he has gone to the country to rest. His sister—that's you, Cynthia—has given him letters of introduction to several people.

CYNTHIA: Framton's sister has only five lines at the beginning of the play. After that, I go back over to sound effects.

TODD: Cynthia, do you think you can walk from the mike to the tape deck in time for the first sound cue?

CYNTHIA: Maybe not. Jess, what if Todd runs the tape of country noises—the birds, rustling leaves, and so on? Then I could do the doorbell effect that comes a few seconds later.

JESSICA: Fine. That's Todd on tape, Cynthia on doorbell. Both of you mark it in your scripts.

model

LUIS: While these effects are going on. I'm doing a voice-over. I tell how Framton is met at the door by "a very self-possessed young lady of fifteen."

JESSICA: That "self-possessed" turns out to be very important, Luis, so be sure the audience hears it.

LUIS: I remember: I'm to narrate everything in a clear, deadpan style.

JESSICA: Yvonne, you play the girl, who's named Vera.

YVONNE: *(as Vera)* "My aunt will be down in a minute, Mr. Nuttell. In the meantime, you must try and put up with me."

CARL: And Framton—that's me—feels very uncomfortable. This is the point where Vera starts telling him about her aunt.

JESSICA: Right. Carl, don't make Framton sound *too* foolish. Remember, the audience has to identify with him if the story is going to work.

CARL: *(marking his script)* "Embarrassed, but not too foolish."

JESSICA: Now, Yvonne, would you do Vera's big narrative speech— the one where she explains why her aunt keeps the French window open in the late afternoon?

YVONNE: *(as Vera)* "Out through that window, three years ago to the day, her husband and her two young brothers went out for their day's shooting. They never came back."

JESSICA: Excuse me, Yvonne, but could you put a little more mystery into that last sentence?

model

YVONNE: *(as Vera)* "They never came back. In crossing the moor to their favorite snipe-shooting ground, they were all three engulfed in a treacherous piece of bog. Their bodies were never recovered. That was the dreadful part of it."

JESSICA: Good. Lower your voice now—this has really got to grip the audience.

YVONNE: *(as Vera)* "Poor aunt always thinks they will come back some day—they and the little brown spaniel that was lost with them—and walk in at that window, just as they used to. That is why the window is kept open every evening till it is quite dusk. Poor dear aunt, she has often told me how they went out, her husband with his white waterproof coat over his arm, and Ronnie—her youngest brother—singing 'Bertie, why do you bound?' as he always did."

JESSICA: Fine. Let's hear your voice tremble now.

YVONNE: *(as Vera)* "Do you know, sometimes on still, quiet evenings like this, I almost get a creepy feeling that they will all walk in through that window—"

JESSICA: That's a sound cue.

(Cynthia opens door with sudden loud noise. Yvonne and Carl, as Vera and Framton, gasp.)

JESSICA: Excellent!

ROGER: That should knock the audience right out of their chairs.

model

JESSICA: Now let's skip the next scene for the time being. The aunt comes in—that's you, Mona—and says hello to Framton. She tells him that her husband and brothers should be home any minute. Framton is horrified, and tries to change the subject of conversation. He talks about his nerves instead, but the aunt is obviously bored, and keeps looking out the window. Suddenly—Mona, will you take the speech?

MONA: *(as the aunt)* "Oh! Here they are at last! Just in time for tea—and don't they look as if they are muddy up to the eyes!"

LUIS: *(as narrator)* "Framton shivered, and turned toward the niece with a look of sympathy. But the girl was staring out through the open window with dazed horror in her eyes. Framton swung round in his seat, and looked in the same direction ..."

CARL: *(as Framton)* *gasps and moans of terror.*

LUIS: *(as narrator)* "In the deepening twilight, three figures were walking across the lawn toward the window. They all carried guns under their arms, and one of them had a white coat over his shoulder. A tired brown spaniel kept close at their heels."

JESSICA: Roger, let's hear that distant voice.

ROGER: *(muffling his voice)* "I said, Bertie, why do you bound?"

CARL: *(as Framton)* "No! No!"

JESSICA: Sound cue!

(Todd and Cynthia make sound of furniture being knocked over. Todd runs tape of footsteps running along hall, door opening, and footsteps running away down gravel path.)

JESSICA: Five seconds' silence—time it.

(Todd imitates heavy footsteps on the floor.)

TODD: *(as the aunt's husband)* "Here we are, my dear! Fairly muddy, but most of it's dry. Who was that who bolted out as we came up?"

MONA: *(as the aunt)* "A most extraordinary man ... could only talk about his illness, and dashed off without a word of apology. One would think he had seen a ghost."

YVONNE: *(as Vera)* "I expect it was the dog. He told me he had a horror of dogs. He was once hunted into a cemetery on the banks of the Ganges by a pack of pariah dogs, and had to spend the night in a newly dug grave, with the creatures snarling and grinning and foaming just above him. Enough to make anyone lose their nerve."

JESSICA: Okay, narrator, give us the punchline.

LUIS: *(as narrator)* "Romance at short notice was her specialty."

JESSICA: Great, just great. But I wonder about that word "romance."

CYNTHIA: Yes, some people might think it means "love story" instead of "adventure."

model

LUIS: Why don't we change it to "drama"?

JESSICA: Good. Does anyone object? All right, everybody change your scripts.

ROGER: Also, I'm not sure many listeners will know what "pariah" dogs are. Shouldn't we change it to "wild"?

JESSICA: I think so. Do we all agree on that? Change "pariah" to "wild" in Vera's last speech.

MONA: Todd, did I catch the sound of an automobile on your last tape?

(Todd reruns tape.)

CARL: Yes, there it is, behind the running footsteps. That doesn't belong in the English countryside of 1900.

JESSICA: Todd, can you record another thirty seconds of footsteps, minus the cars?

TODD: Sure, I'll do it before the final rehearsal.

JESSICA: Fine. Let's take a break now, and then we can run through the play again, without interruption.

QUESTIONS

A. Think about what the group accomplished at its *first* rehearsal.

 1. How did the students divide the work of presenting the play?
 2. What did they do with their scripts during the first rehearsal?
 3. What non-spoken part of the play was prepared between the first and second rehearsals?

B. Think about what the group accomplished during its *second* rehearsal.

 1. What does Jessica do to help the actors understand their parts?
 2. What change in responsibility is made at this rehearsal?
 3. What changes in interpretation are made at this rehearsal?
 4. What technical error is noticed at this rehearsal? When will it be corrected?

C. Think about how the students use their scripts at this rehearsal.

 1. In whose script is the change in the sound effects assignment marked?
 2. In whose script is a change in interpretation marked?
 3. What changes were made in the narration and dialogue of the scripts? Why were these changes made? In whose scripts were they made? Why are these particular changes so important?

D. Think about the work the group will have to complete during this rehearsal and the final rehearsal.

 1. What will occur at the two rehearsals?

2. What changes in the script do you think the students might make at the final rehearsal?

3. What changes in sound effects do you think the students might make?

4. What kind of music, if any, do you think would be appropriate for this play? At what points in the play would you use it?

E. Read Saki's short story "The Open Window." Compare the original story with the portions of the script that were read at the rehearsal. Think about the difference between the printed story and the radio version. Think about how *you* would adapt the story for radio.

Guidelines

Follow this checklist to be sure you complete all the necessary steps when rehearsing a radio play or other drama.

First rehearsal

_____ Distribution of scripts to cast and crew

_____ Talk by director, explaining play and production

_____ Assignment of roles to actors (including doubling, if necessary)

_____ Assignment of music and sound effects to crew (who may also be actors)

_____ First reading of the script, to answer questions and understand basic interpretation

Second rehearsal *(or as many intermediate rehearsals as are necessary)*

_____ Performance of the script, in character and with music and sound effects, if available

_____ Explanation by director of motivation, interpretation, and timing

_____ Marking of scripts to indicate any changes in interpretation

_____ Changing of scripts when necessary for dramatic effect

Final rehearsal

_____ Performance of script in final form, with complete music and sound effects

_____ Checking and adjustment of microphones, speakers, tape recorders, and other equipment

_____ Timing of performance to within fifteen to twenty seconds of allotted time

Preparing and Presenting _____

Working with four to six other students, prepare a script for a radio drama. Your script may be an expanded version of the scene you prepared in lesson 13.3, or it may be an adaptation of a play, short story, or scene from a novel. The play should communicate the action through voice, narration, sound, and music. It should last about ten minutes.

Rehearse the play, following the directions given in this lesson. (If the cast is large and roles cannot be doubled, you may need to add more students to your group.) Time the play, and tell the class how long you expect it to take. Present your play either by playing a tape recording or by acting it in front of a microphone in another room.

Evaluating _____

Give each person in your class a copy of the original scene, story, or play your group adapted. Ask them to answer the following questions about your play:

1. How well was the setting conveyed by sound, dialogue, and narration? How could information about the setting have been better conveyed?

2. How well was the action of the play conveyed by sound and dialogue? Did the play rely excessively on narration? How could the action have been better conveyed?

3. How well were the characters in the play distinguished by their voices and dialogue? How could the presentation of different characters have been improved? If some roles were doubled by the same actors, how easily could the characters be told apart?

4. How effective was the use of music? What music could be changed, added, or deleted to make the play more effective?

5. How appropriate, clear, and convincing were the sound effects? What effects could be changed, added, or deleted to make the play more effective?

6. How close did the performance come to the announced time? Should the performance have been paced differently? What material, if any, could have been added or deleted to bring the performance closer to the ideal length?

Using a Microphone or Public Address System

If you know how to use it, a microphone or public address system can help you communicate with a large audience. Before using such a system, however, you must be prepared. Remember these rules:

1. Test the microphone setup before you begin speaking, preferably before any listeners have arrived. Have another person in the room or auditorium tell you if the level of your voice is appropriate, and if you are speaking clearly.

2. Because most microphone systems do not reproduce sound with high fidelity, you must speak *more slowly and more distinctly* than usual in order to be understood (see Speaking Skills, lesson 13.3).

3. Find the proper distance from your mouth to the microphone, and stay at that distance. If you move too close, your voice will be distorted. If you turn your head away from the microphone, you will be inaudible.

4. Speak at approximately the same voice level. The system has been adjusted for a specific level. Any sound much louder will be painful for your listeners, and any sound much softer will not be heard.

5. Do not touch the microphone with your mouth or fingers, blow into the microphone, or hold the microphone stand.

6. Remember that coughs, rattling papers, muttering under your breath, and other sounds will all be audible to your listeners.

7. If you are using a "body mike" (for a televised interview, for example), be aware of where the microphone is attached to your clothing and where the cord is. Do not touch or disconnect the microphone, or pull or trip over the cord.

ACTIVITY

1. Working with other students, take turns reading the same passage over a microphone system in a large room or auditorium. Have a panel of four to six other students evaluate each reader in terms of articulation, clarity, and proper use of the microphone. After studying your evaluation, practice ways to improve your use of the microphone.

career

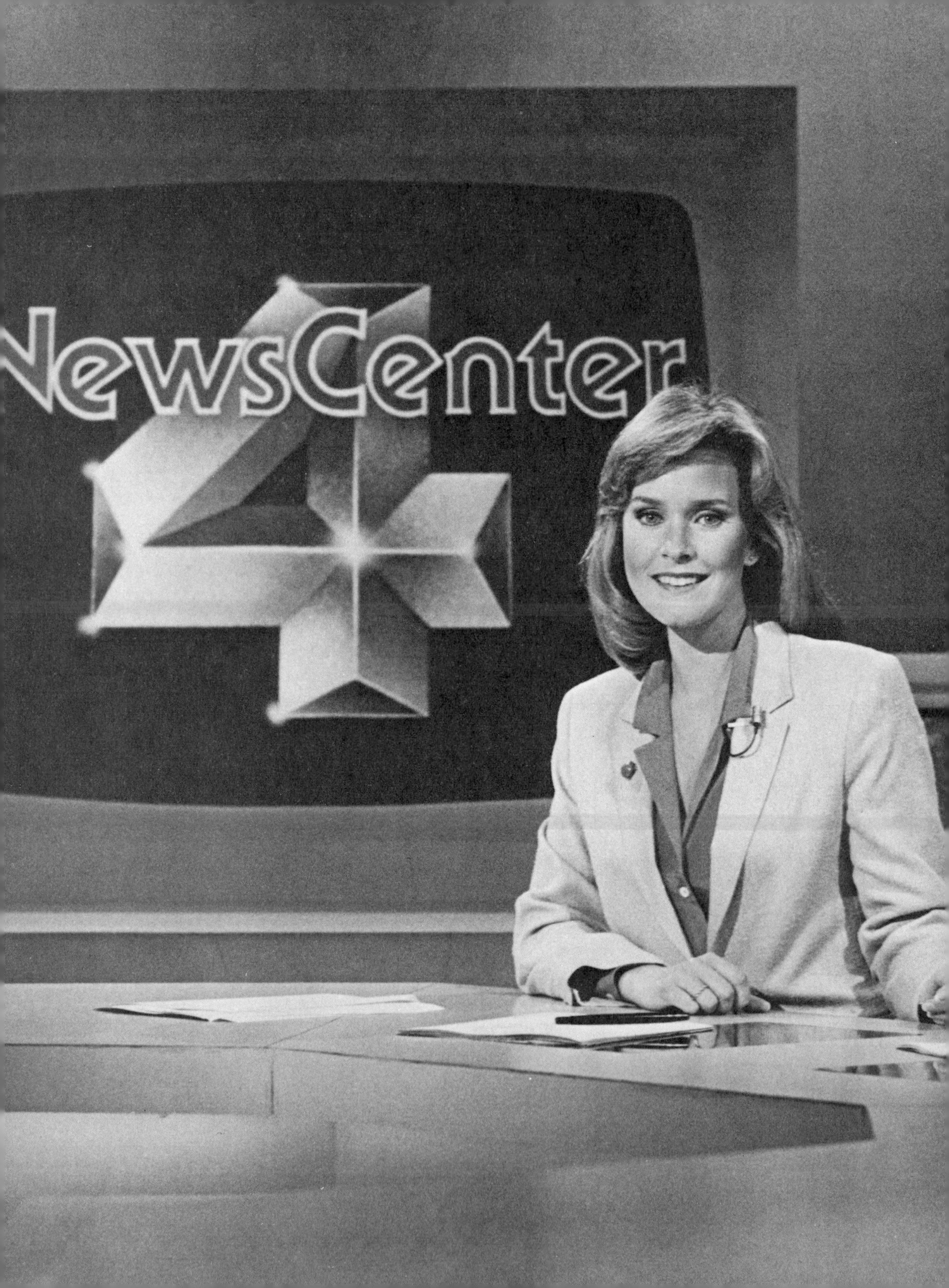
NewsCenter

14 Listening for Enjoyment

According to recent studies, the typical American child has watched 5000 hours of television before entering the first grade. Teenagers and adults continue this pattern, watching an average of more than 30 hours a week throughout their lives. If you are like most people, you have probably asked yourself whether you spend too much time watching television and listening to the radio. Perhaps you have wondered whether television affects the way you look at the world. You may have tried to think of better ways of spending your time.

After working through this chapter, you should be able to

- measure the time you spend watching television
- evaluate the effect of television on your life
- decide how you can benefit the most from electronic media

The Speaking Skills lesson in this chapter will help you evaluate the material you hear and see on television and radio. In the lesson, you will learn to

- distinguish reporting from entertainment
- distinguish reporting from commentary

The Skills for Success lesson will show how you can use speaking and listening skills in your career and as a citizen. You will learn to

- listen critically to documentaries and docudramas
- distinguish fact from fiction in docudramas

14.1 Evaluating Your Radio and Television Listening

Evaluating Television News Broadcasts and Commentaries

When you watch television broadcasts on current events and personalities, ask yourself these three questions:

1. *Is this program entertainment or reporting?* A genuine news program will examine important issues in depth. Although reporters will try to make the news interesting, their primary concern is to present it honestly and accurately. By contrast, a "news" broadcast about alligator farms, flying saucers, and talking dogs is entertainment.

2. *Does the reporter understand the subject?* Reporters who know a great deal about politics may know very little about other subjects. For this reason, they may distort the subject of a report by focusing on aspects that are simple or that photograph well.

3. *Does the broadcast distinguish fact from opinion?* Most news broadcasts try to be objective and neutral when dealing with controversial stories. Some programs, however, openly take sides. Be alert to slanted news stories, and judge the facts for yourself.

Television *commentary* may be a personal opinion presented by an individual reporter, or it may be an editorial by the manager of the station. As you listen to a commentary, ask yourself:

- Does this person show a real knowledge of the facts and issues?
- Is this reporter or manager fair to those who hold opposing views?
- Does this television station, or its management, stand to profit financially if voters and politicians follow their advice? How can I find out who owns the station, and what other interests they have?

ACTIVITY

1. Watch one or more television news broadcasts. Select one story on a current issue that you think was not presented objectively. Decide what position the reporter took on the story, and list evidence to support your findings. Report on your observations to the class.

listening

How to Evaluate Your
Radio and Television Listening

Most Americans spend thousands of hours each year watching television. Many people are unaware of how much time television really takes out of their lives. They turn the set on when they arrive home from school or work, and leave it on until they go to bed. If asked, they might say that they watch very little television, or that they think most programs are bad. Although they may be unaware of it, the time devoted to television is time during which they are not reading, talking, thinking, walking, exercising, meeting people, or earning money.

One way to get more control over your time is to keep a *media diary*. You can find out how much time radio and television actually take out of each week. Then you can decide how much time you want to devote to radio and television.

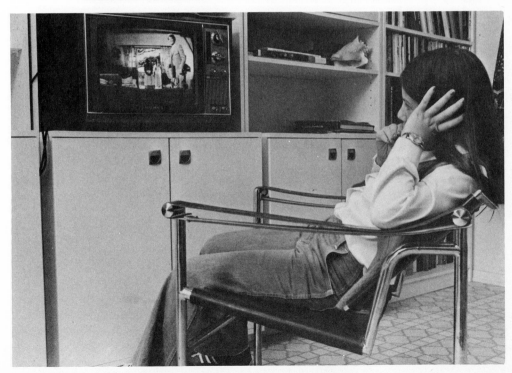

Working with the Model

Two students, Sohalia and Craig, kept media diaries for one week. Here are the portions of their diaries for Monday, Tuesday, and Wednesday. As you read their media diaries, think about how much time you spent listening to radio or television on those days of the week.

MEDIA DIARY: SOHALIA

Day	Medium	6 A.M. to Noon	Noon to 6 P.M.	6 P.M. to 10 P.M.	Total
Mon.	Radio	15 min.	10 min.	——	25 min.
	TV	——	——	1 hr.	1 hr.
Tues	Radio	5 min.	10 min.	——	15 min.
	TV	——	——	30 min.	30 min.
Wed.	Radio	10 min.	15 min.	——	25 min.
	TV	——	30 min.	1 hr.	1½ hrs.

TOTAL RADIO/TV TIME FOR 3 DAYS: 4 hrs. 5 mins.

MEDIA DIARY: CRAIG

Day	Medium	6 A.M. to Noon	Noon to 6 P.M.	6 P.M. to 10 P.M.	Total
Mon.	Radio	30 min.	1 hr.	30 min.	2 hrs.
	TV	——	30 min.	3 hrs.	3½ hrs.
Tues.	Radio	20 min.	1½ hrs.	——	1 hr. 50 mins.
	TV	——	30 min.	4 hrs.	4½ hrs.
Wed.	Radio	20 min.	1 hr.	30 min.	1 hr. 50 mins.
	TV	15 min.	1 hr.	3½ hrs.	4 hrs. 45 mins.

TOTAL RADIO/TV TIME FOR 3 DAYS: 18 hrs. 25 mins.

QUESTIONS

A. Think about Sohalia's media diary.

1. Consider the length of time Sohalia spends listening to the radio in each part of the day. Is she more likely to be listening to specific programs, or using the radio as background to some chore? Explain your answer.

    2. Consider the time Sohalia spends watching television. How careful do you think she is in selecting the programs she wants to watch? Explain your answer.

B. Think about Craig's media diary.

    1. Considering the amount of time Craig spends watching television, how careful do you think he is in selecting the programs he wants to watch? Explain your answer.

    2. Craig's teachers estimate the following amounts of homework are required each evening for his classes:

Math	30 minutes
Spanish	30 minutes
Civics	1 to 2 hours
Speech	30 minutes to 1 hour
Chemistry	0 to 30 minutes

In view of his radio and television habits, when do you think Craig does his homework?

C. Keep a media diary of your own for one week. At the end of the week, add up the amount of time you spent on radio and television. Then list the things you had wanted to do during the week but had no time for. Include

    reading books
    doing homework
    shopping
    sports
    time with friends
    learning job skills

Estimate the time you would have liked to spend on these activities. Compare this time with the time you spent on radio and television. What conclusions do you come to? Report your findings to the class.

Guidelines

A media diary shows you *how much* time you spent, but not how well it was spent. A *media evaluation* records what you watched or listened to, how much you enjoyed each program, and whether or not you learned anything. You may use the following letter ratings:

    A excellent
    B good
    C mediocre
    D bad
    F very bad

Here is a sample media evaluation for one evening:

MEDIA EVALUATION

Time	Program	Rating	Comment
7:00 P.M.	Network News	A-	Made me aware of current events (only one story was silly)
7:30 P.M.	Embarrassing Questions	F	Terrible—wish I'd turned it off.
8:00 P.M.	Gas 'n' 'Gators	D-	Dumb!
8:30 P.M.	Weinstein's Wombats	C+	Some funny jokes, but could have been much better
9:00 P.M.	Bullets in the Bayou	C−	Brainless violence, and pretty dull
10:00 P.M.	Great Expectations, Part 3	A	Excellent BBC series—wish it wasn't on so late!
11:00 P.M.	Local News	B	First 4 stories well done; then I fell asleep.

Record your feelings about a program immediately after watching or listening to it. You will have a record of your reactions to refer to the next time that program, or a similar one, is on the air. If you are wondering whether to listen to a program, ask yourself the following questions:

- Do I have any reason to believe that this program will be worth watching or listening to?
- Have I ever enjoyed any other program in this series?
- The last time I listened to this program, or a similar one, what reaction did I record?
- Will I be glad tomorrow that I listened to this program? Will I be glad next week?
- Is there anything else I either should do or would like to do instead of listening to this program?

Answering such questions will help you take back control over some of the time you once gave to radio and television. This practice in managing your time will become more important as you go on to college or enter the job market. Successful college students, workers, and business people have all learned how to manage their time. First, they allow ample time for the work they *must* do. Then they think about their other activities, including entertainment, very carefully. Finally, they schedule only those activities that they believe they will enjoy or learn from.

ACTIVITY

1. Write a media evaluation of the radio and television programs you listen to during a single week. Give each program a letter grade, and write down your reactions to each in a few words. At the end of the week, count the number of programs you enjoyed and the number you felt were a waste of time. Add up the number of hours you spent on worthless programs. Think about the things you would rather have done during those hours. During the following week, ask yourself the questions in the Guidelines section before you turn on any program. See if you are able to reduce your radio and television time by the number of hours you felt were wasted.

Preparing and Presenting _____

Working with five other students, conduct an experiment to see how well you spend your radio and television time. Each student should keep a media diary and make a media evaluation for one week. At the end of the week, all six students should meet and pass out copies of their diaries and evaluations. The entire group should study and discuss each person's listening and viewing habits. (This group discussion should have a leader and should be conducted according to the guidelines in chapter 7.) At the end of the meeting, each student should decide how, and by how much, he or she will reduce the amount of time spent on radio or television. Each student should also decide on one program that he or she feels is worth watching or listening to regularly.

During the following week, the members of the group should put their resolutions into effect by reducing their radio and television time. Then the group should present the results of its experiment to the class. The presentation should be in two parts. In the first part, the group leader should report on the success of the experiment. (It may be better not to use names. The leader can say, "Student A reduced his time by 4 hours a week," "Student B reduced her time by 2½ hours a week," and so forth.) In the second part, each student should report briefly to the class on the one program he or she believes is really worth watching or listening to. The report should include a description of the program and of the student's reaction to it.

Evaluating

After the presentations, the class should discuss the following questions:

1. In what other ways could a person control the time he or she spends on radio or television?
2. What do the worthless programs watched by group members have in common?
3. What do the outstanding programs described by the group members have in common?
4. What are some other programs on which students would feel they had not wasted their time?

Listening Critically
to Documentaries and Docudramas

A television *documentary* is a program about a historic event or a current issue. It uses authentic films, recordings, and interviews to inform the audience about an event or issue that cannot be covered on a brief news broadcast. Many documentaries are informative and fair, but some are one-sided. When watching a documentary, ask yourself:

- Does this program present all sides of an issue?
- Is it consistent with what I already know about the issue?
- Does it distinguish between fact, opinion, and conjecture?
- Are films, interviews, and other materials presented in a complete, undistorted form?
- Do the reporters appear to understand the issue, and do they present it objectively?

A *docudrama* is a fictional drama based on real events. It uses actors to portray famous people, and is intended primarily as entertainment. (*The Missiles of October, Franklin and Eleanor,* and *Backstairs at the White House* are examples.) As you watch a docudrama, ask yourself:

- Does this program show events that are a matter of public record, or are the authors inventing scenes and events?
- Have the authors tried to make the program more entertaining by presenting people as either heros or villains?
- Have the authors had to suppress events or characters in order to avoid lawsuits from people who are still alive?

ACTIVITY

1. Watch a documentary or docudrama about a current or historical event. Then do independent research on that event. Compare scenes from the documentary or docudrama with the facts you learn. Decide whether the program was essentially accurate or whether it distorted facts in order to be more entertaining or persuasive. Report on your findings to the class, and learn how students who did not research the program reacted to it.

citizenship

Guide to Speaking Skills

How to Use the Guide to Speaking Skills

Each of the 35 **Speaking Skills** in this book precedes one of the numbered lessons. The **Speaking Skills** contain guidelines on researching, planning, and delivering speeches, as well as on listening and problem solving. Each of the 35 **Skills for Success** follows one of the numbered lessons. The **Skills for Success** contain guidelines on choosing a career, communicating at work, and participating in meetings and local government.

The **Guide to Speaking Skills** will enable you to look up any of the skills you want to. To locate one of the Speaking Skills, first decide which part of the communication process you are interested in. For example, the first part is **Research,** the second **Planning,** the third **Attitude,** and so on. Under the name of the part, each skill is listed alphabetically, with the number of the page where you can find it. A brief description of each skill is given to make the **Guide** easier to use. The **Skills for Success** are listed under two categories, **Career** and **Citizenship.**

Speaking Skills

RESEARCH

PLANNING

ATTITUDE

Using the Right Word

In general, you should use concrete and familiar words, active verbs, and few adjectives. Prefer one word to a phrase, and short words to long-winded ones.

Using Transitions

Transitions are words or phrases that connect one sentence or paragraph with the following one. Skillful use of transitions can help your listeners follow your speech more easily.

VOICE

Improving Your Articulation and Pronunciation

Articulation is the art of speaking clearly and distinctly. Good pronunciation means pronouncing your words correctly and in a way your listeners will understand. Good articulation and correct pronunciation will make your audience pay more attention to what you have to say.

Improving Your Voice: Rate, Pitch, and Variety

Controlling the rate and pitch of your voice, and knowing when to pause, will make your speech more interesting. Adding variety to the way you speak helps demonstrate your confidence and intelligence to your listeners.

Knowing When and How to Speak Louder

To be a good speaker, you should learn to control the volume of your voice. Learn when to speak louder, and when to speak more softly. Practice speaking in a relaxed manner in order to gain more control over your voice.

MOVEMENT

Communicating through Posture and Expression

The way you use your face and body can help reinforce your speech. Your expression, posture, and use of eye contact can all hold your audience's attention and underline the points you are making.

Using Gestures to Communicate

Good use of gestures can make your speech more interesting and effective. You must be careful, however, not to distract or irritate your audience. Your gestures should be purposeful, appropriate, smooth, and economical.

Handbook of
Contest Speaking

How to Use the Handbook of Contest Speaking

Contest Debating

Impromptu Speaking

Extemporaneous Speaking

Original Oratory

Oral Interpretation of Prose or Poetry

Dramatic Interpretation

Humorous Interpretation

Specialized Events

EXPOSITORY SPEAKING

RADIO AND TELEVISION SPEAKING

READERS THEATER

COMBINATION EVENTS

DISCUSSION

Student Congress

How to Use the Handbook of Contest Speaking

Speech and debate contests will provide you with opportunities to develop your speaking skills. You will obtain expert opinions about your performance and have the chance to compete with students representing other schools.

This handbook will introduce you to the major activities included in speech tournaments. Colleges, high schools, and other institutions sponsor competitive speaking events. The host of each tournament establishes rules and procedures related to the specific activities; therefore, you will want to become thoroughly familiar with the specific requirements before competing.

In addition to tournaments, you may have an opportunity to participate in specialized speaking contests. Businesses and service organizations offer scholarships and other prizes for the students who win their contests.

The general elements of speech communication discussed throughout this text apply to all contest speaking. You will be most successful if you demonstrate original thought, clear expression, good choice of words, positive attitude, and effective use of voice and gestures.

The National Forensic League provides information and an organizational framework for high school students interested in competitive speaking. Your state probably has its own organization with its own rules. Your speech teacher can help you locate materials that will supplement this handbook and help prepare you to participate in contests.

Contest Debating

Contest debates are conducted according to strict time limits, and on an assigned proposition. The proposition is always worded in positive language, and proposes a change in current policy. (For more about the nature of debate, see chapter 10.) Each debater works with a partner. One or more judges listen to each round and select the winning team.

GUIDELINES

1. The most common format for competitive debating is the cross-examination model. Affirmative speakers are cross-examined by negative speakers, and vice-versa. The time limits vary with different

tournaments; the following times are most common on the national level.

First Affirmative Constructive	8 minutes
Cross-Examination	3 minutes
First Negative Constructive	8 minutes
Cross-Examination	3 minutes
Second Affirmative Constructive	8 minutes
Cross-Examination	3 minutes
Second Negative Constructive	8 minutes
Cross-Examination	3 minutes
First Negative Rebuttal	4 minutes
First Affirmative Rebuttal	4 minutes
Second Negative Rebuttal	4 minutes
Second Affirmative Rebuttal	4 minutes

2. The affirmative team has the burden of analyzing a current problem, and defending the plan for solving it which is expressed in the debate proposition. The debate proposition is usually a national topic debated throughout the country during a specific year.

3. Teams may be allowed preparation time during the debate. This is usually a period of 2 minutes between constructive and rebuttal speeches. Some tournaments establish other rules for preparation time throughout a debate.

4. The purpose of the cross-examination period is to clarify points made by the opposition, and to expose weaknesses in their arguments or evidence. Both the questioner and the witness should speak concisely and to the point. They should avoid showing off or exhibiting personal hostilities.

5. Teams are judged on the basis of analysis, reasoning, evidence, refutation, delivery, and cross-examination skills. Usually, each speaker is rated. The teams are given ratings ranging from *poor* to *superior*, and the winner of each round is identified.

6. Debaters generally participate in several rounds of debate during a tournament. Rounds are scheduled so that the strongest teams eventually face each other, and the entire contest has one winning team.

PREPARING FOR COMPETITION

1. Debate speaking involves the same skills as an expository speech based on analysis (see chapter 5) and a persuasive speech appealing to logic

(see chapter 9). The first step is to analyze the problem and the proposition thoroughly, understanding your opponents' position as well as your own.

2. Research the topic, making sure that your evidence is accurate, complete, and up-to-date. Several publishers and debate associations offer yearly handbooks on the national topic, but a debate handbook is no substitute for doing your own research and background reading.

3. Prepare a brief, outlining your analysis of the problem, the arguments on both sides, and the evidence you will use (see chapter 10).

4. Although preparation is vital to good debating, only the first affirmative speech can be fully prepared in advance. All other speeches will be influenced, both in argument and choice of evidence, by what has been said in other speeches. Debaters must have good listening skills (see chapters 6 and 11). They must be able to think on their feet, and to select and organize evidence while their opponents are speaking.

5. Remember, judges usually vote for the team that gave the most persuasive arguments, rather than one that simply collected the greater amount of evidence.

6. At every stage of the debate, be courteous to your opponents, your partner, and the judges.

ACTIVITIES

1. Invite a pair of students who have participated in an interscholastic debate to speak to your class. Ask them to present an abridged version of the debate. After the debate, ask the students to explain the strategies and techniques they have found most useful in debating.

2. The National Forensic League makes available recordings of championship debates. If your school has these recordings, listen to several of the debates. Compare the various ways in which different affirmative and negative teams approached the topic.

Impromptu Speaking

Impromptu speeches must be delivered with a minimum of preparation. This competition tests the student's ability to rapidly organize an effective speech, and to deliver it smoothly and confidently.

GUIDELINES

1. The speaker does not enter the room until it is his or her turn to speak.

2. The speaker is given a choice of three topics. Topics may be single words or brief phrases, or they may be cartoons or excerpts from editorials. Frequently, the topic will fall into a broad area that has been announced in advance (for example, national events during the first half of the year).

3. The speaker is given 2 or 3 minutes to prepare.

4. The speaker speaks on the topic for 5 or 6 minutes. Time signals are given to help the speaker stay within the limit.

PREPARING FOR COMPETITION

1. Read widely to stay informed about current events. If a topic area is announced, follow developments in newspapers, news magazines, news broadcasts, and public affairs programs. You may find it helpful to keep notecards on current events, although notes will not be permitted during your preparation or speech.

2. Prepare anecdotes, examples, and statistics that you may be able to use in your speech. Don't hesitate to use personal experiences, if they are relevant.

3. Organize your speech into a clear *introduction, body,* and *conclusion.* In the introduction, use an anecdote or idea you have prepared in advance to get the audience's attention.

4. Tell your audience what you will say and why, say it, then summarize what you have said. Stick closely to the topic, and keep your speech simple and concise. Make no more than three points. Concentrate on proving or illustrating those points with specific examples.

5. Try to be original in your approach to the topic. Remember, the judge has to listen to many similar presentations.

6. No matter how nervous you may be, try for a smooth, relaxed, self-confident delivery.

ACTIVITIES

1. With the other members of your class, conduct two rounds of impromptu speaking. For the first round, have the speakers draw quotations from famous authors on such topics as friendship, pride, patriotism, or peace. For the second round, have them draw editorial cartoons on national issues. Evaluate the impromptu speeches on the basis of adherence to the topic, knowledge of the topic, originality, persuasiveness, organization, gestures, and voice.

2. The best preparation for impromptu speaking is to practice it several times a week for at least a month before the contest. Your class can

select a general topic area, and each student can draw a different specific topic each time he or she speaks.

Extemporaneous Speaking

An extemporaneous speech, like an impromptu speech, cannot be prepared in advance. The extemporaneous speaker, however, has been given a more specific topic area beforehand. He or she can do detailed background research, and has a longer preparation time in which to organize the speech. Judges listen for persuasive, factual examples as well as for organization and delivery.

GUIDELINES

1. On the day of the contest, the speaker draws three specific topics from a large number of topics. The speaker chooses one of the three, and is given 30 to 60 minutes in which to prepare a speech.

2. While preparing, the speaker can usually consult research files and other materials he or she has brought.

3. The speaker may be permitted to use one or two notecards while speaking. In some contests, however, notes are prohibited.

4. The speaker delivers a 5- to 7-minute speech on the topic; time signals are usually given.

5. In some contests, the judges may question the contestants after all the speeches have been delivered. Sometimes contestants must question each other.

PREPARING FOR COMPETITION

1. Extemporaneous speaking requires a thorough, up-to-date knowledge of current events. Generally, the topic area is announced in advance (for example, international events related to energy problems). You will have several months in which to do systematic research. This should include reading and taking notes on major newspapers, news magazines, and recent books; watching newscasts and current affairs shows; and interviewing teachers, public officials, and other experts on current problems and issues. Try to find sources of information that the other speakers will probably not use.

2. Keep your notes on cards or in a loose-leaf notebook, and bring them up to date frequently. Have a separate entry and bibliography on each subtopic, and keep a copy of the most informative article or articles on each subtopic. Take these notes and articles with you to the contest.

3. When you draw your three topics, pick the one on which you are best informed, can make the most effective speech, and are best prepared to answer questions. Briefly review your notes and articles on this topic, and analyze the topic. Decide how you can best answer the question or provide the information that is needed.

4. Organize your speech around a single purpose: either to inform or to persuade. Be sure this is the purpose implied in the topic you have chosen. Outline an introduction, a body, and a conclusion for your speech. Keep the parts of your speech clear and distinct. In the introduction, capture your audience's attention by using a personal anecdote, an unusual fact, or an arresting opinion. In the body, follow a clear organizational plan: problem-to-solution, parts-to-whole, chronological, or thesis-proof-proof. In your conclusion, remind your audience of what you have said, and summarize your arguments.

5. Your delivery should be confident and relaxed. Your language should not be too formal; if you use a prepared anecdote or example in your speech, be sure that it does not stand out from the rest of your speech.

6. Answer any questions directly and concisely. Take a few seconds to organize your answer before you speak. Treat the questioner politely, even if you find the question irrelevant or annoying.

ACTIVITIES

1. Conduct an extemporaneous speaking contest with the other students in your speech class. Decide on a general topic area. Each student should have a week in which to do research. On the day of the contest, each speaker should draw a topic and take 10 minutes to prepare. (If your teacher arranges to hold the contest after school or on the weekend, the speakers can have the usual 30 to 60 minutes of preparation.) Each person should speak for 5 to 8 minutes on a topic of national importance. Evaluate the speakers on the basis of adherence to the topic, preparation, use of facts and statistics, originality, persuasiveness, organization, gestures, and voice.

2. Conduct an extemporaneous speaking contest in which every member of the class does research on the speaking topic. After the speeches, the students should question each speaker for 2 to 3 minutes. When evaluating the speeches, take into account how well each speaker was able to answer the questions.

Original Oratory

An oration is a speech that has been carefully written out and memorized. In an original oratory contest, you will be expected to deliver a persuasive speech from memory. You will be judged on the originality, organization, and persuasiveness of the speech, as well as on the quality of your delivery.

GUIDELINES

1. An original oration must be your own work. You must certify that it is original, and you will usually not be permitted to quote more than a certain amount (for example, 100 words) from other sources. The length of the oration may be defined by the total number of words (1200, for example) or the time limit (8 to 10 minutes).

2. You will usually submit a copy of the oration to the judge or judges, who will follow it as you speak.

3. The oration is usually a persuasive speech on a national or international issue. It may offer a solution to a problem, warn of a national danger, or urge the audience to support a particular cause. The speech should be well organized, take a clear position on issues, and be expressed in precise, understandable language.

4. Your words may vary slightly from the prepared text, if you feel the change sounds more natural. Clarity and smooth delivery are more important than absolute accuracy.

PREPARING FOR COMPETITION

1. Select your topic carefully. It should be a contemporary issue that interests you and on which you have strong feelings. It should also interest your audience. As you research the topic and outline your speech, think of the precise thesis that you will be proving in the oration. You need not state this thesis in so many words, but you should keep it in mind as you write. Use specific facts and vivid examples to inform and persuade your listeners. (See chapter 5 and chapter 9 for further guidelines.) Prepare a strong opening and closing for your oration.

2. Take several months to write and rewrite your oration. When you have completed the first draft, read it to as many different listeners as you can. Use their reactions and comments to improve the clarity and persuasiveness of the speech.

3. Do not memorize the oration word-by-word or sentence-by-sentence. Instead, practice reading the entire speech aloud over and over. Gradually, you will find that you no longer need to look at the manuscript, except as an occasional reminder. The final step is to discard the manuscript. If you keep the purpose and shape of the entire speech clearly in your mind, you will probably not lose your place or "freeze up." Even if you forget the exact words, your knowledge of the subject and of your thesis should enable you to keep speaking.

4. Your delivery should sound natural, confident, and spontaneous, not like a recitation. Practice your delivery many times in front of different audiences. Change any sentence in your speech that you cannot say easily and comfortably.

ACTIVITIES

1. Practice original oratory with the other students in your class. Each speaker should prepare a 4- to 5-minute oration on one aspect of a national or international issue. As the student delivers the speech from memory, the other members of the class should follow copies of the speech. Evaluate the speakers on the basis of organization; persuasiveness, use of facts and examples, clarity, quality of memorization, and quality of delivery.

2. In a collection of speeches, find an oration by a famous orator of the past. Memorize and practice a portion of this speech, and deliver it before the class. Have the other students follow a copy of the speech. Ask them to evaluate the quality of your memorization and delivery. Also discuss with them why this oration was effective, and how you think the speaker may have originally delivered it.

Oral Interpretation of Prose or Poetry

In an oral interpretation contest, each speaker prepares a program of several prose passages or poems that are tied together by a common theme. The speaker interprets each selection, reading it so that its meaning is made vividly clear to the audience. Speakers are judged on their understanding of the selections as well as on preparation and delivery.

GUIDELINES

1. The selections should conform to the rules of the contest; for example, there may be a prescribed theme, or certain materials (for example, humorous selections) may be prohibited.

2. You should prepare a spoken introduction to each selection, announcing the author and title and preparing the audience by giving them any necessary information. You should also prepare transitional remarks to bridge selections.

3. Prepare a manuscript of the entire presentation. Often, you will have to submit this manuscript to the judges.

4 Costumes, props, and makeup are not used in interpretive speaking. The purpose is to *suggest* characters and situations by means of your voice, rather than to act them out.

5. The time limit for the event is usually 7 to 10 minutes. Afterwards, the judge may give a spoken critique of your performance.

PREPARING FOR COMPETITION

1. Choose your selections very carefully. They should be of high literary merit, and understandable to a general audience. (Many great works of literature are not suited to reading aloud.) Avoid selections that have been used frequently in speaking contests. Also avoid language or situations that might offend members of your audience.

2. Be sure you understand each selection thoroughly, that you can pronounce all the words and suggest each of the characters. Remember, you are trying to make the author's emotions and ideas clear to the audience, rather than imposing your interpretation on the author's work.

3. Prose selections will probably have to be cut to fit within the time limit. When you cut, be sure that the essential scenes and actions remain, and that the emotional climax of the selection is still effective.

4. When reading poetry, be sure you understand the meter (rhythm) and rhyme scheme. Your delivery, however, should be flexible; do not read line-by-line or with a mechanical rhythm.

5. Your delivery should be clear, confident, accurate, and effective. (For more guidelines on oral interpretation, see chapter 13.)

ACTIVITIES

1. Practice oral interpretation with members of your class. Each student should prepare a brief program (not over 5 minutes) of prose or poetry selections on a given theme. Other students may follow the speaker on their own copies of the selection. Evaluate the oral interpretations on the basis of selection, presentation, understanding of the material, gestures, and vocal delivery.

2. With one or more other students, listen to recordings of prose or poetry as read by professional actors. Discuss the actors' interpretation of each selection, and evaluate it in terms of understanding of the material and effectiveness of interpretation and delivery. Discuss the ways in which your own interpretation would be similar or different.

Dramatic Interpretation

In serious dramatic interpretation, the speaker presents a scene from a play (or sometimes from a work of prose fiction), representing the different characters by means of his or her voice. The presentation is judged on the basis of adaptation, understanding, delineation of characters, and clarity and effectiveness of delivery.

GUIDELINES

1. Depending on the rules, the selections may be limited to adaptations ("cuttings") from published plays, or they may include dramatic passages from novels or short stories. Some contests permit speakers to read their selections; others require that they speak from memory. Humorous scenes are usually excluded.

2. Props, costumes, and makeup are not used. The speaker is interpreting the scene to the audience, not acting it out for them. You should use your voice to *suggest,* rather than impersonate, the different characters.

3. You should prepare an introduction announcing the author and title and setting the scene. You may need to deliver further remarks during the course of the scene in order to clarify the stage directions or dramatic situation.

4. The time limit for this event is usually 10 minutes. Afterwards, the judge may give a spoken critique of your performance.

PREPARING FOR COMPETITION

1. Choose the scene carefully. You may use a "cutting" made especially for speaking contests, or you may prepare your own. Be sure that your adaptation can be clearly understood and does not distort the author's intentions. Avoid language or situations that might offend your audience.

2. Be sure you understand the characters and situation thoroughly. Create a different voice characterization for each person (two or three is the best number), but do not do imitations. Practice your presentation in front of different audiences to be sure it is effective. Tape-record the scene as well, and listen carefully to be sure that the characters and conflicts come across distinctly.

3. As you speak, try to create and sustain a dramatic mood. Do not allow your gestures or delivery to break that mood or to distract your listeners. Try to let the mood linger for a few moments after you have completed your presentation.

ACTIVITIES

1. Prepare a dramatic scene from a play, story, or novel, and present it before the class. Use your voice and a few gestures to distinguish the

characters and to interpret the action for your listeners. The presentation should last about 3 to 5 minutes. Afterwards, ask the members of your class to evaluate your presentation in terms of your understanding of the scene, the clarity of your presentation, the distinctness of the characters, and the effectiveness of your delivery.

2. Listen to a recording of a professional actor reading dramatic scenes from novels or short stories. Notice how the actor is able to suggest distinct characters by very slight alterations in his or her voice and delivery. Record your own reading of the selection, and compare it with the professional's.

Humorous Interpretation

Like prose interpretation and dramatic interpretation, humorous interpretation is the presentation of a selection adapted from a published work. Besides interpreting the actions, emotions, and characters, the speaker must also make the audience laugh. Speakers are judged on timing and comic ability, as well as on understanding, preparation, and delivery.

GUIDELINES

1. The rules are similar to those for other oral interpretation events. The speaker may read the selection, or may be required to recite from memory. The material may be limited to selections from published plays, or it may be chosen from any written source.

2. As in other oral interpretation, the speaker must prepare an introduction and transitions. The different characters are suggested, rather than acted out.

3. The time limit for this event is generally 10 minutes. The judge usually gives a critique of the performance afterwards.

PREPARING FOR COMPETITION

1. Choose and adapt your selection (or "cutting") with the same care you would give to serious material (see "Oral Interpretation of Prose or Poetry" and "Dramatic Interpretation," above). Be sure the selection is suited to you and to your audience, and is genuinely funny. Avoid humor that is cruel, offensive, or aimed at racial or religious groups.

2. Prepare your interpretation with the aim of conveying the author's meaning to your listeners (see chapter 13). Pay close attention to the humor in the material and how you can make it most effective. Practice your timing; that is, the rate at which you speak, the way you deliver funny lines, and the length of time you allow for audience laughter.

3. Practice your selection in front of as many different audiences as you can. Notice where and why they laugh, and change your material or your interpretation to produce the response you want. (For a professional viewpoint, read Woody Allen's description of the way he tries out jokes, in lesson 4.2.)

4. Pace your performance so that it builds towards a humorous climax. Don't defuse the laughter by mugging, exaggerating, or overemphasizing minor jokes at the expense of the total effect.

ACTIVITIES

1. Prepare a 3- to 5-minute presentation of one of your favorite humorous stories, anecdotes, or speeches. Practice your interpretation before friends or members of your family, then deliver it before the class. Observe the places where the audience laughed—or failed to laugh— and change your interpretation accordingly.

2. Listen to a recording of an actor or a comedian telling a humorous anecdote. Observe the way this person paces the performance and times the jokes. Practice delivering the same material, and see if you can duplicate or improve on the professional's delivery.

Specialized Events

The following specialized events are found in speaking contests at various local and state levels.

EXPOSITORY SPEAKING

In the expository speaking event, the student delivers a prepared speech explaining an institution, concept, or process. The rules may permit or prohibit notes. Speakers select their own topics from general categories that have been announced in advance. The time limit is usually 8 minutes. (See chapter 5 for guidelines on expository speaking.)

RADIO AND TELEVISION SPEAKING

In the most common format, students in the radio and television speaking event are given 10 to 15 minutes' worth of teletype news copy. Each student has 30 minutes in which to edit this copy down to 4 minutes' delivery time, check the accuracy of the copy, and practice delivery. Carefully timed practice sessions are essential. In some broadcast speaking events, students read editorials they have written on assigned topics. (For guidelines on radio speaking, see chapter 13.)

READERS THEATER

Readers theater is oral interpretation, by a small group of readers, of adapted prose or drama selections. Two to six performers (generally) sit or stand on the stage; lighting effects and backdrops may be permitted. The time limit is usually 30 to 40 minutes. Performances are judged on suitability, adaptation, understanding, gestures, and delivery. An imaginative director and many rehearsals give a performance the smoothness and unity needed to win.

COMBINATION EVENTS

A combination event requires a speaker to take part in a series of different speaking competitions; for example, one round of impromptu speaking, one round of extemporaneous speaking, and one round of original oratory. (These events are described in detail above.) Besides careful preparation and practice for all of the events, the contestant must pay close attention to the different rules of each.

DISCUSSION

In a group discussion event, students participate either as members or as leaders of a problem-solving group. Participants are judged on preparation and on the quality of their contributions. Some events include panel discussions on topics of national importance, with each participant offering a different perspective or opinion. (For guidelines on group discussions, see chapter 7.)

Student Congress

The National Forensic League sponsors regional and national student congresses. These events give students an opportunity to learn about legislative procedures, and to develop their skills in parliamentary procedure as well as in speaking.

GUIDELINES

1. The participants may form a unicameral congress (with a single house), or a bicameral congress (with two houses: a senate and a house of representatives). The National Forensic League recommends a membership of 20 to 45 participants in each house.

2. The following officials are needed for each student congress session:
   - a *general director,* who makes practical arrangements for the congress

- an *official scorer,* who awards merit points for each speech and who nominates two congress members for honors
- a *parliamentarian,* who makes sure that the appropriate rules of parliamentary procedure are followed, and who nominates two congress members for honors
- a *page,* who carries messages between student congress participants
- a *timekeeper,* who makes sure that no speaker exceeds the official time limits.

3. The members of each session of the student congress elect a presiding officer, whose main responsibility is to provide strong, thoughtful leadership for the congress.

4. All bills and resolutions are submitted to congress members before the student congress convenes.

5. Parliamentary procedure is used in conducting all congressional debate.

6. The National Forensic League requires that each legislative day consist of at least four hours, not counting the time spent in elections. The N.F.L. suggests the following order of business:
   - call to order
   - roll call of members
   - consideration of the calendar
   - election of presiding officer
   - committee meetings (optional)
   - calendar; debate of bills and resolutions
   - selection of superior congressman or congresswoman
   - awarding of congress gavel to presiding officer
   - fixing time for next meeting
   - adjournment

7. Before the end of each session, the scorer and the parliamentarian each nominate two students for the title of Most Outstanding Representative. The three students who received the highest scores are also nominated (if they have not already been). Then all the students vote for the most outstanding member of the congress.

PREPARING FOR COMPETITION

1. Prepare for a student congress by studying the bills and resolutions carefully. Do careful research on the topic of each bill and resolution, gathering arguments and evidence on both sides. Take notes during your research; then organize your notes (either on cards or in a loose-leaf notebook) so that you will be able to refer to them during the congress.

2. If you submit a bill or resolution for a student congress, carefully plan the speech in which you will introduce that bill or resolution. Prepare to give a well-organized persuasive speech developed with appeals to logic (see lesson 9.1).

3. Before the congress begins, be sure you are familiar with the use of parliamentary procedure (see chapter 8).

4. Always show your respect both for the congress and for the other participants.

ACTIVITIES

1. Attend a student congress sponsored by the National Forensic League. Write a short essay in response to one of the following questions:
   - Select one bill. How was that bill introduced, debated, and voted upon during the congress? In what ways could the participants have improved the process of dealing with that bill?
   - Who was chosen the outstanding member of the student congress? What particular qualities made that student outstanding? In what ways might other students have improved their contributions to the student congress?

2. With the other members of your class, form and conduct a practice student congress. You may debate specific issues that you have studied in a civics, history, or government class. If you conduct the congress at the level of the entire school, you may invite local government officials or community leaders to testify during the sessions.

For Further Reading

COLLECTIONS OF SPEECHES

Copeland, Lewis, ed. *The World's Great Speeches*. Garden City, N.Y.: Garden City Publishing Company, 1942.

Crossup, Richard, ed. *Classic Speeches*. New York: Philosophical Library, 1965.

Hibbitt, George W., ed. *The Dolphin Book of Speeches*. Garden City, N.Y.: Doubleday, 1965.

Parrish, Wayland, and Hochmuth, Marie, eds. *American Speeches, 1741–1944*. New York: Longmans, Green, 1954.

Wrage, Ernest, and Baskerville, Barnet, eds. *American Forum: Speeches on Historic Issues, 1788–1900*. New York: Harper, 1960.

1. You the Communicator

KNOWING YOURSELF AS A COMMUNICATOR

Krupar, Karen. *Communication Games*. New York: The Free Press, 1973.

Luft, Joseph. *Of Human Interaction*. Palo Alto, Calif.: National Press, 1969.

Postman, Neil. *Crazy Talk, Stupid Talk: How We Defeat Ourselves by the Way We Talk and What to Do about It*. New York: Delacorte, 1976.

Ratliffe, Sharon, and Harmon, Deldee. *Adventures in the Looking Glass*. Skokie, Ill.: National Textbook Co., 1972.

USING YOUR VOICE

Bender, J. F., and Crowell, Thomas L., Jr., eds. *NBC Handbook of Pronunciation*. 3rd ed. New York: Crowell, 1964.

Horner, A. Musgrave. *Movement, Voice, and Speech*. London: Methuen, 1970.

Linklater, Kristin. *Freeing the Natural Voice*. New York: Drama Book Specialists, 1976.

2. Communicating with Others

Fast, Julius. *Body Language.* New York: Simon & Schuster, 1971.

Hall, Edward T. *The Silent Language.* Garden City, N.Y.: Doubleday, 1959.

Johnson, David. *Reaching Out.* Englewood Cliffs, N.J.: Prentice-Hall, 1972.

Johnson, Kenneth, et al. *Nothing Never Happens.* Beverly Hills: Glencoe, 1974.

Mehrabian, Albert. *Silent Messages.* Belmont, Calif.: Wadsworth, 1971.

Work, Jane, and Work, William. *Relating: Everyday Communication.* Boston: Houghton Mifflin, 1975.

3. Active Listening

Galvin, Kathleen, and Book, Cassandra. *Person to Person.* Skokie, Ill.: National Textbook Co., 1978.

Nichols, Ralph G., and Stevens, Leonard. *Are You Listening?* New York: McGraw-Hill, 1957.

Wilkinson, Charles A. *Speaking of . . . Communication.* Glenview, Ill.: Scott, Foresman, 1975.

4. Interviewing

Brady, John Joseph. *The Craft of Interviewing.* Cincinnati: Writer's Digest, 1976.

Brian, Denis. *Murderers and Other Friendly People: The Public and Private Worlds of Interviewers.* New York: McGraw-Hill, 1973.

Keefe, John. *The Teenager and the Interview.* New York: Richards Rosen Press, 1970.

Sherwood, Hugh C. *The Journalistic Interview.* New York: Harper & Row, 1969.

Walters, Barbara. *How to Talk with Practically Anybody about Practically Anything.* New York: Doubleday, 1970.

5. Expository Speaking

The following list includes the most useful reference works for preparing expository speeches. Most of them are brought up to date periodically. Your reference librarian can direct you to the lastest edition and to other sources.

GENERAL

Collier's Encyclopedia
Encyclopaedia Britannica
New Columbia Encyclopedia

SCIENCE

McGraw-Hill Encyclopedia of Science and Technology
Van Nostrand's Scientific Encyclopedia

BIOGRAPHY AND HISTORY

American Men and Women of Science
Contemporary Authors
Current Biography
Dictionary of American Biography
Dictionary of National Biography (British)
International Who's Who
Who's Who in the World (with editions for different countries and professions)

STATISTICS AND CURRENT EVENTS

Facts on File
Hammond Almanac
World Almanac

PERIODICAL INDEXES

Access
Biography Index
Book Review Index
Readers' Guide to Periodical Literature

6. Listening to Understand

See the list of books for chapter 3.

7. Group Discussion

Potter, David, and Andersen, Martin P. *Discussion in Small Groups*. 3rd ed. Belmont, Calif.: Wadsworth, 1976.

Scheidel, Thomas M., and Crowell, Laura. *Discussing and Deciding*. New York: Macmillan, 1979.

8. Parliamentary Discussion

Robert, H. H. *Robert's Rules of Order, Newly Revised*. Glenview, Ill.: Scott, Foresman, 1970.

Sturgis, A. F. *Sturgis' Standard Code of Parliamentary Procedure*. 2nd ed. New York: McGraw-Hill, 1966.

9. Persuasive Speaking

Boettinger, Henry M. *Moving Mountains; or The Art and Craft of Letting Others See Things Your Way*. New York: Macmillan, 1969.

Newman, Robert P. and Newman, Dale R. *Evidence*. Boston: Houghton Mifflin, 1969.

10. Debates

Buys, William E., et al. *Contest Speaking Manual*. Skokie, Ill.: National Textbook Co., 1968.

Fryar, Maridell, and Thomas, David A. *Basic Debate*. Skokie, Ill.: National Textbook Co., 1979.

McBurney, J. R., et al. *Argumentation and Debate*. 3rd ed. New York: Macmillan, 1969.

Musgrave, G. M. *Competitive Debate: Rules and Techniques*. 3rd ed. New York: Wilson, 1965.

Wood, Roy V. *Strategic Debate*. 2nd ed. Skokie, Ill.: National Textbook Co., 1977.

11. Critical Listening

Hayakawa, S. I. *Language in Thought and Action*. 4th ed. New York: Harcourt Brace Jovanovich, 1978.

Orwell, George. *Nineteen Eighty-four.* New York: New American Library, 1971.

Orwell, George. "Politics and the English Language," in *A Collection of Essays by George Orwell.* New York: Harcourt Brace Jovanovich, 1972.

Pei, Mario. *Weasel Words: The Art of Saying What You Don't Mean.* New York: Harper & Row, 1978.

12. Narrative Speaking

Baker, Augusta, and Greene, Ellin. *Storytelling: The Oral Tradition.* New York: Bowker, 1977.

Pomeroy, Ralph S. *Speaking from Experience.* New York: Harper & Row, 1977.

13. Oral Interpretation

Buys, William E., et al. *Creative Speaking.* Skokie, Ill.: National Textbook Co., 1974.

Lee, Charlotte. *Oral Interpretation.* 4th ed. Boston: Houghton Mifflin, 1971.

Lee, Charlotte. *Speaking of . . . Interpretation.* Glenview, Ill.: Scott, Foresman, 1975.

Mattingly, Alethea Smith, and Grimes, Wilma H. *Interpretation: Writer, Reader, Audience.* 2nd ed. Belmont, Calif.: Wadsworth, 1970.

Parrish, W. M. *Reading Aloud.* 4th ed. New York: Ronald, 1966.

14. Listening for Enjoyment

Berger, Arthur A. *The TV Guided American.* New York: Walker, 1976.

Goldsen, Rose. *The Show and Tell Machine.* New York: Dial, 1977.

Newcomb, Horace. *TV: The Most Popular Art.* Garden City, N.Y.: Doubleday-Anchor, 1974.

Index